ROME

TOP SIGHTS, AUTHENTIC EXPERIENCES

D0269071

HED BY

Contents

Plan Your Trip

This Year in Rome..................................4
Need to Know.......................................18
Top Days in Rome 20
Hotspots for:...28
What's New 30
For Free..31
Family Travel.......................................32

Top Experiences........................ 35

Colosseum 36
Vatican Museums.............................. 40
St Peter's Basilica 46
Pantheon.. 50
Museo e Galleria Borghese 54
Palatino...58
Piazza Navona 62
Museo Nazionale Romano:
Palazzo Massimo alle Terme 66
Capitoline Museums...........................70
Via Appia Antica 74
Roman Forum.....................................78
Trevi Fountain 84
Basilica di Santa Maria del Popolo... 86
Basilica di San Giovanni
in Laterano...................................... 88
Spanish Steps.................................. 90
Day Trip:
Ostia Antica 92
Basilica di San Clemente 94
Terme di Caracalla 96
Modern Architecture........................... 98
Basilica di Santa Maria Maggiore....102
Basilica di Santa Maria
in Trastevere 104
Galleria Doria Pamphilj......................106
Via Margutta.....................................108
Day Trip: Tivoli 110
Walking Tour:
Centro Storico Piazzas......................112
Walking Tour:
Literary Footsteps............................ 114

Dining Out.................................. 117

The Best 120
Ancient Rome...................................122
Centro Storico...................................122
Tridente, Trevi &
the Quirinale....................................127
Vatican City,
Borgo & Prati...................................129
Monti, Esquilino &
San Lorenzo.....................................132
Trastevere & Gianicolo..........................134
San Giovanni & Testaccio 138
Villa Borghese & Northern Rome....... 139
Southern Rome..................................... 140

Treasure Hunt 143

The Best 146
Centro Storico...................................148
Tridente, Trevi &
the Quirinale....................................153
Vatican City, Borgo & Prati 156
Monti, Esquilino &
San Lorenzo 157
Trastevere & Gianicolo..........................159
San Giovanni & Testaccio 161
Villa Borghese & Northern Rome..........161

Bar Open 163

The Best 166
Ancient Rome................................... 168
Centro Storico................................... 168
Tridente, Trevi &
the Quirinale....................................170
Vatican City, Borgo & Prati 170
Monti, Esquilino &
San Lorenzo 171
Trastevere & Gianicolo..........................175
San Giovanni & Testaccio 177
Villa Borghese & Northern Rome..........178
Southern Rome...................................179

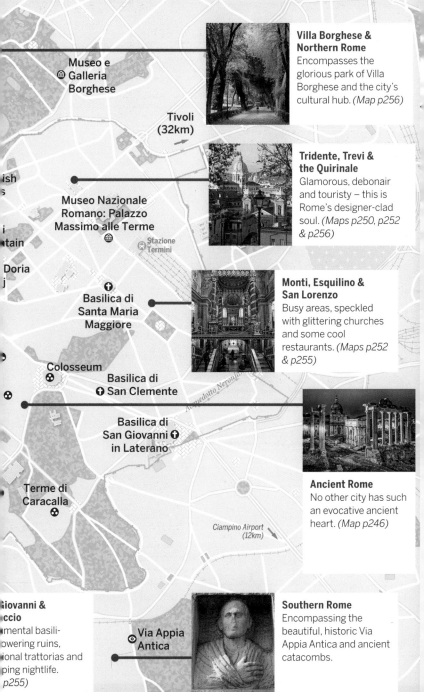

Villa Borghese & Northern Rome
Encompasses the glorious park of Villa Borghese and the city's cultural hub. (Map p256)

Museo e Galleria Borghese

Tivoli (32km)

Tridente, Trevi & the Quirinale
Glamorous, debonair and touristy – this is Rome's designer-clad soul. (Maps p250, p252 & p256)

Museo Nazionale Romano: Palazzo Massimo alle Terme

Stazione Termini

ish s

i tain

Doria j

Monti, Esquilino & San Lorenzo
Busy areas, speckled with glittering churches and some cool restaurants. (Maps p252 & p255)

Basilica di Santa Maria Maggiore

Colosseum

Basilica di San Clemente

Acquedotto Neroniano

Basilica di San Giovanni in Laterano

Ancient Rome
No other city has such an evocative ancient heart. (Map p246)

Terme di Caracalla

Ciampino Airport (12km)

Giovanni & ccio
mental basili- owering ruins, ional trattorias and ping nightlife. p255)

Via Appia Antica

Southern Rome
Encompassing the beautiful, historic Via Appia Antica and ancient catacombs.

Welcome to Rome

A heady mix of haunting ruins, breath-taking art, vibrant street life and incredible food, Italy's hot-blooded capital is one of the world's most romantic and inspiring cities.

The result of 3000 years of ad hoc urban development, Rome's cityscape is an exhilarating spectacle. Ancient icons such as the Colosseum, Roman Forum and Pantheon recall the city's golden age as *caput mundi* (capital of the world), while monumental basilicas testify to the role that great popes have played in its history.

Rome's astonishing artistic heritage is almost unrivalled. Throughout history, the city has starred in the great upheavals of Western art, drawing the top artists of the day and inspiring them to push the boundaries of creative achievement. The result is a city awash with priceless treasures. A walk around the centre will have you encountering masterpieces by the giants of Western art: sculptures by Michelangelo, canvases by Caravaggio, frescoes by Raphael and fountains by Bernini.

A trip to Rome is as much about lapping up the dolce vita lifestyle as gorging on art and culture. Idling around picturesque streets, whiling away hours at street-side cafes and people-watching on pretty piazzas are all an integral part of the Roman experience. Eating out is one of the great pleasures here, and a combination of romantic alfresco settings and superlative food guarantees good times. For a truly Roman meal head to a boisterous pizzeria or a convivial neighbourhood trattoria.

Ancient icons recall the city's golden age as caput mundi *(capital of the world)*

Porta del Popolo (p87)
FELIPE RODRIGUEZ/500PX ©

★ ROME ★

Basilica di Santa Maria del Popolo ✛

Via Margut*

Sp
St

Vatican Museums 🏛

St Peter's Basilica ✛

Tiber

T
F

Vatican City, Borgo & Prati
Home to a stunning wealth of artistic treasures. *(Map p253)*

Piazza Navona ◉

Pantheon ✛

Galle
Pam

Basilica di Santa Maria in Trastevere ✛

Capitoline Museums 🏛

Isola Tiberina

Roma
Forur

Palati

Centro Storico
The city's tangled historic centre is packed with incredible sights. *(Map p250)*

Ostia Antica (22km)
Leonardo da Vinci (Fiumicino) International Airport (26km) ↓

Stazione
Roma-Os

Trastevere & Gianicolo
Enchantingly pretty, with tangled lanes, ochre palazzi (palaces) and a boho vibe. *(Map p254)*

PIZZERIE

Sa
Te
M
ca
tra
th
(M

Showtime 181

The Best **183**
Centro Storico.................................. 184
Tridente, Trevi &
the Quirinale.................................... 184
Vatican City, Borgo & Prati 184
Monti, Esquilino &
San Lorenzo 186
Trastevere & Gianicolo........................ 186
San Giovanni & Testaccio 187
Villa Borghese & Northern Rome..........187
Southern Rome.................................. 188

Active Rome 191

The Best **193**
Spectator Sports 194
Tours.. 194
Courses 197
Spas..197

Rest Your Head 199

Accommodation Types.........................202
Seasons & Rates.................................203
Getting There 203
Useful Websites.................................204
Where to Stay....................................205

In Focus

Rome Today...................................... 208
History 210
The Arts 218
Architecture 222
The Roman Way of Life....................227

Survival Guide

Directory A–Z 230
Transport 233
Language.. 238
Index 240
Rome Maps 245
Symbols & Map Key..........................257

This Year in Rome

2018

Rome

From saints' days and neighbourhood shindigs to shopping bonanzas and major cultural festivals, Rome's calendar bursts with events. History, architecture and art might have called you here, but food, wine, music, theatre and parades will etch Rome into your memory.

Above: Festa della Madonna delle Neve (p13)

2018

ANDREAS SOLARO/AFP/GETTY IMAGES ©

★ **Top Festivals & Events**

Carnevale Romano Feb (p7)

Natale di Roma Apr (p9)

Lungo il Tevere Jun–Aug (p13)

Estate Romana Jun–Oct (p11)

RomaEuropa Late Sep–Nov (p14)

CF IMAGES/ALAMY STOCK PHOTO ©

Plan Your Trip
This Year in Rome

January

As New Year celebrations fade, the winter cold digs in. It's a quiet time of year, but the winter sales are a welcome diversion.

🔒 Shopping Sales   Early Jan
From early January to mid-February, the winter sales offer savings of between 20% and 50%, with bargain hunters descending on the shops in droves.

🎊 Epiphany   6 Jan
A witch known as La Befana delivers gifts to Italian kids for Epiphany (pictured above), the last day of the Christmas holidays. To mark the occasion, a costumed procession makes its way down Via Conciliazione to St Peter's Square.

🎊 Festa di Sant'Antonio Abate   17 Jan
Animal-lovers take their pets to be blessed at the Chiesa di Sant'Eusabio on Piazza Vittorio Emanuele in honour of the patron saint of animals.

⊙ Alta Roma   Late Jan
Fashionistas swan in for the winter outing of Rome's top fashion event. Catwalk shows, held in venues across town, provide sneak previews of seasonal collections by local and international designers.

2018

POCOSTABALDI/GETTY IMAGES ©

February

02

Rome's winter quiet is shattered by high-spirited carnival celebrations and weekend invasions of cheerful rugby fans in town for the annual Six Nations rugby tournament.

★ Six Nations Rugby   Feb & Mar
The Stadio Olimpico (pictured above) hosts Italy's home games during the Six Nations rugby tournament, held each year from early February to late March. (pictured above)

🎭 Valentine's Day   14 Feb
Valentine was a Roman priest before being martyred, and Valentine's Day in Rome is widely celebrated. Some museums and galleries offer two-for-one ticket discounts, while restaurants prepare special romance-themed menus.

★ Equilibrio   Mid-Feb
Taking place over three weeks at the Auditorium Parco della Musica, Equilibrio presents emerging talents and affirmed international choreographers at this festival of contemporary dance.

🎭 Carnevale Romano   6–13 Feb
Rome really goes to town for Carnevale (www.carnevaleroma.com), with leaping horse shows on Piazza del Popolo, costumed parades down Via del Corso, street performers on Piazza Navona and crowds of kids in fancy dress.

LUIGI DE POMPEIS/ALAMY STOCK PHOTO ©

Plan Your Trip
This Year in Rome

March

03

The onset of spring brings blooming flowers, rising temperatures and unpredictable rainfall. With Good Friday falling on 30 March 2018, prices increase as the end of the month approaches.

✱ Festa di Santa Francesca Romana
9 Mar

Traffic jams galore! Every year on the feast day of Francesca Romana, patron saint of drivers, devout motorists drive their cars to the Monastero della Oblate di Santa Francesca Romana for a vehicular blessing.

✱ Festa di San Giuseppe
19 Mar

Previously an official public holiday, the Feast of St Joseph is still a cherished event, particularly in the Trionfale district near the Vatican City, where local *pasticcerie* (pastry shops) prepare delicious cream puffs known as *bignè di san Giuseppe* (pictured above).

◉ Giornate FAI di Primavera
Late Mar

Palazzi (mansions), churches and archaeological sites that are generally closed to the

✱ Easter
30 Mar–2 Apr

In the capital of the Catholic world, Easter is a big deal. On Good Friday, the pope leads a candlelit procession around the Colosseum. At noon on Easter Sunday he blesses the crowds in St Peter's Square.

public unbolt their doors for a weekend of special openings, courtesy of Italy's main conservation body, the Fondo Ambiente Italiano (www.fondoambiente.it).

2018

GIUSEPPE CICCIA/PACIFIC PRESS/ALAMY LIVE NEWS ©

04

April

April will reward your visit with sunny weather, fervent Easter celebrations, a week of free museums, azaleas on the Spanish Steps and Rome's birthday festivities. Expect high-season prices.

🏃 Maratona di Roma   8 Apr

Sightseeing becomes sport at Rome's annual marathon (www.maratonadiroma. it; pictured above). The 42km route starts and finishes near the Colosseum, taking in many of the city's big sights.

☉ Mostra
delle Azalee   Mid-Apr–Early May

From mid-April into May the Spanish Steps are decorated with hundreds of vases full of fragrant blooms in the Exhibition of Azaleas.

🎊 Festa della Liberazione   25 Apr

Schools, shops and offices shut as Rome commemorates the WWII liberation of Italy by Allied troops and resistance forces in 1945.

🎊 Natale di Roma   21 Apr

Rome celebrates its birthday on 21 April with music, historical recreations and fireworks. Events are staged throughout the city but the focus is on Campidoglio and Circo Massimo.

LUIGI DE POMPEIS/ALAMY STOCK PHOTO ©

This Year in Rome

05

May

May is a busy high-season month. The weather's perfect – usually warm enough for you to eat outside – and the city is looking gorgeous with blue skies and spring flowers.

☆ Primo Maggio   1 May
Thousands of fans troop to Piazza di San Giovanni in Laterano for Rome's free May Day rock concert (www.primomaggio.net). It's a mostly Italian affair with big-name local performers, but you might catch the occasional foreign star.

☆ Italian Open   14 May
The world's top tennis stars bash it out on the clay courts of the Foro Italico at the Internazionali BNL d'Italia (www.internaz-ionalibnlditalia.com; pictured above), one of Europe's major tournaments.

☆ Show Jumping   Late May
Villa Borghese sets the attractive stage for Rome's annual horse-jumping event, known officially as the Concorso Ippico Internazionale di Piazza di Siena (http://piazzadisiena.it).

☆ Coppa Italia Final   21 May
Football fans fill the Stadio Olimpico for the final of Italy's main football cup, with the winner of the competition automatically qualifying for the Europa League.

2018

ERNESTO RUSCIO/GETTY IMAGES ©

06

June

Summer has arrived and with it hot weather, the Italian school holidays and a number of open-air celebrations.

🎎 Festa della Repubblica   2 Jun

A big military parade along Via dei Fori Imperiali is the highlight of ceremonial events held to commemorate the birth of the Italian Republic in 1946. Presiding is the President of the Republic and other assorted worthies.

☆ Isola del Cinema   Jun & Jul

The Isola Tiberina provides the picturesque backdrop for this open-air film festival (www.isoladelcinema.com), which screens a range of Italian and international films with a focus on independent productions.

☆ Rock in Roma   Jun & Jul

Dust down the denims for Rome's big rock fest (www.rockinroma.com). Headline acts from recent editions have included the Red Hot Chili Peppers, the XX, Bruce Springsteen, Primal Scream, the Chemical Brothers and Arcade Fire (pictured above).

☆ Estate Romana   Jun–Oct

Rome's big summer festival (www.estate romana.comune.roma.it) hosts hundreds of cultural events and activities across the capital. It showcases everything from concerts and dance performances to book fairs, puppet shows and late-night museum openings.

☆ Concerti del Tempietto   Jun–Sep

The ancient Teatro di Marcello and the lovely Villa Torlonia form marvellous venues for a summer concert series (www.tempietto.it).

🎎 Festa dei Santi Pietro e Paolo   29 Jun

Rome celebrates its two patron saints, Peter and Paul, with a mass at St Peter's Basilica and a street fair on Via Ostiense near the Basilica di San Paolo Fuori-le-Mura.

Plan Your Trip
This Year in Rome

07

July

Hot summer temperatures make sightseeing a physically challenging endeavour, but come the cool of evening, the city's streets burst into life as locals emerge to enjoy summer festivities.

☆ Luglio Suona Bene   Jul
Music legends from Sting to Santana take to the outdoor stage at the Auditorium Parco della Musica for a month-long series of concerts held as part of the Luglio Suona Bene (July Sounds Good) festival.

☆ Opera at the
Terme di Caracalla   Jul
The hulking ruins of a vast 2nd-century baths complex provide the spectacular setting for the Teatro dell'Opera di Roma's summer season. The complex also hosts ballet and the occasional rock concert.

☆ Roma Incontra
il Mondo   Jul & Aug
Villa Ada (www.villaada.org; pictured above) is transformed into a colourful multi-ethnic village for this popular annual event.

There's a laid-back party vibe and an excellent program of concerts, ranging from Roman rap to jazz and world music.

⚜ Gay Village   Jul–Sep
The big annual event in Rome's gay calendar is usually held at the Parco del Ninfeo in EUR. Expect huge crowds, DJs, dance music, film screenings, cabaret and theatrical performances.

⚜ Festa de'Noantri   Late Jul
Trastevere celebrates its roots with a raucous street party in the last two weeks of the month. Centred on Piazza Santa Maria, events kick off with a religious procession and continue with much eating, drinking, dancing and praying.

2018

August

Rome melts in the heat as locals flee the city for their summer holidays. Many businesses shut down around 15 August, but hoteliers offer discounts and there are loads of summer events to enjoy.

⚘ Festa della Madonna della Neve   5 Aug
On this day in August rose petals are showered on celebrants in the Basilica di Santa Maria Maggiore to commemorate a miraculous 4th-century snowfall.

⚘ Ferragosto   15 Aug
The Festival of the Assumption holiday is celebrated with almost total shutdown, as what seems like Rome's entire population decamps to the seaside.

♟ Lungo il Tevere   Jun–Aug
Nightly crowds converge on the river Tiber for this popular summer-long event (www.lungoiltevereroma.it; pictured above). Stalls, clubs, bars, restaurants and dance floors line the riverbank as Rome's nightlife goes alfresco.

⚘ Ferragosto   15 Aug
The Festival of the Assumption holiday is celebrated with almost total shutdown, as what seems like Rome's entire population decamps to the seaside.

JANE SWEENEY/GETTY IMAGES ©

Plan Your Trip
This Year in Rome

September

09

In the dying days of summer, the weather is still pleasantly warm, but cooler nights mean the city starts to shrug off its heat-induced torpor. The kids go back to school and locals return to work.

◉ Evening Openings   Jun–Sep

A number of Rome's headline sights offer night visits over the summer and through September. In past years, these have included the Colosseum (pictured above) and Vatican Museums.

♟ City Clubbing   Late Sep

The end of the month is a good time for party-goers as the city's main clubs return to town after their summer exodus. Curtain-raiser events are a guarantee of big nights and sweaty dance floors.

☆ RomaEuropa   Late Sep–Nov

Established international performers join emerging stars at Rome's premier dance and drama festival (http://romaeuropa.net).

✗ Taste of Roma   Mid-Sep

Foodies flock to the Auditorium Parco della Musica to revel in world food. Join Rome's top chefs for tastings, performances and three days of food-related events (www.tasteof roma.it).

Events range from avant-garde dance performances to installations, multimedia shows, recitals and readings.

2018

October

Autumn is a good time to visit – the warm weather is holding, RomaEuropa continues to ensure plenty of cultural action and, with the schools back, there are far fewer tourists around.

☆ Start of Santa Cecilia Symphony Season   Early Oct

Rome's premier orchestra, the Orchestra dell'Accademia Nazionale di Santa Cecilia (www.santacecilia.it), returns for the start of the symphonic season to its home stage at the Auditorium Parco della Musica (pictured above; designed by Renzo Piano Building Workshop Architects).

☆ Chamber Music Concerts   Late Oct–Mid-Dec

Designed by baroque genius Francesco Borromini, the Chiesa di Sant'Agnese in Agone on Piazza Navona hosts a series of chamber music concerts.

☆ Festival Internazionale del Film di Roma   Mid-Oct

Held at the Auditorium Parco della Musica, Rome's film festival (www. romacinemafest.it) rolls out the red carpet for Hollywood hotshots and Italian cinema bigwigs.

This Year in Rome

November

Although this is the wettest month, November has its compensations: low-season prices, excellent jazz concerts and no queues outside the big sights. Autumn is also great for foodies.

⚶ Festa di Ognisanti 1 Nov
Celebrated as a national holiday, All Saints' Day (pictured above) commemorates the Saint Martyrs, while All Souls' Day, on 2 November, is set aside to honour the deceased. Many Romans leave flowers on tombs at the Cimitero di Campo Verano.

☆ Festival Internazionale di Musica e Arte Sacra Early Nov
Over several days in early November, the Vienna Philharmonic Orchestra and other top ensembles perform a series of classical concerts in Rome's four papal basilicas and other churches. Check the program online: www.festivalmusicaeartesacra.net.

☆ Roma Jazz Festival Nov
The Auditorium Parco della Musica is the place to be in mid-November for jazz fans, as performers from around the world play

☆ Start of the Opera Season Late Nov
Towards the end of November the opera season gets underway at the Teatro dell'Opera di Roma, the city's opera house. The theatre is also home to Rome's principal ballet corps, with the dance season starting in December.

to appreciative audiences during this three-week festival (www.romajazzfestival.it).

2018

FRANCKREPORTER/GETTY IMAGES ©

December

The build-up to Christmas creates a festive atmosphere as the city, decked out in festive lights, twinkles in anticipation. Every church has a presepe *(nativity scene) on display, from small tableaux to life-sized extravaganzas.*

⊙ Christmas Lights   Early Dec
Crowds fill Via del Corso for the annual switching-on of the Christmas lights. Over the river in the Vatican a huge Christmas tree and life-sized nativity scene adorn St Peter's Square.

🎎 Festa dell'Immacolata Concezione   8 Dec
Tradition dictates that the pope, in his capacity as the Bishop of Rome, celebrates the Feast of the Immaculate Conception in Piazza di Spagna. Earlier in the day Rome's fire brigade places a garland of flowers atop the Colonna dell'Immacolata in adjacent Piazza Mignanelli.

🗗 Piazza Navona Christmas Fair   Dec
Rome's most beautiful baroque square becomes a big, brash marketplace as brightly lit market stalls set up shop, selling everything from nativity scenes to stuffed toys and teeth-cracking *torrone* (nougat).

BETTINA STRENSKE/ALAMY STOCK PHOTO ©

🎎 Capodanno   31 Dec
Rome is a noisy place to be on New Year's Eve (pictured above) as big fireworks displays usher in the new year and outdoor concerts are held across town, most notably on Piazzas del Quirinale and del Popolo.

18

Plan Your Trip
Need to Know

Daily Costs
Budget
Less than €100

- Dorm bed: €20–35
- Double room in a budget hotel: €60–110
- Pizza plus beer: €15

Midrange
€100–250

- Double room in a hotel: €110–200
- Lunch and dinner in local restaurants: €25–45
- Museum admission: €5–15
- Three-day Roma Pass covering museum entry and public transport: €38.50

Top end
More than €250

- Double room in a four- or five-star hotel: €200–450
- Top restaurant dinner: €45–150
- Opera ticket: €17–150
- City-centre taxi ride: €10–15
- Auditorium concert ticket: €25–90

Advance Planning
Two months before Book high-season accommodation.

Three to four weeks before Check for concerts at www.auditorium.com and www.operaroma.it.

One to two weeks before Reserve tables at A-list restaurants. Sort tickets to the pope's weekly audience at St Peter's.

A few days before Book for the Museo e Galleria Borghese (compulsory) and for the Vatican Museums (advisable to avoid queues).

Useful Websites

- **Lonely Planet** (lonelyplanet.com/rome) Destination low-down, hotel bookings and traveller forum.
- **060608** (www.060608.it) Rome's official tourist website.
- **Coopculture** (www.coopculture.it) Information and ticket booking for Rome's monuments.
- **Vatican Museums** (www.vatican.va) Book tickets and avoid the queues.
- **Auditorium** (www.auditorium.com) Check concert listings.

Currency
Euro (€)

Language
Italian

Visas
Not required by EU citizens. Not required by nationals of Australia, Canada, New Zealand and the USA for stays of up to 90 days.

Money
ATMs are widespread. Major credit cards are widely accepted but some smaller shops, trattorias and *pensioni* may not take them.

Mobile Phones
Local SIM cards can be used in unlocked European, Australian and US phones. Other phones must be set to roaming.

Time
Western European Time (GMT/UTC plus one hour)

Tourist Information
Information points around town are open from 9.30am to 7pm for maps, brochures and the Roma Pass.

For more, see the **Survival Guide** (p229)

When to Go

Spring and early autumn see good weather and many outdoor festivals. It's a busy period, and peak rates apply. Summer is stifling, but rates can be lower.

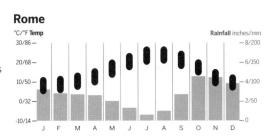

Arriving in Rome

Leonardo da Vinci (Fiumicino) Airport Direct trains to Stazione Termini run from 6.23am to 11.23pm, €14; slower trains run to Trastevere, Ostiense and Tiburtina stations from 5.57am to 10.42pm, €8; buses to Stazione Termini run from 5.35am to midnight, €4 to €9; private transfers cost from €13 per person; taxis cost €48 (fixed fare to stops within the Aurelian Walls).

Ciampino Airport Buses to Stazione Termini run from 7.45am to 11.59pm, €4; private transfers cost from €13 per person; taxis cost €30 (fixed fare to stops within the Aurelian Walls).

Stazione Termini Airport buses and trains as well as international trains arrive at Stazione Termini. From here, continue by bus, metro or taxi.

Getting Around

Rome's public transport system includes buses, trams, metro and a suburban train network. The main hub is Stazione Termini, the only point at which the city's two main metro lines cross. The metro is quicker than surface transport, but the network is limited and the bus is often a better bet. Children under 10 travel free.

⚬ Metro The main lines: A (orange; 5.30am to 9.30pm Thursday to Sunday, replacement buses MA1–MA2 to 11.30pm, to 1.30am Saturday) and B (blue; 5.30am to 11.30pm Monday to Thursday, to 1.30am Friday and Saturday). New line C runs between Monte Compatri, about 19km southeast of the city, and Parco di Centocelle; it is as yet of little use to tourists.

⚬ Bus Most routes pass through Stazione Termini. Buses run 5.30am to midnight, with limited services throughout the night.

Sleeping

Rome is expensive, and with the city busy year-round you'll want to book as far ahead as you can to secure the best deal and the place you want.

Accommodation options range from palatial five-star hotels to hostels, B&Bs, convents, *pensioni,* and various Airbnb options. Hostels are the cheapest option, offering both dorm beds and private rooms. B&Bs range from simple home-style set-ups to chic boutique outfits with prices to match, while religious institutions provide basic, value-for-money accommodation, but may insist on a curfew. Hotels are plentiful, and there are many budget family-run *pensioni* in the Termini area.

Top Days in Rome

VIACHESLAV LOPATIN/SHUTTERSTOCK ©

Ancient Rome

The Colosseum is an appropriate high on which to start your odyssey in Rome. Next, head to the nearby crumbling scenic ruins of the Palatino, followed by the Roman Forum. After lunch enjoy 360-degree views from Il Vittoriano and classical art at the Capitoline Museums.

Day

01

❶ Colosseum (p36)

More than any other monument, it's the Colosseum that symbolises the power and glory of ancient Rome. Visit its broken interior and imagine the roar of the 50,000-strong crowd as the gladiators fought for their entertainment.

➲ Colosseum to Palatino

🏃 Head south down the Via di San Gregorio to the Palatino.

❷ Palatino (p58)

The gardens and ruins of the Palatino (included with the Colosseum ticket) are an atmospheric place to explore, with great views across Circo Massimo and the Roman Forum. The Palatino was the most exclusive part of ancient Rome, home of the imperial palace, and is still today a hauntingly beautiful site.

➲ Palatino to Roman Forum

🏃 Still in the Palatino, follow the path down past the Vigna Barberino to enter the Roman Forum near the Arco di Tito.

VIACHESLAV LOPATIN/SHUTTERSTOCK ©

❸ Roman Forum (p78)

Sprawled beneath the Palatino, the Forum was the empire's nerve centre, a teeming hive of law courts, temples, piazzas and shops. See where the vestal virgins lived and senators debated matters of state in the Curia.

➲ Roman Forum to Terre e Domus

🏃 Exit the Forum onto Via dei Fori Imperiali and head up Via Alessandrina through the Imperial Forums to Terre e Domus near Trajan's Column.

❹ Lunch at Terre e Domus (p122)

Lunch on earthy Lazio food at this bright modern restaurant just off Piazza Venezia.

➲ Terre e Domus to Il Vittoriano

🏃 Return to Piazza Venezia and follow up to the mountainous monument Il Vittoriano.

❺ Il Vittoriano (p73)

Il Vittoriano is an ostentatious, overpow-ering mountain of white marble; love it or hate it, it's an impressive sight. For an

even more mind-blowing vista, take the glass lift to the top and you'll be rewarded with 360-degree views across the whole of Rome.

➲ Il Vittoriano to the Capitoline Museums

🏃 Descend from Il Vittoriano and head left to the sweeping staircase, La Cordonata. Climb the stairs to reach Piazza del Campidoglio and the Capitoline Museums.

❻ Capitoline Museums (p70)

With wonderful views over the Forum, the piazza atop the Capitoline Hill (Campi-doglio) was designed by Michelangelo and is flanked by the world's oldest national museums. The Capitoline Museums harbour some of Rome's most spectacular ancient art, including the iconic depiction of Romulus and Remus sat under a wolf, the *Lupa capitolina*.

From left: Colosseum (p36); Capitoline Museums (p70)

Top Days in Rome

DAVID ASCHKENAS/GETTY IMAGES ©

Vatican City & Centro Storico

With some ancient monuments under your belt, it's time to hit the Vatican. Have your mind blown at the Sistine Chapel and Vatican Museums, then complete your tour at St Peter's Basilica. Dedicate the afternoon to sniffing around the historic centre, including Piazza Navona and the Pantheon.

❶ Vatican Museums (p40)

There are more than 7km of exhibits, so it's difficult to see it all in a morning, but make a beeline for the Pinacoteca, the Museo Pio-Clementino, Galleria delle Carte Geografiche, Stanze di Raffaello (Raphael Rooms) and the Sistine Chapel.

◑ Vatican Museums to Fa-Bio

🏃 From the Vatican Museums entrance, turn downhill and follow the walls towards Piazza del Risorgimento. Take a left down Via Vespasiano and then the first right to Via Germanico and Fa-Bio.

❷ Lunch at Fa-Bìo (p130)

Grab a light lunch bite at this tiny takeaway. It's very popular so you'll need to squeeze through to the counter to order your *panino,* salad or smoothie, all made with quality organic ingredients.

◑ Fa-Bio to St Peter's Basilica

🏃 Double back to Piazza del Risorgimento, then follow the crowds to reach St Peter's Basilica.

Day

02

❸ St Peter's Basilica (p46)

Approaching St Peter's Square from the side, you'll see it as Bernini intended: a surprise. Visit this beautiful public square and the church itself, home to Michelangelo's *Pietà*. The church's breathtaking dome is worth climbing for astounding views.

⊘ St Peter's Basilica to Castel Sant'Angelo

🏃 From near St Peter's Square, walk along the Borgo Sant'Angelo, following the fortified wall of the elevated walkway, to reach Castel Sant'Angelo.

❹ Castel Sant'Angelo (p49)

If you've still more energy for sightseeing, visit the interior of this ancient Roman tomb that became a fortress.

⊘ Castel Sant'Angelo to Piazza Navona

🏃 Cross the river via Ponte Sant'Angelo, then follow the river eastwards for around 300m before turning right down Via G Zanardelli to reach Piazza Navona.

❺ Piazza Navona (p62)

This vast baroque square is a showpiece of the *centro storico* (historic centre), and full of vibrant life. The space is an echo of its ancient origins as the site of a stadium.

⊘ Piazza Navona to the Pantheon

🏃 It's a short walk eastwards from Piazza Navona to Piazza della Rotonda, where you'll find the Pantheon.

❻ Pantheon (p50)

This 2000-year-old temple, now a church, is an extraordinary building; its innovative design has served to inspire generations of architects and engineers.

⊘ Pantheon to Casa Coppelle

🏃 It's a short walk north via Via del Pantheon and Via della Maddalena, then a hop and a skip west to Piazza delle Coppelle and Casa Coppelle.

❼ Dinner at Casa Coppelle (p127)

Savour an evening at Casa Coppelle, with its plush furnishings and gorgeous Gallic-Roman cuisine.

From left: Vatican Museums (p40); Pantheon (p50)

Plan Your Trip
Top Days in Rome

LA CHRIST7/GETTY IMAGES ©

Villa Borghese, Tridente & Trevi

Start your day at the brilliant Museo e Galleria Borghese and then ramble around the shady avenues of the surrounding park of Villa Borghese. Next, explore the Tridente neighbourhood, including the Spanish Steps and Via dei Condotti, before heading to the Trevi Fountain.

❶ Museo e Galleria Borghese (p54)

Book ahead and start your day at the Museo e Galleria Borghese, one of Rome's best art museums. The highlight is a series of astonishing sculptures by baroque genius Gian Lorenzo Bernini.

➲ Museo e Galleria Borghese to Villa Borghese

🏃 Work your way through the leafy paths of Villa Borghese.

❷ Villa Borghese (p56)

Meander through the lovely, rambling park of Villa Borghese, formerly the playground of the mighty Borghese family. En route you'll pass the Piazza di Siena and walk along tree-shaded lanes to reach the Pincio, a panoramic terrace offering great views across Rome.

➲ Villa Borghese to the Spanish Steps

🏃 From the Pincio, exit along Viale Gabriele d'Annunzio and continue on to the top of the Spanish Steps.

Day
03

MICHELE FALZONE/GETTY IMAGES ©

❸ Spanish Steps (p90)

This glorious flight of ornamental rococo steps gives views out over Piazza di Spagna and the glittering, designer-store-packed streets of the Tridente district.

➲ Spanish Steps to Via dei Condotti

🏃 Make your way down the Spanish Steps to Via dei Condotti.

❹ Via dei Condotti (p91)

Via dei Condotti is Rome's most exclusive shopping street, lined with big-name designers and jewellers. Even if you haven't got cash to splash, it's well worth a wander to window-shop and people-watch.

➲ Via dei Condotti to Palatium

🏃 From Via Condotti turn south along Via Belsiana to reach Palatium.

❺ Lunch at Palatium (p129)

Specialising in produce from Lazio, this sleek wine bar is a great place to try local wines and artisanal delicacies.

➲ Palatium to Piazza del Popolo

🏃 Returning along Via Belsiana, turn right at Via Vittoria, then left at Via del Babuino to reach Piazza del Popolo.

❻ Piazza del Popolo (p87)

The huge, oval Piazza del Popolo dates from the 16th century. It's overlooked by Chiesa di Santa Maria del Popolo, home to a remarkable array of masterpieces.

➲ Piazza del Popolo to Trevi Fountain

🏃 From Piazza del Popolo walk back along Via del Corso, then turn left up Via Sabini to reach the Trevi Fountain.

❼ Trevi Fountain (p84)

End your day at this fantastical baroque fountain, where you can toss in a coin to ensure a return visit to Rome.

From left: Villa Borghese (p56); Trevi Fountain (p84)

Top Days in Rome

Southern Rome, Monti & Trastevere

On your fourth day, venture out to Via Appia Antica and the catacombs. Start the afternoon by visiting the Museo Nazionale Romano: Palazzo Massimo alle Terme, then drop by the Basilica di Santa Maria Maggiore. Finish with an evening in Trastevere.

❶ Catacombe di San Sebastiano (p76)

Start your day underground on a tour of one of the three networks of catacombs open to the public. It's a fascinating and chilling experience to see the tunnels where early Christians buried their dead.

➲ Catacombe di San Sebastiano to Villa di Massenzio

🏃 Head south about 100m along Via Appia and you'll see Villa di Massenzio on your left.

❷ Villa di Massenzio (p77)

The best-preserved part of Maxentius' 4th-century ruined palace is the Circo di Massenzio, once a racetrack boasting arena space for 10,000 people.

➲ Villa di Massenzio to Mausoleo di Cecilia Metella

🏃 Walk Via Appia 50m to the tomb of Cecilia Metella.

❸ Mausoleo di Cecilia Metella (p77)

With travertine walls and an interior decorated with a sculpted frieze bearing Gaelic

Day
04

CATARINA BELOVA/SHUTTERSTOCK ©

shields, ox skulls and festoons, this great, rotund tomb is an imposing sight.

⊙ Mausoleo di Cecilia Metella to Qui Nun Se More Mai

🏃 From the tomb, continue up the road for a few metres to Qui Nun Se More Mai.

❹ Lunch at Qui Nun Se More Mai (p141)

Fortify yourself for the afternoon ahead with a lunch of hearty Roman pasta and expertly grilled meat at this rustic restaurant.

⊙ Qui Nun Se More Mai to Palazzo Massimo alle Terme

🚌 After lunch, hop on a bus to Termini station to visit the Palazzo Massimo alle Terme.

❺ Palazzo Massimo alle Terme (p66)

This light-filled museum holds part of the Museo Nazionale Romano collection, including a splendid array of classical carving and an unparalleled selection of ancient Roman frescoes.

⊙ Palazzo Massimo alle Terme to Basilica di Santa Maria Maggiore

🏃 From the museum walk 200m southwest along Via Massimo d'Azeglio to reach Santa Maria Maggiore.

❻ Basilica di Santa Maria Maggiore (p102)

One of Rome's four patriarchal basilicas, this monumental church stands on the summit of the Esquiline Hill, on the spot where snow is said to have miraculously fallen in the summer of AD 358.

⊙ Basilica di Santa Maria Maggiore to Trastevere

🚌 From Termini Station, which is a short walk from the basilica, take a bus to Trastevere.

❼ Trastevere

Spend the evening wandering the charismatic streets of Trastevere. This district is a beguiling place for an evening stroll before settling on a place for dinner.

From left: Circo di Massenzio (p77); Trastevere district

Plan Your Trip
Hotspots for...

GLITZ & GLAMOUR

HISTORY BUFFS

◉ **Pantheon** This awe-inspiring temple has served as an architectural blueprint for millennia. (p50)

◉ **Via Appia Antica** The first great superhighway of the Roman world, built in the 4th century BC. (p74)

✕ **La Ciambella** A laid-back eatery situated over an ancient baths complex. (p125)

☆ **Terme di Caracalla** These 2nd-century baths provide a spectacular setting for opera and ballet. (p187; pictured below)

🚗 **Bici & Baci** Climb into a classic Fiat 500 for a tour of Rome's historical sites. (p237)

◉ **Basilica di Santa Maria in Trastevere** An ancient basilica celebrated for its golden apse mosaics. (p104; pictured above)

🍸 **Zuma Bar** Sophistication finds its home on the rooftop terrace of Palazzo Fendi. (p170)

🛍 **Gente** Requisite fashionista stop with an array of international luxury designers. (p153)

🛍 **Fendi** Dazzling flagship store of Italy's luxury behemoth. (p154)

☆ **Teatro dell'Opera di Roma** A plush interior sets the stage for dazzling operas. (p186)

ROMANCE

◉ **Via Margutta** Imagine your own Roman Holiday in this ivy-draped lane. (p108)

🍫 **Confetteria Moriondo & Gariglio** With crimson walls and glass cabinets, this historic chocolate shop is sweet decadence. (p148)

◉ **Chiesa di Santa Maria della Vittoria** Home to Bernini's daringly erotic sculpture *Santa Teresa trafitta dall'amore di Dio* (Ecstasy of St Teresa; p69)

✖ **Imàgo** Bold eats and stunning views set the scene for an intimate evening. (p129)

🍷 **Stravinskij Bar** Hotel de Russie's courtyard bar exudes effortless dolce vita style. (p170)

ACTIVE OUTDOORS

◉ **Villa Adriana** With 40 hectares to explore, this sprawling estate is great for stretching those legs. (p111; pictured above)

✖ **Aromaticus** Creative salads and inventive smoothies to fuel the adventure. (p133)

🐴 **A Friend in Rome** Saddle up for a horse ride along Via Appia Antica. (p194)

🚲 **Red Bicycle** Pick up a bike and helmet and discover Rome on two wheels. (p196)

🛍 **AS Roma Store** Clad yourself in Roma-branded kit. (p153)

CULTURE VULTURES

◉ **Vatican Museums** Home to the Sistine Chapel and kilometres of awesome art. (p40)

◉ **Museo e Galleria Borghese** The greatest gallery you've never heard of, with some of Rome's most spectacular works of art. (p54)

✖ **La Veranda** A location in Paolo Sorrentino's art drama *The Great Beauty*. (p132; pictured above)

☆ **Auditorium Parco della Musica** State-of-the-art Renzo Piano–designed cultural complex. (p187)

🛍 **Casali** Stop by for an original etching or a 16th-century botanical manuscript. (p150)

Plan Your Trip
What's New

Pizza

In a city that prides itself on its pizza, new-comers need to be pretty special to stand out. Sbanco (p138), Don (p135), Emma Pizzeria (p125) and Trieste Pizza (p133) have all risen to the top in a crowded market of delicious offerings.

Triumphs & Laments

This huge frieze (p65), charting Rome's history from mythology to modern times, was created using stencils and by power-washing the travertine walls along the Tiber river to create shadows against the white-grey stone background.

Desserts Galore

Fuel an afternoon's exploration or pencil in an evening of indulgence at one of Rome's chic new dessert bars. Go vegan at Grezzo Raw Chocolate (p132), swoon at the epony-mous offering of Tiramisù Zum (p123) or try wine ice cream at Locanda del Gelato (p136).

Yellow Square

Yellow Hostel has been open for more than a decade, but the sunny brand has been slowly colonising its surrounding area, with pop-ups such as a hair salon and tattoo lab, a fun bar (p172) and a new bike shop.

Craft Beer

Local beers go from strength to strength, with brewers reflecting seasonality; look for winter beers made from chestnuts. New players on the scene include BrewDog Roma (p168) and good-looking Be.re (p170).

Pianostrada

Pianostrada (p125) offers a *centro storico* (historic centre) follow-up to its Trastevere outlet, cementing the brand as a glorious must-visit. The friendly all-female team, gorgeous summer courtyard and fresh, seasonal fare ensure a memorable visit.

Above: Craft beers are growing in popularity

Plan Your Trip
For Free

Need to Know

Transport Holders of the Roma Pass are entitled to free public transport.

Wi-fi Free wi-fi is available in many hostels, hotels, bars and cafes.

Tours To take a free tour, check out www.newrome freetour.com.

Art & Architecture

Feast on fine art in Rome's churches. They're all free and many contain priceless treasures by big-name artists such as Michelangelo, Raphael, Bernini and Caravaggio. Major art churches include St Peter's Basilica (p46), Basilica di San Pietro in Vincoli (p103), Chiesa di San Luigi

dei Francesi (p65) and Basilica di Santa Maria del Popolo (p86).

All of the state-run museums are free on the first Sunday of the month, including the Museo Carlo Bilotti (p57). The Vatican Museums (p40) are free on the last Sunday of the month.

A pagan temple turned church, the Pantheon (p50) is a staggering work of architecture with a record-breaking dome and echoing interior.

Piazzas & Parks

Hanging out and people-watching on Rome's piazzas is a signature city experience. Top spots include Piazza Navona (p62), Campo de' Fiori (p65) and Piazza di Spagna (p91).

It doesn't cost a thing to enjoy Rome's parks. The most famous is Villa Borghese (p56), but you'll also find greenery at Villa Celimontana (p97) and Gianicolo.

Monuments

You don't have to spend a penny to admire the Trevi Fountain (p84), although most people throw a coin in to ensure their return to Rome.

According to legend, if you tell a lie with your hand in the gaping maw of the *Bocca della Verità* (p73), it will bite your hand off.

Above: *Bocca della Verità* (p73)

Family Travel

STEFAN CIOATA/GETTY IMAGES ©

The Low-Down

Despite a reputation as a highbrow cultural destination, Rome has a lot to offer kids. Child-specific sights might be thin on the ground, but if you know where to go there's plenty to keep the little ones occupied and parents happy.

Need to Know

○ **Eating out** In a restaurant ask for a *mezza porzione* (child's portion) and *seggiolone* (high chair).

○ **Getting around** Cobbled streets can make getting around with a pram difficult.

○ **Supplies** Buy baby formula and sterilising solutions at pharmacies. Disposable nappies (diapers; *pannolini*) are available from supermarkets and pharmacies.

○ **Transport** Under 10s travel free on all public transport.

History for Kids

Everyone wants to see the **Colosseum** (p36) and it doesn't disappoint, especially if accompanied by tales of bloodthirsty gladiators and hungry lions. For maximum effect prep your kids beforehand with a Rome-based film.

Spook your teens with a trip to the catacombs on **Via Appia Antica** (p74). These pitch-black tunnels, full of tombs and ancient burial chambers, are fascinating, but not suitable for children under about seven.

Hands-On Activities

Kids love throwing things, so they'll enjoy flinging a coin into the **Trevi Fountain** (p84). And if they ask, you can tell them that about €3000 is thrown in on an average day.

Another favourite is putting your hand in the **Bocca della Verità** (p73), the Mouth of Truth. It's said if you tell a fib, the mouth will bite your hand off.

A Family Day Out

Many of Rome's ancient ruins can be boring for children – they just look like piles of old stones – but **Ostia Antica** (p92) is different. Here your kids can run along the ancient town's streets, among shops, and up the tiers of its impressive amphitheatre. A trip to Ostia also means a quick ride on a train. Note that there's little shade on the site, so bring water and hats, and take all the usual precautions.

Run in the Park

When the time comes to let the kids off the leash, head to **Villa Borghese** (p56), the most central of Rome's main parks. There's plenty of space to run around in – though it's not absolutely car-free – and you can hire family bikes.

Best Food Stops for Kids

La Ciambella (p125)

Necci dal 1924 (p133)

Cups (p138)

Pizzarium (p129)

Porto Fluviale (p141)

Food for Kids

Pizza al taglio (by the slice) is a saviour for parents. It's cheap (about €1 buys two slices of pizza *bianca* – with salt and olive oil), easy to get hold of (there are hundreds of takeaways around town) and works wonders on flagging spirits.

Gelato is also a guaranteed winner, served in *coppette* (tubs) or *coni* (cones). Child-friendly flavours include *fragola* (strawberry), *cioccolato* (chocolate) and *bacio* (with hazelnuts).

From left: Piazza Navona (p62); Villa Borghese (p56)

Colosseum...................................36

Vatican Museums.......................40

St Peter's Basilica......................46

Pantheon....................................50

Museo e Galleria Borghese........54

Palatino......................................58

Piazza Navona............................62

Museo Nazionale Romano:
Palazzo Massimo alle Terme......66

Capitoline Museums...................70

Via Appia Antica.........................74

Roman Forum.............................78

Trevi Fountain............................84

Basilica di Santa Maria
del Popolo...................................86

Basilica di San Giovanni
in Laterano.................................88

Spanish Steps.............................90

Day Trip: Ostia Antica................92

Basilica di San Clemente............94

Terme di Caracalla......................96

Modern Architecture..................98

Basilica di Santa
Maria Maggiore.........................102

Basilica di Santa Maria
in Trastevere.............................104

Galleria Doria Pamphilj.............106

Via Margutta.............................108

Day Trip: Tivoli.........................110

Walking Tour: Centro
Storico Piazzas..........................112

Walking Tour:
Literary Footsteps.....................114

TOP
EXPERIENCES

The very best to see and do

Colosseum

A monument to raw, merciless power, the Colosseum is the most thrilling of Rome's ancient sights. It was here that gladiators met in mortal combat and condemned prisoners fought off wild beasts in front of baying, bloodthirsty crowds. Two thousand years on and it's Italy's top tourist attraction, drawing more than five million visitors a year.

Great For...

ℹ **Need to Know**

Colosseo; Map p246; ☎06 3996 7700; www. coopculture.it; Piazza del Colosseo; adult/ reduced incl Roman Forum & Palatino €12/7.50; ⊙8.30am-1hr before sunset; Ⓜ Colosseo

★ **Top Tip**
Beat the queues by buying your ticket at the Palatino (Via di San Gregorio 30).

Built by Vespasian (r AD 69–79) in the grounds of Nero's vast Domus Aurea complex, the arena was inaugurated in AD 80, eight years after it had been commissioned. To mark the occasion, Vespasian's son and successor Titus (r AD 79–81) staged games that lasted 100 days and nights, during which 5000 animals were slaughtered. Trajan (r AD 98–117) later topped this, holding a marathon 117-day killing spree involving 9000 gladiators and 10,000 animals.

The 50,000-seat arena was originally known as the Flavian Amphitheatre, and although it was Rome's most fearsome arena it wasn't the biggest – the Circo Massimo could hold up to 250,000 people. The name Colosseum, when introduced in medieval times, was a reference not to its size but to the Colosso di Nerone, a giant statue of Nero that stood nearby.

With the fall of the Roman Empire in the 5th century, the Colosseum was abandoned and gradually became overgrown. In the Middle Ages it served as a fortress for two of the city's warrior families, the Frangipani and the Annibaldi. Later, during the Renaissance and baroque periods, it was plundered of its precious travertine, and the marble stripped from it was used to make huge palaces such as Palazzo Venezia, Palazzo Barberini and Palazzo Cancelleria.

More recently, pollution and vibrations caused by traffic and the metro have taken their toll, but the first stage of a €25-million clean-up, the first in its 2000-year history, has once again revealed the creamy hues of the Colosseum walls.

Interior view of the Colosseum

Exterior

The outer walls have three levels of arches, framed by Ionic, Doric and Corinthian columns. These were originally covered in travertine, and marble statues filled the niches on the 2nd and 3rd storeys. The upper level, punctuated with windows and slender Corinthian pilasters, had supports for 240 masts that held up a huge canvas awning over the arena, shielding spectators from sun and rain. The 80 entrance arches, known as vomitoria, allowed the spectators to enter and be seated in a matter of minutes.

☑ **Don't Miss**

The hypogeum's network of dank tunnels beneath the main arena. Visits require advance booking and cost an extra €9.

JUSTIN FOULKES/LONELY PLANET ©

Arena

The arena originally had a wooden floor covered in sand to prevent the combatants from slipping and to soak up the blood. It could also be flooded for mock sea battles. Trapdoors led down to the hypogeum, a subterranean complex of corridors, cages and lifts beneath the arena floor.

Stands

The *cavea*, for spectator seating, was divided into three tiers: magistrates and senior officials sat in the lowest tier, wealthy citizens in the middle, and the plebeians in the highest tier. Women (except for vestal virgins) were relegated to the cheapest sections at the top. As in modern stadiums, tickets were numbered and spectators assigned a seat in a specific sector – in 2015, restorers uncovered traces of red numerals on the arches, indicating how the sectors were numbered. The podium, a broad terrace in front of the tiers of seats, was reserved for the emperor, senators and VIPs.

Hypogeum

The hypogeum served as the stadium's backstage area. Sets for the various battle scenes were prepared here and hoisted up to the arena by a complicated system of pulleys. Caged animals were kept here and gladiators would gather here before show time, having come in through an underground corridor from the nearby Ludus Magnus (gladiator school).

✕ **Take a Break**

Cafè Cafè (p138) is the perfect venue for a post-arena break, for tea and cake or a light meal.

Vatican Museums gallery

Vatican Museums

Founded in the 16th century, the Vatican Museums boast one of the world's greatest art collections. Highlights include spectacular classical statuary, rooms frescoed by Raphael, and the Michelangelo-decorated Sistine Chapel.

Housing the museums are the lavishly decorated halls and galleries of the Palazzo Apostolico Vaticano. This vast 5.5-hectare complex consists of two palaces – the Vatican Palace and the Belvedere Palace – joined by two long galleries. Inside are three courtyards: the Cortile della Pigna, the Cortile della Biblioteca and, to the south, the Cortile del Belvedere. You'll never cover it all in one day, so it pays to be selective.

Great For...

☑ **Don't Miss**

The Museo Gregoriano Egizio's fascinating 3rd-century linen 'Shroud of the Lady of the Vatican'.

Pinacoteca

Often overlooked by visitors, the papal picture gallery contains Raphael's last work, *La Trasfigurazione* (Transfiguration; 1517–20), and paintings by Giotto, Fra Angelico, Filippo Lippi, Perugino, Titian, Guido Reni, Guercino, Pietro da Cortona, Caravaggio and Leonardo da Vinci, whose haunting *San Gerolamo* (St Jerome; c 1480) was never finished.

Apollo Belvedere, Museo Pio-Clementino

❶ Need to Know

Musei Vaticani; Map p253; ☎06 6988 4676; www.museivaticani.va; Viale Vaticano; adult/reduced €16/8, last Sun of the month free; ⏱9am-6pm Mon-Sat, 9am-2pm last Sun of the month, last entry 2hr before close; 🚊Piazza del Risorgimento, ⓂOttaviano-San Pietro

✖ Take a Break

Snack on a scissor-cut square of pizza or a rice croquette from Pizzarium (p129).

★ Top Tip

Avoid queues by booking tickets online (http://biglietteriamusei.vatican.va/musei/tickets/do); the booking fee costs €4.

Museo Chiaramonti & Braccio Nuovo

The Museo Chiaramonti is effectively the long corridor that runs down the eastern side of the Belvedere Palace. Its walls are lined with thousands of statues and busts representing everything from immortal gods to playful cherubs and unattractive Roman patricians. Near the end of the hall, off to the right, is the Braccio Nuovo (New Wing), which contains a famous statue of the Nile as a reclining god covered by 16 babies.

Museo Pio-Clementino

This stunning museum contains some of the Vatican Museums' finest classical statuary, including the peerless *Apollo Belvedere* and the 1st-century *Laocoön,* both in the **Cortile Ottagono** (Octagonal Courtyard). Before you go into the courtyard, take a moment to admire the 1st-century *Apoxyomenos,* one of the earliest known sculptures to depict a figure with a raised arm.

To the left as you enter the courtyard, the *Apollo Belvedere* is a 2nd-century Roman copy of a 4th-century-BC Greek bronze. A beautifully proportioned representation of the sun god Apollo, it's considered one of the great masterpieces of classical sculpture. Nearby, the *Laocoön* depicts a muscular Trojan priest and his two sons in mortal struggle with two sea serpents.

Back inside, the **Sala degli Animali** is filled with sculpted creatures and some magnificent 4th-century mosaics. Continuing on, you come to the **Sala delle Muse**, centred on the *Torso Belvedere*, another of the museum's must-sees. A fragment of a muscular 1st-century-BC Greek sculpture, it was found in Campo de' Fiori and used by Michelangelo as a model for his *ignudi* (male nudes) in the Sistine Chapel. It's currently undergoing restoration.

The next room, the **Sala Rotonda**, contains a number of colossal statues, including a gilded-bronze *Ercole* (Hercules) and an exquisite floor mosaic. The enormous basin in the centre of the room was found at Nero's Domus Aurea and is made out of a single piece of red porphyry stone.

Museo Gregoriano Egizio

Founded by Gregory XVI in 1839, this museum contains pieces taken from Egypt in Roman times. The collection is small, but there are fascinating exhibits including the *Trono di Ramses II* (part of a statue of the seated king), vividly painted sarcophagi dating from around 1000 BC, and some macabre mummies.

Museo Gregoriano Etrusco

At the top of the 18th-century Simonetti staircase, the Museo Gregoriano Etrusco contains artefacts unearthed in the Etruscan tombs of northern Lazio, as well as a superb collection of vases and Roman antiquities. Of particular interest is the *Marte di Todi* (Mars of Todi), a black bronze of a warrior dating to the late 5th century BC.

Galleria delle Carte Geografiche & Sala Sobieski

The last of three galleries on the upper floor – the other two are the **Galleria dei Candelabri** (Gallery of the Candelabra) and the **Galleria degli Arazzi** (Tapestry Gallery) – this 120m-long corridor is hung with 40 huge topographical maps. These were created between 1580 and 1583 for Pope Gregory

Galleria delle Carte Geografiche

XIII based on drafts by Ignazio Danti, one of the leading cartographers of his day.

Beyond the gallery, the **Sala Sobieski** is named after an enormous 19th-century painting depicting the victory of the Polish king John III Sobieski over the Turks in 1683.

Stanze di Raffaello

These four frescoed chambers, currently undergoing partial restoration, were part of Pope Julius II's private apartments. Raphael himself painted the Stanza della Segnatura (1508–11) and the Stanza d'Eliodoro (1512–14),

> ⓘ **Local Knowledge**
>
> Tuesdays and Thursdays are the quietest days to visit, Wednesday mornings are also good, and afternoons are better than mornings. Avoid Mondays, when many other museums are shut.

while the Stanza dell'Incendio (1514–17) and Sala di Costantino (1517–24) were decorated by students following his designs.

The first room you come to is the **Sala di Costantino**, which features a huge fresco depicting Constantine's defeat of Maxentius at the battle of Milvian Bridge.

The **Stanza d'Eliodoro**, which was used for private audiences, takes its name from the *Cacciata d'Eliodoro* (Expulsion of Heliodorus from the Temple), an allegorical work reflecting Pope Julius II's policy of forcing foreign powers off Church lands. To its right, the *Messa di Bolsena* (Mass of Bolsena) shows Julius paying homage to the relic of a 13th-century miracle at the lakeside town of Bolsena. Next is the *Incontro di Leone Magno con Attila* (Encounter of Leo the Great with Attila) by Raphael and his school, and, on the fourth wall, the *Liberazione di San Pietro* (Liberation of St Peter), a brilliant work illustrating Raphael's masterful ability to depict light.

The **Stanza della Segnatura**, Julius' study and library, was the first room that Raphael painted, and it's here that you'll find his great masterpiece, *La Scuola di Atene* (The School of Athens), featuring philosophers and scholars gathered around Plato and Aristotle. The seated figure in front of the steps is believed to be Michelangelo, while the figure of Plato is said to be a portrait of Leonardo da Vinci, and Euclide (the bald man bending over) is Bramante. Raphael also included a self-portrait in the lower right corner – he's the second figure from the right.

The most famous work in the **Stanza dell'Incendio di Borgo** is the *Incendio di Borgo* (Fire in the Borgo), which depicts Pope Leo IV extinguishing a fire by making the sign of the cross. The ceiling was painted by Raphael's master, Perugino.

Sistine Chapel

The jewel in the Vatican's crown, the Sistine Chapel (Cappella Sistina) is home to two of the world's most famous works of art: Michelangelo's ceiling frescoes and his *Giudizio Universale* (Last Judgment).

GONZALO AZUMENDI/GETTY IMAGES ©

The chapel was originally built for Pope Sixtus IV, after whom it's named, and was consecrated on 15 August 1483. However, apart from the wall frescoes and floor, little remains of the original decor, which was sacrificed to make way for Michelangelo's two masterpieces. The first, the ceiling, was commissioned by Pope Julius II and painted between 1508 and 1512; the second, the spectacular *Giudizio Universale* was painted between 1535 and 1541.

Michelangelo's ceiling design, which is best viewed from the chapel's main entrance in the far east wall, covers the entire 800-sq-m surface. With painted architectural features and a cast of colourful biblical characters, it's centred on nine panels depicting scenes from the Creation, the story of Adam and Eve, the Fall, and the plight of Noah.

As you look up from the east wall, the first panel is the *Drunkenness of Noah,* followed by *The Flood* and the *Sacrifice of Noah*. Next, *Original Sin and Banishment from the Garden of Eden* famously depicts Adam and Eve being sent packing after accepting the forbidden fruit from Satan, represented by a snake with the body of a woman coiled around a tree. The *Creation of Eve* is then followed by the *Creation of Adam*. This, one of the most famous images in Western art, shows a bearded God pointing his finger at Adam, thus bringing him to life. Completing the sequence are the *Separation of Land from Sea;* the *Creation of the Sun, Moon and Plants;* and the *Separation of Light from Darkness,* featuring a fearsome God reaching out to touch the sun. Set around the central panels are 20 athletic male nudes, known as *ignudi*.

Stanza della Segnatura (p43)

Opposite, on the west wall is Michelangelo's mesmeric *Giudizio Universale*, showing Christ – in the centre near the top – passing sentence over the souls of the dead as they are torn from their graves to face him. The saved get to stay in heaven (in the upper right); the damned are sent down to face the demons in hell (in the bottom right).

Near the bottom, on the right, you'll see a man with donkey ears and a snake wrapped around him. This is Biagio de Cesena, the papal master of ceremonies, who was a fierce critic of Michelangelo's composition. Another famous figure is St Bartholomew, just beneath Christ, holding his own flayed skin. The face in the skin is said to be a self-portrait of Michelangelo, its anguished look reflecting the artist's tormented faith.

The chapel's walls also boast superb frescoes. Painted between 1481 and 1482 by a crack team of Renaissance artists, including Botticelli, Ghirlandaio, Pinturicchio, Perugino and Luca Signorelli, they represent events in the lives of Moses (to the left looking at the *Giudizio Universale*) and Christ (to the right). Highlights include Botticelli's *Temptations of Christ* and Perugino's *Handing over of the Keys*.

As well as providing a showcase for priceless art, the Sistine Chapel serves an important religious function as the place where the conclave meets to elect a new pope.

★ Top Tip

Most exhibits are not well labelled. Consider hiring an audio guide (€7) or buying the excellent *Guide to the Vatican Museums* and City (€14).

ALERY VOENNY/ALAMY STOCK PHOTO ©

Interior of St Peter's Basilica

St Peter's Basilica

In this city of outstanding churches, none can hold a candle to St Peter's, Italy's largest, richest and most spectacular basilica.

Great For...

☑ **Don't Miss**

Climbing the (numerous, steep and tiring but worth it) steps of the dome for views over Rome.

The original church was commissioned by the emperor Constantine and built around 349 on the site where St Peter is said to have been buried between AD 64 and 67. But like many medieval churches, it eventually fell into disrepair. It wasn't until the mid-15th century that efforts were made to restore it, first by Pope Nicholas V and then, rather more successfully, by Julius II.

In 1506 construction began on a design by Bramante, but ground to a halt when the architect died in 1514. In 1547 Michelangelo stepped in to take on the project. He simplified Bramante's plans and drew up designs for what was to become his greatest architectural achievement: the dome. He didn't live to see it built, though, and it was left to Giacomo della Porta, Domenico Fontana and Carlo Maderno to complete the basilica, which was finally consecrated in 1626.

Nuns resting at St Peter's Square (p49)

❶ Need to Know

Basilica di San Pietro; Map p253; ☎06 6988 5518; www.vatican.va; St Peter's Square; ⊙7am-7pm summer, to 6.30pm winter; ☒Piazza del Risorgimento, Ⓜ Ottaviano-San Pietro FREE

✕ Take a Break

With more than 200 teas to choose from, you'll find the perfect cuppa at Makasar Bistrot (p171).

★ Top Tip

Strict dress codes are enforced, which means no shorts, miniskirts or bare shoulders.

Facade

Built between 1608 and 1612, Maderno's immense facade is 48m high and 118.6m wide. Eight 27m-high columns support the upper attic on which 13 statues stand representing Christ the Redeemer, St John the Baptist and the 11 apostles. The central balcony, the **Loggia della Benedizione**, is where the pope stands to deliver his *Urbi et Orbi* blessing at Christmas and Easter.

Interior

At the beginning of the right aisle is Michelangelo's beautiful *Pietà*. Sculpted when the artist was 25 (in 1499), it's the only work he ever signed; his signature is etched into the sash across the Madonna's breast.

On a pillar just beyond the *Pietà,* Carlo Fontana's gilt and bronze **monument to Queen Christina of Sweden** commemo-

rates the far-from-holy Swedish monarch who converted to Catholicism in 1655.

Moving on, you'll come to the **Cappella di San Sebastiano**, home of Pope John Paul II's tomb, and the **Cappella del Santissimo Sacramento**, a sumptuously decorated baroque chapel.

Dominating the centre of the basilica is Bernini's 29m-high **baldachin**. Supported by four spiral columns and made with bronze taken from the Pantheon, it stands over the **high altar**, which itself sits on the site of St Peter's grave.

Above the baldachin, Michelangelo's **dome** soars to a height of 119m. Based on Brunelleschi's cupola in Florence, it's supported by four massive stone **piers** named after the saints whose statues adorn the Bernini-designed niches – Longinus, Helena, Veronica and Andrew.

At the base of the **Pier of St Longinus** is Arnolfo di Cambio's much-loved 13th-century bronze **statue of St Peter**, whose right foot has been worn down by centuries of caresses.

Dominating the tribune behind the altar is Bernini's extraordinary **Cattedra di San Pietro**, centred on a wooden seat that was once thought to have been St Peter's, but in fact dates to the 9th century.

Situated to the right of the throne, Bernini's **monument to Urban VIII** depicts the pope flanked by the figures of Charity and Justice.

Near the head of the left aisle are the so-called **Stuart monuments**. On the right is the monument to Clementina Sobieska, wife of James Stuart, by Filippo Barigioni, and on the left is Canova's vaguely erotic monument to the last three members of the Stuart clan, the pretenders to the English throne who died in exile in Rome.

Dome

From the **dome** (with/without lift €8/6; ☼8am-6pm summer, to 5pm winter) entrance on the right of the basilica's main portico, you can walk the 551 steps to the top or take a small lift halfway and then follow on foot for the last 320 steps. Either way, it's a long, steep climb and not recommended for anyone who suffers from claustrophobia or vertigo. Make it to the top, though, and you're rewarded with stunning views.

Museo Storico Artistico

Accessed from the left nave, the **Museo Storico Artistico** (Tesoro, Treasury; adult/ reduced €7/5; ☼8am-6.50pm summer, to 5.50pm winter) sparkles with sacred relics. Highlights include a tabernacle by Donatello and the 6th-century *Crux Vaticana* (Vatican Cross).

St Peter's dome and city skyline

Vatican Grottoes

Extending beneath the basilica, the **Vatican Grottoes** (☺8am-6pm summer, to 5.30pm winter) FREE contain the tombs and sarcophagi of numerous popes, as well as several columns that were retained from the original 4th-century basilica. The entrance is located in the Pier of St Andrew.

★ Free Tours

Between October and late May, free English-language tours of the basilica are run by seminarians from the Pontifical North American College, usually departing 2.15pm Monday to Friday from Centro Servizi Pellegrini e Turisti.

JUSTIN FOULKES/LONELY PLANET ©

St Peter's Tomb

Excavations beneath the basilica have uncovered part of the original church and what archaeologists believe is the **Tomb of St Peter** (☎06 6988 5318; www.scavi.va; admission €13, over 15s only).

The excavations can only be visited by guided tour. To book a spot, email the Ufficio Scavi (scavi@fsp.va) as far in advance as possible.

What's Nearby?

St Peter's Square   Piazza

(Piazza San Pietro; Map p253; ℳ Ottaviano-San Pietro) Overlooked by St Peter's Basilica, the Vatican's central square was laid out between 1656 and 1667 to a design by Gian Lorenzo Bernini. Seen from above, it resembles a giant keyhole with two semicircular colonnades, each consisting of four rows of Doric columns, encircling a giant ellipse that straightens out to funnel believers into the basilica. The effect was deliberate – Bernini described the colonnades as representing 'the motherly arms of the church'.

Castel Sant'Angelo   Museum, Castle

(Map p250; ☎06 681 91 11; www.castelsantangelo. beniculturali.it; Lungotevere Castello 50; adult/reduced €10/5; ☺9am-7.30pm, ticket office to 6.30pm; ☒ Piazza Pia) With its chunky round keep, this castle is an instantly recognisable landmark. Built as a mausoleum for the emperor Hadrian, it was converted into a papal fortress in the 6th century and named after an angelic vision that Pope Gregory the Great had in 590. Nowadays, it houses the **Museo Nazionale di Castel Sant'Angelo** and its eclectic collection of paintings, sculpture, military memorabilia and medieval firearms.

---

❶ Local Knowledge

Near the main entrance of St Peter's, a red floor disk marks the spot where Charlemagne and later Holy Roman Emperors were crowned by the pope.

Pantheon

A striking 2000-year-old temple that's now a church, the Pantheon is Rome's best-preserved ancient monument and one of the most influential buildings in the Western world. Its greying, pockmarked exterior may look its age, but inside it's a different story. It's a unique and exhilarating experience to pass through the vast bronze doors and gaze up at the largest unreinforced concrete dome ever built.

Great For...

ⓘ Need to Know

Map p250; www.pantheonroma.com; Piazza della Rotonda; ☺8.30am-7.15pm Mon-Sat, 9am-5.45pm Sun; ☒Largo di Torre Argentina
`FREE`

★ **Top Tip**

Mass is celebrated at the Pantheon at 5pm on Saturdays and 10.30am on Sundays.

In its current form the Pantheon dates to around AD 125. The original temple, built by Marcus Agrippa in 27 BC, burnt down in AD 80, and although it was rebuilt by Domitian, it was struck by lightning and destroyed for a second time in AD 110. The emperor Hadrian had it reconstructed between AD 118 and 125, and it's this version that you see today.

Hadrian's temple was dedicated to the classical gods – hence the name Pantheon, a derivation of the Greek words *pan* (all) and *theos* (god) – but in 608 it was consecrated as a Christian church. It's now officially known as the Basilica di Santa Maria ad Martyres.

Thanks to this consecration, it was spared the worst of the medieval plundering that reduced many of Rome's ancient buildings to near dereliction. But it didn't escape entirely unscathed – its gilded-bronze roof tiles were removed and bronze from the portico was used by Bernini for the baldachin at St Peter's Basilica.

Exterior

The dark-grey pitted exterior faces onto busy, cafe-lined Piazza della Rotonda. And while its facade is somewhat the worse for wear, it's still an imposing sight. The monumental entrance **portico** consists of 16 Corinthian columns, each 13m high and made of Egyptian granite, supporting a triangular **pediment**. Behind the columns, two 20-tonne **bronze doors** – 16th-century restorations of the original portal – give onto the central rotunda. Rivets and holes in the building's brickwork indicate where marble-veneer panels were originally placed.

Oculus in the Pantheon's dome

Inscription

For centuries the inscription under the pediment – M:AGRIPPA.L.F.COS.TERTIUM. FECIT or 'Marcus Agrippa, son of Lucius, consul for the third time built this' – led scholars to think that the current building was Agrippa's original temple. However, 19th-century excavations revealed traces of an earlier temple and historians realised that Hadrian had simply kept Agrippa's original inscription.

Interior

Although impressive from outside, it's only when you get inside that you can really appreciate the Pantheon's full size. With light streaming in through the **oculus** (the 8.7m-diameter hole in the centre of the dome), the cylindrical marble-clad interior seems vast.

Opposite the entrance is the church's main **altar**, over which hangs a 7th-century icon of the *Madonna col Bambino* (Madonna and Child). To the left are the tombs of the artist Raphael, King Umberto I and Margherita of Savoy. Over on the opposite side of the rotunda is the tomb of King Vittorio Emanuele II.

Dome

The Pantheon's dome, considered to be the Romans' most important architectural achievement, was the largest dome in the world until Brunelleschi beat it with his Florentine cupola. Its harmonious appearance is due to a precisely calibrated symmetry – its diameter is exactly equal to the building's interior height of 43.3m. At its centre, the oculus, which symbolically connected the temple with the gods, plays a vital structural role by absorbing and re-distributing the dome's huge tensile forces.

What's Nearby?

Basilica di Santa Maria Sopra Minerva   Basilica

(Map p250; www.santamariasopraminerva.it; Piazza della Minerva 42; ☺6.40am-7pm Mon-Fri, 6.40am-12.30pm & 3.30-7pm Sat, 8am-12.30pm & 3.30-7pm Sun; ⊠Largo di Torre Argentina) Built on the site of three pagan temples, including one to the goddess Minerva, the Dominican Basilica di Santa Maria Sopra Minerva is Rome's only Gothic church. However, little remains of the original 13th-century structure and these days the main drawcard is a minor Michelangelo sculpture and the colourful, art-rich interior.

> ☑ **Don't Miss**
> The 7m-high bronze doors provide a suitably grand entrance to your visit.

VIACHESLAV LOPATIN/GETTY IMAGES ©

> ✕ **Take a Break**
> Get caffeinated at Caffè Sant'Eustachio (p122), known to serve some of the best coffee in town.

Bernini's *Rape of Proserpina*, Sala IV

DE AGOSTINI/A. DE GREGORIO/GETTY IMAGES ©

Museo e Galleria Borghese

Housing what's often referred to as the 'queen of all private art collections', this spectacular gallery boasts some of the city's finest art treasures.

Great For...

☑ **Don't Miss**

Canova's *Venere Vincitrice,* his sensual portrayal of Paolina Bonaparte Borghese.

Including a series of sensational sculptures by Gian Lorenzo Bernini and important paintings by the likes of Caravaggio, Titian, Raphael and Rubens, the museum's collection was formed by Cardinal Scipione Borghese (1579–1633), the most knowledgeable and ruthless art collector of his day. It was originally housed in his residence near St Peter's, but in the 1620s he had it transferred to his new villa just outside Porta Pinciana. And it's here, in the villa's central building, the Casino Borghese, that you'll see it today.

Over the centuries the villa has undergone several overhauls, most notably in the late 1700s when Prince Marcantonio Borghese added much of the neoclassical decor.

The villa is divided into two parts: the ground-floor museum and the upstairs picture gallery.

Museo e Galleria Borghese

❶ Need to Know

Map p256; ☏06 3 28 10; www.galleriaborgh-ese.it; Piazzale del Museo Borghese 5; adult/reduced €15/8.50; ⏱9am-7pm Tue-Sun; 🚇Via Pinciana

✕ Take a Break

Stroll through Villa Borghese for a cocktail at Hotel de Russie's Stravinskij Bar (p170).

★ Top Tip

Remember to prebook your ticket, and take ID when you pick it up.

Entrance & Ground Floor

The **entrance hall** features 4th-century floor mosaics of fighting gladiators and a 2nd-century *Satiro Combattente* (Fighting Satyr). High on the wall is a gravity-defying bas-relief of a horse and rider falling into the void by Pietro Bernini (Gian Lorenzo's father).

Sala I is centred on Antonio Canova's daring depiction of Napoleon's sister, Paolina Bonaparte Borghese, reclining topless as *Venere Vincitrice* (Venus Victrix; 1805–08). Its suggestive pose and technical virtuosity is typical of Canova's elegant, mildly erotic neoclassical style.

But it's Gian Lorenzo Bernini's spectacular sculptures – flamboyant depictions of pagan myths – that really steal the show. Just look at Daphne's hands morphing into leaves in the swirling *Apollo e Dafne* (1622–25) in

Sala III, or Pluto's hand pressing into the seemingly soft flesh of Persephone's thigh in the *Ratto di Proserpina* (Rape of Proserpina; 1621–22) in **Sala IV**.

Caravaggio, one of Cardinal Scipione's favourite artists, dominates **Sala VIII**. You'll see a dissipated *Bacchino malato* (Young Sick Bacchus; 1593–94), the strangely beautiful *La Madonna dei Palafrenieri* (Madonna of the Palafrenieri; 1605–06), and *San Giovanni Battista* (St John the Baptist; 1609–10), probably the artist's last work.

Picture Gallery

Upstairs, the **pinacoteca** offers a wonderful snapshot of Renaissance art.

In **Sala IX** don't miss Raphael's extraordinary *La Deposizione di Cristo* (The Deposition; 1507) and his charming *Dama con Liocorno* (Lady with a Unicorn; 1506). In the same room you'll find Fra Bartolomeo's superb *Adorazione del Bambino* (Adoration of the Christ Child; 1499) and Perugino's

Madonna col Bambino (Madonna and Child; early 16th century).

Next door, Correggio's *Danäe* (1530–31) shares wall space with a willowy Venus, as portrayed by Cranach in his *Venere e Amore che Reca Il Favo do Miele* (Venus and Cupid with Honeycomb; 1531).

Other highlights include Correggio's erotic *Danae* (1530–31) in **Sala X**, Bernini's self-portraits in **Sala XIV**, and Titian's early masterpiece, *Amor Sacro e Amor Profano* (Sacred and Profane Love; 1514) in **Sala XX**.

What's Nearby?

Villa Borghese   Park

(Map p256; www.sovraintendenzaroma.it; entrances at Piazzale San Paolo del Brasile, Piazzale Flaminio, Via Pinciana, Via Raimondo, Largo Pablo Picasso; ⊙sunrise-sunset; 🚍Via Pinciana)

Villa Borghese

Locals, lovers, tourists, joggers – no one can resist the lure of Rome's most celebrated park. Originally the 17th-century estate of Cardinal Scipione Borghese, it covers about 80 hectares of wooded glades, gardens and grassy banks. Among its attractions are several excellent museums, the landscaped **Giardino del Lago** (Map p256; Villa Borghese; boat hire per 20min €3; ⊙7am-9pm summer, to 6pm winter; 🚍Via Pinciana), and **Piazza di Siena** (Map p256; Villa Borghese; 🚍Via Pinciana), a dusty arena used for Rome's top equestrian event in May.

Museo Nazionale
Etrusco di Villa Giulia   Museum

(Map p256; ☎06 322 65 71; www.villagiulia. beniculturali.it; Piazzale di Villa Giulia; adult/ reduced €8/4; ⊙8.30am-7.30pm Tue-Sun; 🚍Via delle Belle Arti) Pope Julius III's 16th-century

villa provides the charming setting for Italy's finest collection of Etruscan and pre-Roman treasures. Exhibits, many of which came from burial tombs in the surrounding Lazio region, range from bronze figurines and black *bucchero* tableware to temple decorations, terracotta vases and a dazzling display of sophisticated jewellery.

Must-sees include a polychrome terracotta statue of Apollo, the 6th-century-BC *Sarcofago degli Sposi* (Sarcophagus of the Betrothed), and the *Euphronios Krater,* a celebrated Greek vase.

★ Top Tip

Monday is not a good time for exploring Villa Borghese. Sure, you can walk in the park, but its museums and galleries are all shut – they are only open Tuesday to Sunday.

PHANT/GETTY IMAGES ©

La Galleria Nazionale   Gallery

(Map p256; ☎06 3229 8221; http://lagalleria nazionale.com; Viale delle Belle Arti 131, accessible entrance Via Antonio Gramsci 71; adult/reduced €10/5; ⊗8.30am-7.30pm Tue-Sun; 🚊Piazza Thorvaldsen) Housed in a vast belle époque palace, this oft-overlooked gallery is an unsung gem. Its superlative collection runs the gamut from neoclassical sculpture to abstract expressionism with works by many of the most important exponents of 19th- and 20th-century art.

Pincio Hill Gardens   Gardens

(Map p256; Ⓜ Flaminio) Overlooking Piazza del Popolo, the 19th-century Pincio Hill is named after the Pinci family, who owned this part of Rome in the 4th century. It's quite a climb up from the piazza, but at the top you're rewarded with lovely views over to St Peter's and the Gianicolo Hill. Alternatively, you can approach from the top of the Spanish Steps. From the gardens you can strike out to explore Villa Borghese, the Villa dei Medici, or the Chiesa della Trinità dei Monti at the top of the Spanish Steps.

Museo Carlo Bilotti   Gallery

(Map p256; ☎06 06 08; www.museocarlobilotti. it; Viale Fiorello La Guardia; ⊗10am-4pm Tue-Fri, 10am-7pm Sat & Sun winter, 1-7pm Tue-Fri, 10am-7pm Sat & Sun summer; 🚊Via Pinciana) FREE The Orangery of Villa Borghese provides the handsome setting for the art collection of billionaire cosmetics magnate Carlo Bilotti. The main focus are 18 works by Giorgio de Chirico (1888–1978), one of Italy's foremost modern artists, but also of note is a Warhol portrait of Bilotti's wife and daughter.

❶ Local Knowledge

For unforgettable views over Rome's rooftops and domes, make your way to the Pincio Hill Gardens in the southwest of Villa Borghese.

Palatino

Rising above the Roman Forum, the Palatino (Palatine Hill) is an atmospheric area of towering pine trees, majestic ruins and memorable views. According to legend, this is where Romulus and Remus were saved by a wolf and where Romulus founded Rome in 753 BC. Archaeological evidence can't prove the myth, but it has dated human habitation here to the 8th century BC.

Great For...

❶ Need to Know

Palatine Hill; Map p246; ☏06 3996 7700; www.coopculture.it; Via di San Gregorio 30, Piazza di Santa Maria Nova; adult/reduced incl Colosseum & Roman Forum €12/7.50; ⊙8.30am-1hr before sunset; Ⓜ Colosseo

★ **Top Tip**

The best spot for a picnic is the grassy Vigna Barberini near the Orti Farnesiani.

The Palatino was ancient Rome's most exclusive neighbourhood. The emperor Augustus lived here all his life and successive emperors built increasingly opulent palaces. But after Rome's fall, it fell into disrepair, and in the Middle Ages churches and castles were built over the ruins. Later, wealthy Renaissance families established gardens on the hill.

Most of the Palatino as it appears today is covered by the ruins of the emperor Domitian's 1st-century complex, which served as the main imperial palace for 300 years.

Stadio

On entering the Palatino from Via di San Gregorio, head uphill until you come to the first recognisable construction, the *stadio*. This sunken area, which was part

of the main imperial palace, was used by the emperor for private games. To the southeast of the stadium are the remains of a complex built by Septimius Severus, comprising baths – **Terme di Settimio Severo** – and a palace – **Domus Severiana** – where, if they're open, you can visit the **Arcate Severiane** (Severian Arches; ☎06 3996 7700; www.coopculture.it; admission incl in Palatino ticket; ⏱8.30am-4pm Tue, Thu & Fri), a series of arches built to facilitate further development.

Domus Augustana, Museo Palatino & Domus Flavia

Next to the *stadio* are the ruins of the **Domus Augustana** (Emperor's Residence), the emperor's private quarters in the imperial palace. Over two levels, rooms lead off a *peristilio* (porticoed courtyard) on

Domus Augustana

each floor. You can't get to the lower level, but from above you can see the basin of a fountain.

The grey building next to the Domus Augustana houses the **Museo Palatino** (admission incl in Palatino ticket; ◔8.30am-1½hr before sunset), which holds a small collection of finds from the Palatino. The downstairs section illustrates the history of the hill from its origins to the Republican age, while upstairs you'll find artefacts from the Imperial age, including a beautiful 1st-century bronze, the *Erma di Canefora*.

MARCPO/GETTY IMAGES ©

Over on the other side of the Museo Palatino is the **Domus Flavia**, the public part of the palace. The Domus was centred on a grand columned peristyle – the grassy area with the base of an octagonal fountain – off which the main halls led.

Casa di Livia & Casa di Augusto

Among the best-preserved buildings on the Palatino is the **Casa di Livia** (☎06 3996 7700; www.coopculture.it; incl Casa di Augusto visit/guided tour €4/9; ◔visits 12.45pm daily, pre-booking necessary), northwest of the Domus Flavia. Home to Augustus' wife Livia, it was built around an atrium leading onto what were once frescoed reception rooms. Nearby, the **Casa di Augusto**, Augustus' separate residence, contains superb frescoes in vivid reds, yellows and blues.

Criptoportico

Northeast of the Casa di Livia lies the **criptoportico**, a 128m tunnel where Caligula is said to have been murdered, and which Nero used to connect his Domus Aurea with the Palatino. It is now used for temporary exhibitions.

Orti Farnesiani

Covering the Domus Tiberiana (Tiberius' palace) in the northwest of the Palatino, the **Orti Farnesiani** is one of Europe's earliest botanical gardens. Named after Cardinal Alessandro Farnese, who had it laid out in the mid-16th century, it commands breathtaking views over the Roman Forum.

✕ **Take a Break**

On the Circo Massimo, 0,75 (p168) is an attractive spot for an evening *aperitivo*.

Piazza Navona

With its ornate fountains, exuberant baroque palazzi (mansions) and pavement cafes, Piazza Navona is central Rome's elegant showcase square. Long a hub of local life, it hosted Rome's main market for close on 300 years, and today attracts a colourful daily circus of street performers, hawkers, artists, tourists, fortune-tellers and pigeons.

Great For...

ⓘ Need to Know

Map p250; 🚇Corso del Rinascimento

★ **Top Tip**
Each December the piazza hosts a
traditional Christmas market.

Stadio di Domiziano

Like many of Rome's landmarks, the piazza sits over an ancient monument. The 30,000-seat **Stadio di Domiziano** (Domitian's Stadium; ☎06 4568 6100; www.stadio domiziano.com; Via di Tor Sanguigna 3; adult/reduced €8/6; ⏰10am-7pm Sun-Fri, to 8pm Sat), the subterranean remains of which can be accessed from Via di Tor Sanguigna, once hosted athletic meets – hence the name Navona, a corruption of the Greek word *agon,* meaning public games.

Fountains

The piazza's grand centrepiece is Bernini's **Fontana dei Quattro Fiumi** (Fountain of the Four Rivers), a showy fountain featuring four muscular personifications of the rivers Nile, Ganges, Danube and Rió de la Plata.

The **Fontana del Moro** at the southern end of the square was designed by Giacomo della Porta in 1576.

At the northern end of the piazza, the 19th-century **Fontana del Nettuno** depicts Neptune fighting with a sea monster, surrounded by sea nymphs.

Main Buildings

Overlooking Bernini's Fontana dei Quattro Fiumi, is the **Chiesa di Sant'Agnese in Agone** (Map p250; ☎06 6819 2134; www.santagneseinagone.org; concerts €13; ⏰9.30am-12.30pm & 3.30-7pm Tue-Sat, 9am-1pm & 4-8pm Sun; 🚌Corso del Rinascimento), an elaborate baroque church designed by Francesco Borromini.

Located further down, the 17th-century **Palazzo Pamphilj** (Map p250; http://roma.itamaraty.gov.br/it; ⏰by reservation only; 🚌Corso del Rinascimento) was built for Pope Innocent X and now houses the Brazilian Embassy.

What's Nearby?

Chiesa di San Luigi dei Francesi
Church

(Map p250; Piazza di San Luigi dei Francesi 5; ⊗9.30am-12.45pm & 2.30-6.30pm Mon-Fri, 9.30am-12.15pm & 2.30-6.45pm Sat, 11.30am-12.45pm & 2.30-6.45pm Sun; ⊡Corso del Rinascimento) Church to Rome's French community since 1589, this opulent baroque *chiesa* is home to a celebrated trio of Caravaggio paintings: the *Vocazione di San Matteo* (The Calling of Saint Matthew), the *Martirio di San Matteo* (The Martyrdom of Saint Matthew) and *San Matteo e l'angelo* (Saint Matthew and the Angel), known collectively as the St Matthew cycle.

> ☑ **Don't Miss**
> Bernini's Fontana dei Quattro Fiumi, the piazza's high-camp central fountain.

S.BORISOV/SHUTTERSTOCK ©

Museo Nazionale Romano: Palazzo Altemps
Museum

(Map p250; ☑06 3996 7700; www.coopculture. it; Piazza Sant'Apollinare 44; adult/reduced €7/3.50; ⊗9am-7.45pm Tue-Sun; ⊡Corso del Rinascimento) Just north of Piazza Navona, Palazzo Altemps is a beautiful late-15th-century *palazzo*, housing the best of the Museo Nazionale Romano's formidable collection of classical sculpture. Many pieces come from the celebrated Ludovisi collection, amassed by Cardinal Ludovico Ludovisi in the 17th century.

Campo de' Fiori
Piazza

(Map p250; ⊡Corso Vittorio Emanuele II) Noisy, colourful 'Il Campo' is a major focus of Roman life: by day it hosts one of Rome's best-known markets, while at night it morphs into a raucous open-air pub. For centuries the square was the site of public executions, and it was here that the philosopher Giordano Bruno was burned at the stake for heresy in 1600. The spot is marked by a sinister statue of the hooded monk, created by Ettore Ferrari and unveiled in 1889.

Triumphs and Laments
Public Art

(Map p250; Lungotevere della Farnesina; ⊡Lungotevere dei Tebaldi) A bold new addition to Rome's cityscape, this vast frieze adorns the Tiber river walls between Ponte Sisto and Ponte Mazzini. The creation of South African artist William Kentridge, it stretches for 550m and comprises more than 80 figures, some that are up to 12m high, illustrating episodes from Rome's history. Look for depictions of Roman emperor Marcus Aurelius, Mussolini, and actor Marcello Mastroianni who's shown kissing Anita Ekberg in a recreation of the famous Trevi Fountain scene from *La Dolce Vita*.

> ✗ **Take a Break**
> Stroll south to view the *Triumphs and Laments* mural, with a stop en route at gorgeous Pianostrada (p125).

Fresco from Villa Livia (p68)

Museo Nazionale Romano: Palazzo Massimo alle Terme

Every day, thousands of tourists, commuters and passers-by hurry past this neo-Renaissance palazzo without giving it a second glance. They don't know what they're missing. This is one of Rome's great museums, and a treasure trove of classical art. The sculpture here is truly impressive, but what really takes the breath away is the collection of vibrantly coloured frescoes and mosaics.

Great For...

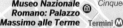

ℹ **Need to Know**

Map p252; ☎06 3996 7700; www.coopculture.it; Largo di Villa Peretti 1; adult/reduced €7/3.50; ⊙9am-7.45pm Tue-Sun; Ⓜ Termini

★ **Top Tip**
Your ticket (valid for three days) also gives admission to the other three sites of the Museo Nazionale Romano.

Sculpture

The ground and 1st floors are devoted to sculpture, examining imperial portraiture as propaganda and including some breathtaking works of art.

Ground-floor show-stoppers include the 5th-century-BC *Niobide morente* (Dying Niobid) and two 2nd-century Greek bronzes – the *Pugile* (Boxer) and the *Principe ellenistico* (Hellenistic Prince). Upstairs, look out for *Il discobolo* (Discus Thrower), a muscular 2nd-century copy of an ancient Greek work. Another admirable body belongs to the graceful *Ermafrodite dormiente* (Sleeping Hermaphrodite).

Also fascinating are the elaborate bronze fittings that belonged to Caligula's ceremonial ships.

Frescoes & Mosaics

On the 2nd floor you'll find the museum's thrilling exhibition of ancient mosaics and frescoes. These vibrantly coloured panels were originally used as interior decor and provide a more complete picture of the inside of a grand ancient Roman villa than you'll see anywhere else in the world. There are intimate *cubicula* (bedroom) frescoes focusing on nature, mythology, domestic and sensual life, and delicate landscape paintings from the winter triclinium (dining room).

The museum's crowning glory is a room of **frescoes from Villa Livia**, one of the homes of Augustus' wife Livia Drusilla. The frescoes depict a paradisiacal garden full of a wild tangle of roses, violets, pomegranates, irises and camomile under a deep-blue sky. These decorated a summer triclinium, a large living and

Below left: *Abduction of Hylas* panel detail; Below right: *Sleeping Hermaphrodite*

DEA/ARCHIVIO J. LANGE/CONTRIBUTOR/GETTY IMAGES ©

dining area built half underground to provide protection from the heat. The lighting mimics the modulation of daylight and highlights the richness of the millennia-old colours.

Basement

The basement contains a coin collection tracing the Roman Empire's use of coins for propaganda purposes; it's far more absorbing than you might expect. There's also jewellery dating back several millennia that looks as good as new, and the disturbing remains of a mummified eight-year-old girl, the only known example of mummification dating from the Roman Empire.

☑ Don't Miss

The athletic pose of the discus thrower, *Il Discobolo,* an aborbing homage to the male physique.

DEA/ARCHIVIO J. LANGE/CONTRIBUTOR/GETTY IMAGES ©

What's Nearby?

Museo Nazionale Romano: Terme di Diocleziano   Museum

(Map p252; ☑06 3996 7700; www.coopculture.it; Viale Enrico de Nicola 78; adult/reduced €7/3.50; ☺9am-7.30pm Tue-Sun; Ⓜ Termini) The Terme di Diocleziano was ancient Rome's largest bath complex, covering about 13 hectares and with a capacity for 3000 people. Today its ruins constitute part of the impressive Museo Nazionale Romano. This branch of the National Roman Museum supplies a fascinating insight into Roman life through memorial inscriptions and other artefacts. Outside, the vast, elegant cloister was constructed from drawings by Michelangelo.

Chiesa di Santa Maria della Vittoria   Church

(Map p252; ☑06 4274 0571; Via XX Settembre 17; ☺8.30am-noon & 3.30-6pm; Ⓜ Repubblica) This modest church is an unlikely setting for an extraordinary work of art – Bernini's extravagant and sexually charged *Santa Teresa trafitta dall'amore di Dio* (Ecstasy of St Teresa). This sculpture depicts Teresa, engulfed in the folds of a cloak, floating in ecstasy on a cloud while a teasing angel pierces her repeatedly with a golden arrow.

Palazzo Barberini   Gallery

(Galleria Nazionale d'Arte Antica; Map p252; ☑06 481 45 91; www.barberinicorsini.org; Via delle Quattro Fontane 13; adult/reduced €5/2.50, incl Palazzo Corsini €10/5; ☺8.30am-7pm Tue-Sun; Ⓜ Barberini) Commissioned to celebrate the Barberini family's rise to papal power, Palazzo Barberini is a sumptuous baroque palace that impresses even before you go inside and start on the breathtaking art. Many high-profile architects worked on it, including rivals Bernini and Borromini: the former contributed a large squared staircase, the latter a helicoidal one.

✕ Take a Break

Head to the recently opened Mercato Centrale (p133) for a range of tempting snack stalls.

Capitoline Museums

Dating to 1471, the Capitoline Museums are the world's oldest public museums. Their collection of classical sculpture is one of Italy's finest, including crowd-pleasers such as the iconic Lupa capitolina (Capitoline Wolf), and the formidable picture gallery includes masterpieces by the likes of Titian, Tintoretto, Rubens and Caravaggio.

Great For...

ⓘ Need to Know

Musei Capitolini; Map p246; ☑06 06 08; www. museicapitolini.org; Piazza del Campidoglio 1; adult/reduced €11.50/9.50; ⊙9.30am-7.30pm, last admission 6.30pm; ⎅Piazza Venezia

★ **Top Tip**

In a tunnel between the two *palazzi*, the Tabularium commands inspiring views over the Roman Forum.

The museums occupy two stately *palazzi* on **Piazza del Campidoglio**. The entrance is in **Palazzo dei Conservatori**, where you'll find the original core of the sculptural collection and the Pinacoteca (picture gallery).

Palazzo dei Conservatori: 1st Floor

Before you start on the sculpture collection proper, check out the marble body parts littered around the ground-floor **courtyard**. The mammoth head, hand and feet all belonged to a 12m-high statue of Constantine that stood in the Basilica di Massenzio in the Roman Forum.

Of the sculpture on the 1st floor, the Etruscan *Lupa capitolina* (Capitoline Wolf) is the most famous. Dating to the 5th century BC, the bronze wolf stands over her

suckling wards, Romulus and Remus, who were added in 1471.

Other popular pieces include the *Spinario,* a delicate 1st-century-BC bronze of a boy removing a thorn from his foot, and Gian Lorenzo Bernini's *Medusa* bust.

Also on this floor, in the modern **Esedra di Marco Aurelio**, is the original of the equestrian statue that stands outside in Piazza del Campidoglio.

Palazzo dei Conservatori: 2nd Floor

The 2nd floor is given over to the **Pinacoteca**, the museum's picture gallery. Each room harbours masterpieces, but two stand out: the **Sala Pietro da Cortona**, which features Pietro da Cortona's famous depiction of the *Ratto delle sabine* (Rape of the Sabine Women; 1630), and the **Sala di**

Detail of sculpted wall figures

Santa Petronilla, named after Guercino's huge canvas *Seppellimento di Santa Petronilla* (The Burial of St Petronilla; 1621–23). This airy hall also boasts two works by Caravaggio: *La Buona Ventura* (The Fortune Teller; 1595) and *San Giovanni Battista* (John the Baptist; 1602).

Tabularium

A tunnel links Palazzo dei Conservatori to Palazzo Nuovo via the Tabularium, ancient Rome's central archive, beneath **Palazzo Senatorio**.

☑ **Don't Miss**

The touching depiction of the *Galata morente* (Dying Gaul) in the Sala del Gladiatore in Palazzo Nuovo.

JUSTIN FOULKES/LONELY PLANET ©

Palazzo Nuovo

Palazzo Nuovo contains some unforgettable show-stoppers. Chief among them is the *Galata morente* (Dying Gaul), a Roman copy of a 3rd-century-BC Greek original that movingly depicts the anguish of a dying Gaul warrior. Another superb figurative piece is the *Venere capitolina* (Capitoline Venus), a sensual yet demure portrayal of the nude goddess.

What's Nearby?

Il Vittoriano　　　　　　Monument
(Victor Emmanuel Monument; Map p246; Piazza Venezia; ⊘9.30am-5.30pm summer, to 4.30pm winter; 🚊Piazza Venezia) FREE Love it or loathe it, as most locals do, you can't ignore Il Vittoriano (aka the Altare della Patria; Altar of the Fatherland), the massive mountain of white marble that towers over Piazza Venezia. Begun in 1885 to honour Italy's first king, Victor Emmanuel II, it incorporates the **Museo Centrale del Risorgimento** (Map p246; ☏06 679 35 98; www.risorgimento.it; Vittoriano, Piazza Venezia; adult/reduced €5/2.50; ⊘9.30am-6.30pm; 🚊Piazza Venezia), a small museum documenting Italian unification, and the **Tomb of the Unknown Soldier**. For Rome's best 360-degree views, take the **Roma dal Cielo** (Map p246; Vittoriano, Piazza Venezia; adult/reduced €7/3.50; ⊘9.30am-7.30pm, last admission 7pm; 🚊Piazza Venezia) lift to the top.

Bocca della Verità　　　　Monument
(Mouth of Truth; Map p254; Piazza Bocca della Verità 18; ⊘9.30am-5.50pm; 🚊Piazza Bocca della Verità) A bearded face carved into a giant marble disc, the *Bocca della Verità* is one of Rome's most popular curiosities. Legend has it that if you put your hand in the mouth and tell a lie, the Bocca will slam shut and bite your hand off. The mouth now lives in the **Chiesa di Santa Maria in Cosmedin**.

✗ **Take a Break**

Head up to the 2nd floor of Palazzo dei Conservatori for a bite at the panoramic Terrazza Caffarelli (p122).

Via Appia Antica

Ancient Rome's regina viarum (queen of roads) is now one of Rome's most exclusive addresses, a beautiful cobbled thoroughfare flanked by grassy fields, ancient ruins and towering pine trees. But it has a dark history – it was here that Spartacus and 6000 of his slave rebels were crucified, and also here that the early Christians buried their dead in the underground catacombs.

Great For...

❶ Need to Know

Appian Way; ☎ 06 513 53 16; www.parcoappia antica.it; ⏱ Info Point 9.30am-sunset summer, 9.30am-1pm & 2-5pm Mon-Fri, 9.30am-5pm Sat & Sun winter; 🚍 Via Appia Antica

★ **Top Tip**

The stretch of road near the Basilica di San Sebastiano is traffic-free on Sundays.

Heading southeast from Porta San Sebastiano, Via Appia Antica was named after Appius Claudius Caecus, who laid the first 90km section in 312 BC. It was later extended in 190 BC to reach Brindisi, some 540km away on the southern Adriatic coast.

Catacombe di San Sebastiano

The **Catacombe di San Sebastiano** (06 785 03 50; www.catacombe.org; Via Appia Antica 136; adult/reduced €8/5; 10am-5pm Mon-Sat Jan-Nov) were the first burial chambers to be called catacombs, the name deriving from the Greek *kata* (near) and *kymbas* (cavity), because they were located near a cave. During the persecutory reign of Vespasian from AD 258, they are said to have provided a safe haven for the remains of Sts Peter and Paul.

The 1st level is now almost completely destroyed, but frescoes, stucco work and epigraphs can be seen on the 2nd level. There are also three perfectly preserved mausoleums and a plastered wall with hundreds of invocations to Peter and Paul, engraved by worshippers in the 3rd and 4th centuries.

Above the catacombs, the **Basilica di San Sebastiano** preserves one of the arrows allegedly used to kill St Sebastian, and the column to which he was tied.

Catacombe di San Callisto

These are the largest and busiest of Rome's catacombs. Founded at the end of the 2nd century and named after Pope Calixtus I, the **Catacombe di San Callisto** (06 513 01 51; www.catacombe.roma.it; Via Appia Antica 110-126; adult/reduced €8/5; 9am-noon &

Bas relief along Via Appia Antica

2-5pm Thu-Tue Mar-Jan; ☐Via Appia Antica) became the official cemetery of the newly established Roman Church. In the 20km of tunnels explored to date, archaeologists have found the tombs of 16 popes, dozens of martyrs and thousands upon thousands of Christians.

The patron saint of music, St Cecilia, was also buried here, though her body was later removed to the Basilica di Santa Cecilia in Trastevere. When her body was exhumed in 1599, more than a thousand years after her death, it was apparently perfectly preserved.

☑ Don't Miss

The ruins of Villa di Massenzio, which litter the green fields by the side of the cobbled road.

Catacombe di Santa Domitilla

Among Rome's largest and oldest, the **Catacombe di Santa Domitilla** (☏06 511 03 42; www.domitilla.info; Via delle Sette Chiese 282; adult/reduced €8/5; ⊙9am-noon & 2-5pm Wed-Mon mid-Jan–mid-Dec) were established on the private burial ground of Flavia Domitilla, niece of the emperor Domitian. They contain Christian wall paintings and the haunting underground **Chiesa di SS Nereus e Achilleus**, a 4th-century church dedicated to two Roman soldiers martyred by Diocletian.

What's Nearby?

Mausoleo di Cecilia Metella   Ruins

(☏06 3996 7700; www.coopculture.it; Via Appia Antica 161; adult/reduced incl Terme di Caracalla & Villa dei Quintili €6/3; ⊙9am-1hr before sunset Tue-Sun; ☐Via Appia Antica) Dating to the 1st century BC, this great drum of a mausoleum encloses a burial chamber, now roofless. In the 14th century it was converted into a fort by the Caetani family, who were related to Pope Boniface VIII, and used to frighten passing traffic into paying a toll.

Villa di Massenzio   Ruins

(☏06 06 08; www.villadimassenzio.it; Via Appia Antica 153; ⊙10am-4pm Tue-Sun; ☐Via Appia Antica) **FREE** The outstanding feature of Maxentius' enormous 4th-century palace complex is the **Circo di Massenzio** (Via Appia Antica 153; ☐Via Appia Antica), Rome's best-preserved ancient racetrack – you can still make out the starting stalls used for chariot races. The 10,000-seat arena was built by Maxentius around 309, but he died before ever seeing a race here.

ALESSANDRO0770/GETTY IMAGES ©

✕ Take a Break

Fill your belly at the elegant L'Archeologia Ristorante (p141), housed in a 19th-century inn.

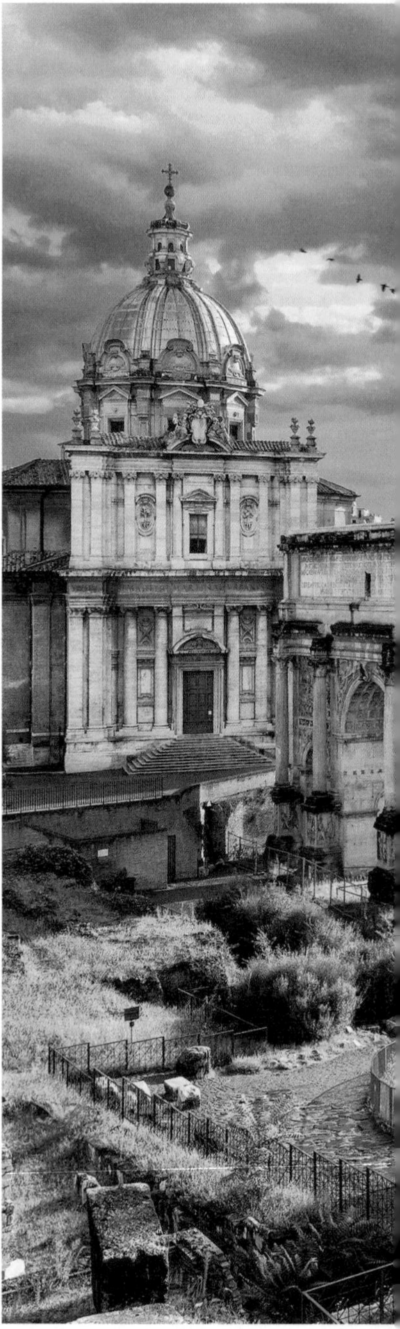

Roman Forum

The Roman Forum was ancient Rome's showpiece centre, a grandiose district of temples, basilicas and vibrant public spaces. Nowadays, it's a collection of impressive but poorly labelled ruins that can leave you drained and confused. But if you can get your imagination going, there's something wonderfully compelling about walking in the footsteps of Julius Caesar and other legendary figures of Roman history.

Great For...

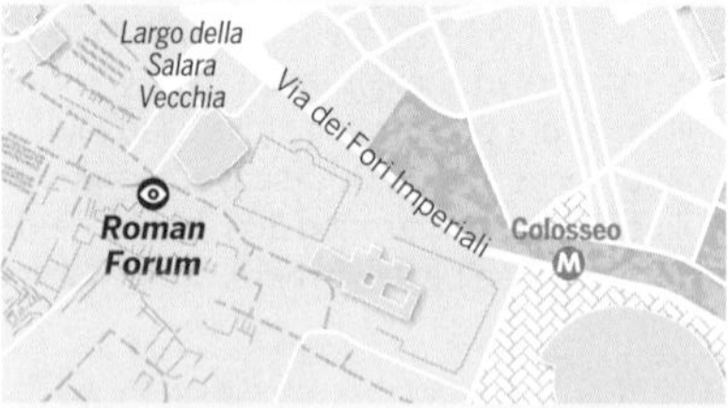

Need to Know

Foro Romano; Map p246; ☎06 3996 7700; www.coopculture.it; Largo della Salara Vecchia, Piazza di Santa Maria Nova; adult/reduced incl Colosseum & Palatino €12/7.50; ⊙8.30am-1hr before sunset; 🚌Via dei Fori Imperiali

★ **Top Tip**
Exit near the Arco di Settimio Severo to continue up to Campidoglio and the Capitoline Museums.

Originally an Etruscan burial ground, the Forum was first developed in the 7th century BC, growing over time to become the social, political and commercial hub of the Roman Empire. In the Middle Ages it was reduced to pasture land and extensively plundered for its marble. The area was systematically excavated in the 18th and 19th centuries and work continues to this day.

Via Sacra to Campidoglio

Entering the Forum from Largo della Salara Vecchia, you'll see the **Tempio di Antonino e Faustina** ahead to your left. Erected in AD 141, this was transformed into a church in the 8th century, the **Chiesa di San Lorenzo in Miranda**. To your right is the 179 BC **Basilica Fulvia Aemilia**.

At the end of the path, you'll come to **Via Sacra**, the Forum's main thoroughfare, and the **Tempio di Giulio Cesare** (Tempio del Divo Giulio), which stands on the spot where Julius Caesar was cremated.

Heading right brings you to the **Curia**, the original seat of the Roman Senate, though what you see today is a reconstruction of how it looked in the reign of Diocletian (r 284–305).

At the end of Via Sacra, the **Arco di Settimio Severo** (Arch of Septimius Severus) is dedicated to the eponymous emperor and his sons, Caracalla and Geta. Close by, the **Colonna di Foca** (Column of Phocus) rises above what was once the Forum's main square, **Piazza del Foro**.

The eight granite columns that rise behind the Colonna are all that survive of the **Tempio di Saturno** (Temple of Saturn), an important temple that doubled as the state treasury.

Tempio di Castore e Polluce & Casa delle Vestali

From the path that runs parallel to Via Sacra, you'll pass the stubby ruins of the **Basilica Giulia**. At the end of the basilica, three columns remain from the 5th-century-BC **Tempio di Castore e Polluce** (Temple of Castor and Pollux).

Back towards Via Sacra is the **Casa delle Vestali** (House of the Vestal Virgins), home of the virgins who tended the flame in the adjoining **Tempio di Vesta**.

Via Sacra Towards the Colosseum

Heading up Via Sacra past the **Tempio di Romolo** (Temple of Romulus; Largo della Salara Vecchia, 🚌Via dei Fori Imperiali), you'll come to the **Basilica di Massenzio** (Basilica di Costantino; Map p246; Piazza di Santa Maria Nova; 🚌Via dei Fori Imperiali), the largest building on the forum.

Beyond the basilica, the **Arco di Tito** (Arch of Titus; Map p246; Piazza di Santa Maria Nova; 🚌Via dei Fori Imperiali) was built in AD 81 to celebrate Vespasian and Titus' victories against rebels in Jerusalem.

What's Nearby?

Imperial Forums   Archaeological Site
(Fori Imperiali; Map p246; Via dei Fori Imperiali; 🚌Via dei Fori Imperiali) The forums of Trajan, Augustus, Nerva and Caesar are known collectively as the Imperial Forums. These were largely buried when Mussolini bulldozed Via dei Fori Imperiali through the area in 1933, but excavations have since unearthed much of them. The standout sights are the Mercati di Traiano (Trajan's Markets), accessible through the Museo dei Fori Imperiali, and the landmark **Colonna di Traiano** (Trajan's Column).

Mercati di Traiano Museo dei Fori Imperiali   Museum
(Map p246; 📞06 06 08; www.mercatiditraiano.it; Via IV Novembre 94; adult/reduced €11.50/9.50; ⏰9.30am-7.30pm, last admission 6.30pm; 🚌Via IV Novembre) This striking museum brings to life the Mercati di Traiano, emperor Trajan's great 2nd-century market complex, while also providing a fascinating introduction to the Imperial Forums with multimedia displays, explanatory panels and a smattering of archaeological artefacts.

> ☑ **Don't Miss**
> The Basilica di Massenzio, to get some idea of the scale of ancient Rome's mammoth buildings.

TREVOR COLLENS/ALAMY STOCK PHOTO ©

> ✕ **Take a Break**
> Alongside its views of the Colonna di Traiano, Terre e Domus (p122) offers regional dishes and Lazio wines.

Roman Forum

A HISTORICAL TOUR

In ancient times, a forum was a market place, civic centre and religious complex all rolled into one, and the greatest of all was the Roman Forum (Foro Romano). Situated between the Palatino (Palatine Hill), ancient Rome's most exclusive neighbourhood, and the Campidoglio (Capitoline Hill), it was the city's busy, bustling centre. On any given day it teemed with activity. Senators debated affairs of state in the **❶ Curia**, shoppers thronged the squares and traffic-free streets and crowds gathered under the **❷ Colonna di Foca** to listen to politicians holding forth from the **❷ Rostrum**. Elsewhere, lawyers worked the courts in basilicas including the **❸ Basilica di Massenzio**, while the Vestal Virgins quietly went about their business in the **❹ Casa delle Vestali**.

Special occasions were also celebrated in the Forum: religious holidays were marked with ceremonies at temples such as **❺ Tempio di Saturno** and **❻ Tempio di Castore e Polluce**, and military victories were honoured with dramatic processions up Via Sacra and the building of monumental arches like **❼ Arco di Settimio Severo** and **❽ Arco di Tito**.

The ruins you see today are impressive but they can be confusing without a clear picture of what the Forum once looked like. This spread shows the Forum in its heyday, complete with temples, civic buildings and towering monuments to heroes of the Roman Empire.

TOP TIPS

➡ Get grandstand views of the Forum from the Palatino and Campidoglio.

➡ Visit first thing in the morning or late afternoon; crowds are worst between 11am and 2pm.

➡ In summer it gets hot in the Forum and there's little shade, so take a hat and plenty of water.

Colonna di Foca & Rostrum

The free-standing, 13.5m-high Column of Phocus is the Forum's youngest monument, dating to AD 608. Behind it, the Rostrum provided a suitably grandiose platform for pontificating public speakers.

Campidoglio (Capitoline Hill)

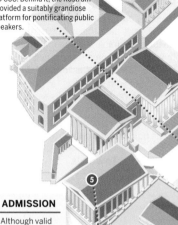

ADMISSION

Although valid for two days, admission tickets only allow for one entry into the Forum, Colosseum and Palatino.

Tempio di Saturno

Ancient Rome's Fort Knox, the Temple of Saturn was the city treasury. In Caesar's day it housed 13 tonnes of gold, 114 tonnes of silver and 30 million sestertii worth of silver coins.

IASCIC/SHUTTERSTOCK ©

VIACHESLAV LOPATIN/SHUTTERSTOCK ©

Tempio di Castore e Polluce

Only three columns of the Temple of Castor and Pollux remain. The temple was dedicated to the Heavenly Twins after they supposedly led the Romans to victory over the Latin League in 496 BC.

Arco di Settimio Severo

One of the Forum's signature monuments, this imposing triumphal arch commemorates the military victories of Septimius Severus. Relief panels depict his campaigns against the Parthians.

Curia

This big barn-like building was the official seat of the Roman Senate. Most of what you see is a reconstruction, but the interior marble floor dates to the 3rd-century reign of Diocletian.

Basilica di Massenzio

Marvel at the scale of this vast 4th-century basilica. In its original form the central hall was divided into enormous naves; now only part of the northern nave survives.

JULIUS CAESAR

Julius Caesar was cremated on the site where the Tempio di Giulio Cesare now stands.

①

⑦

②

Via Sacra

③

⑥

Tempio di Giulio Cesare

④

⑧

Arco di Tito

Said to be the inspiration for the Arc de Triomphe in Paris, the well-preserved Arch of Titus was built by the emperor Domitian to honour his elder brother Titus.

Casa delle Vestali

White statues line the grassy atrium of what was once the luxurious 50-room home of the Vestal Virgins. The virgins played an important role in Roman religion, serving the goddess Vesta.

Trevi Fountain

The Fontana di Trevi is Rome's largest and most celebrated fountain. A foaming ensemble of mythical figures, wild horses and cascading rock falls, it takes up the entire side of the 17th-century Palazzo Poli.

Great For...

☑ Don't Miss

The contrasting horses – one tempestuous, one calm – which depict the moods of the sea.

Immortalised by Federico Fellini's film *La Dolce Vita* – apparently Anita Ekberg wore waders under her iconic black ballgown when she took her famous dip – the Trevi Fountain is one of Rome's must-see sights. It was completed in 1762 and named Trevi in reference to the *tre vie* (three roads) that converge on it.

Today the water continues to be sourced from the Aqua Virgo, an underground aqueduct built by General Agrippa during the reign of Augustus some 2000 years ago. The water flows in from the Salone springs around 19km away.

The Design

The fountain's design, conceived by Nicola Salvi in 1732, depicts Neptune, the god of the sea, in a shell-shaped chariot being led by Tritons and two sea horses, one wild,

Statue of Neptune

Via del Corso · Via del Tritone · Via del Traforo · Barberini Ⓜ · Piazza Colonna · **Trevi Fountain** · Giardino del Quirinale · Via delle Muratte

❶ Need to Know

Fontana di Trevi; Map p252; Piazza di Trevi; ⓂBarberini

✖ Take a Break

For a top-notch gourmet lunch, make for Le Tamerici (p129).

★ Top Tip

Come at the crack of dawn to avoid the crowds, or late afternoon when the fountain's dazzling white stone photographs best.

one docile, representing the moods of the sea. In the niche to the left of Neptune, a statue represents Abundance; to the right is Salubrity.

On the eastern side is a strange conical urn. Known as the *Assso di coppe* (Ace of Cups), this was supposedly placed by Nicola Salvi to block the view of a busybody barber who had been a vocal critic of Salvi's design during the fountain's construction.

Throw In Your Money

The famous tradition (since the 1954 film *Three Coins in the Fountain*) is to toss a coin into the water and thus ensure you'll one day return to Rome. About €3000 is thrown in on an average day. For years much of this was scooped up by local thieves, but in 2012 the city authorities clamped down, making it illegal to remove coins from the water. The money is now collected daily and handed over to the Catholic charity Caritas.

What's Nearby?
Palazzo del Quirinale   Palace

(Map p252; ☎06 3996 7557; www.quirinale.it; Piazza del Quirinale; 1¼hr tour €1.50, 2½hr tour adult/reduced €10/5; ⊙9.30am-4pm Tue, Wed & Fri-Sun, closed Aug; ⓂBarberini) Overlooking Piazza del Quirinale, this immense palace is the official residence of Italy's head of state, the Presidente della Repubblica. For almost three centuries it was the pope's summer residence, but in 1870 Pope Pius IX begrudgingly handed the keys over to Italy's new king. Later, in 1948, it was given to the Italian state.

MARIA GOLOVIANKO/SHUTTERSTOCK ©

Basilica di Santa Maria del Popolo

A magnificent repository of art, this is one of Rome's earliest and richest Renaissance churches, with lavish chapels decorated by artists including Caravaggio, Bernini, Raphael and Pinturicchio.

Great For...

☑ Don't Miss

As all eyes are turned on Caravaggio's canvases, don't miss Pinturicchio's wonderful frescoes.

The first chapel was built here in 1099 to exorcise the ghost of Nero, who was secretly buried on this spot and whose spectre was thought to haunt the area. The church's most important makeover came when Bramante renovated the presbytery and choir in the early 16th century and Pinturicchio added a series of frescoes. Bernini further reworked the church in the 17th century.

Cerasi Chapel

The church's highlight is the Cappella Cerasi, which has two works by Caravaggio: the *Conversion of Saul* and the *Crucifixion of St Peter,* dramatically spotlit via the artist's use of light and shade. The former is the second version, as the first was rejected by the patron. The central altarpiece painting is the *Assumption* by Annibale Carracci.

SONNET SYLVAIN/GETTY IMAGES ©

❶ Need to Know

Map p256; www.smariadelpopolo.com;
Piazza del Popolo 12; ☙10.30am-12.30pm &
4-6.30pm Mon-Thu, 10.30am-6.30pm Fri &
Sat, 4.30-6.30pm Sun; Ⓜ Flaminio

✕ Take a Break

Treat yourself to an ice cream from the
magnificent Fatamorgana Corso (p127).

★ Top Tip

Look out for the oldest stained-glass
windows in Rome.

Chigi Chapel

Raphael designed the Cappella Chigi,
dedicated to his patron Agostino Chigi,
but never lived to see it completed. Bernini
finished the job more than 100 years
later, contributing statues of Daniel and
Habakkuk to the altarpiece. Only the floor
mosaics were retained from Raphael's
original design, including that of a kneeling
skeleton, placed there to remind the living
of the inevitable.

Delle Rovere Chapel

This 15th-century chapel features works by
Pinturicchio and his school. Frescoes in the
lunettes depict episodes from the life of St
Jerome, while the main altarpiece shows
the Nativity with St Jerome.

What's Nearby?

Piazza del Popolo   Piazza

(Map p256; Ⓜ Flaminio) This dazzling piazza
was laid out in 1538 to provide a grandiose entrance to what was then Rome's
main northern gateway. It has since been
remodelled several times, most recently by
Giuseppe Valadier in 1823.

Guarding its southern approach are
Carlo Rainaldi's twin 17th-century churches,
Chiesa di Santa Maria dei Miracoli (Via
del Corso 528; ☙6.45am-12.30pm & 4.30-7.30pm
Mon-Sat, 8am-1.15pm & 4.30-7.45pm Sun) and
Chiesa di Santa Maria in Montesanto
(Chiesa degli Artisti; www.chiesadegliartisti.it;
Via del Babuino 198; ☙5.30-8pm Mon-Fri, 11am-
1.30pm Sun). In the centre, the 36m-high
obelisk was brought by Augustus from
ancient Egypt and originally stood in Circo
Massimo.

Porta del Popolo   Gate

(Map p256; Ⓜ Flaminio) On the north flank of
the Piazza, the Porta del Popolo was created
by Bernini in 1655 to celebrate Queen Christina of Sweden's defection to Catholicism.

JULIAN ELLIOTT PHOTOGRAPHY/GETTY IMAGES ©

Basilica di San Giovanni in Laterano

Dating to the 4th century, this monumental cathedral was the first Christian basilica built in the city, and until the late 14th century it was the pope's main place of worship.

The oldest of Rome's four papal basilicas, it was commissioned by Emperor Constantine and consecrated by Pope Sylvester I in 324. From then until 1309, when the papacy moved to Avignon, it was the principal pontifical church, and the adjacent Palazzo Laterano was the pope's official residence. Both buildings fell into disrepair during the papacy's French interlude, and when Pope Gregory XI returned to Rome in 1377 he preferred to decamp to the fortified Vatican rather than stay in the official papal digs.

Over the centuries the basilica has been revamped several times, most notably by Borromini in the 17th century, and by Alessandro Galilei, who added the immense white facade in 1735.

Great For...

☑ Don't Miss

The serene cloister is well worth the small entrance fee; it's a lovely spot to collect your thoughts.

❶ Need to Know

Map p255; Piazza di San Giovanni in Laterano 4; basilica/cloister free/€5 with audio guide; ⏱7am-6.30pm, cloister 9am-6pm; Ⓜ San Giovanni

✕ Take a Break

There's a dearth of good eateries right by the basilica, but there's phenomenal pizza a 20-minute walk south at Sbanco (p138).

★ Top Tip

Look down as well as up – the basilica has a beautiful inlaid marble floor.

The Facade

Surmounted by 15 7m-high statues – Christ with St John the Baptist, John the Evangelist and the 12 Apostles – Galilei's huge facade is an imposing work of late-baroque classicism. The **central bronze doors** were moved here from the Curia in the Roman Forum. On the far right, the **Holy Door** is opened only in Jubilee years.

The Interior

The interior owes much of its present look to Francesco Borromini, who redecorated it for the 1650 Jubilee. Divided into a central nave and four minor aisles, it's a breathtaking sight with a **gilt ceiling**, a 15th-century **mosaic floor**, and a wide central nave lined with 4.6m-high sculptures of the apostles.

At the head of the nave, an elaborate Gothic **baldachin** stands over the papal altar. Dating to the 14th century, this towering ensemble is said to contain the relics of the heads of Sts Peter and Paul. In front, a double staircase leads down to the **confessio** and the Renaissance **tomb of Pope Martin V**.

Behind the altar, the massive **apse** is decorated with sparkling mosaics. Parts of these date to the 4th century, but most were added in the 1800s.

At the other end of the basilica, on the first pillar in the right-hand nave, is an incomplete Giotto fresco.

The Cloister

To the left of the altar, the basilica's 13th-century cloister is a lovely, peaceful place with graceful twisted columns set around a central garden. Lining the ambulatories are marble fragments from the original church, including the remains of a 5th-century papal throne and inscriptions of two papal bulls.

Spanish Steps

Rising above Piazza di Spagna, the Spanish Steps provide a perfect people-watching perch, and you'll almost certainly find yourself taking stock here at some point in your visit to Rome.

The Spanish Steps area has long been a magnet for foreigners. In the late 1700s, it was much loved by English travellers on the Grand Tour, and was known locally as 'er ghetto de l'inglesi' (the English ghetto). Poet John Keats lived for a short time in some rooms overlooking the Spanish Steps. Later, in the 19th century, Charles Dickens visited, noting how artists' models would hang around in the hope of being hired to sit for a painting.

Great For...

☑ Don't Miss

The sweeping rooftop views from the top of the steps.

The Steps

Although Piazza di Spagna was named after the nearby Spanish Embassy to the Holy See, the monumental 135-step staircase – the *Scalinata della Trinità dei Monti* – was designed by an Italian, Francesco de Sanctis, and built in 1725 with money bequeathed by a French diplomat.

🛈 Need to Know

Map p252; Ⓜ Spagna

✖ Take a Break

Treat yourself to excellent regional cuisine at nearby Palatium (p129).

★ Top Tip

Visit in late April or early May to see the steps ablaze with brightly coloured azaleas.

Chiesa della Trinità dei Monti

The landmark **Chiesa della Trinità dei Monti** (🗷 06 679 41 79; Piazza Trinità dei Monti 3; ⏰ 7.30am-8pm Tue-Fri, 10am-5pm Sat & Sun) was commissioned by King Louis XII of France and consecrated in 1585. In addition to great rooftop views, it boasts some wonderful frescoes by Daniele da Volterra. His *Deposizione* (Deposition), in the second chapel on the left, is regarded as a masterpiece of mannerist painting.

Piazza di Spagna

At the foot of the steps, the fountain of a sinking boat, the **Barcaccia** (1627), is believed to be by Pietro Bernini, father of the more famous Giani Lorenzo. The bees and suns that decorate the structure,

which is sunken to compensate for the low pressure of the feeder aqueduct, represent the Barbarini family who commissioned the fountain.

Opposite the steps lies **Via dei Condotti**, Rome's most exclusive shopping strip, and to the southeast, **Piazza Mignanelli** is dominated by the Colonna dell'Immacolata, built in 1857 to celebrate Pope Pius IX's declaration of the Immaculate Conception.

What's Nearby?

Keats-Shelley House   Museum

(Map p252; 🗷 06 678 42 35; www.keats-shelley-house.org; Piazza di Spagna 26; adult/reduced €5/4; ⏰ 10am-1pm & 2-6pm Mon-Sat; Ⓜ Spagna) The Keats-Shelley House is where Romantic poet John Keats died of TB at the age of 25, in February 1821. A year later, fellow poet Percy Bysshe Shelley drowned off the coast of Tuscany. The small apartment evokes the impoverished lives of the poets, and is now a small museum crammed with memorabilia, from faded letters to death masks.

JON LOVETTE/GETTY IMAGES ©

Day Trip: Ostia Antica

Rome's answer to Pompeii, the Scavi Archeologici di Ostia Antica is one of Italy's most under-appreciated archaeological sites. The amazingly preserved ruins of Rome's main seaport provide a thrilling glimpse into the workings of an ancient town.

Great For...

☑ Don't Miss

The views over the site from atop the Terme di Nettuno.

Founded in the 4th century BC, Ostia (which refers to the mouth, or *ostium,* of the Tiber) grew to become a great port and commercial centre with a population of around 50,000.

Decline set in after the fall of the Roman Empire, and by the 9th century the city had largely been abandoned, its citizens driven off by barbarian raids and outbreaks of malaria. Over subsequent centuries, it was plundered of marble and building materials, and its ruins were gradually buried in river silt, hence their survival.

To get to the site from Rome, take the Ostia Lido train from Stazione Porta San Paolo (next to Piramide metro station) and get off at Ostia Antica.

The Ruins

Near the entrance, **Porta Romana** gives onto the **Decumanus Maximus**, the site's central strip, which runs over 1km to Porta Marina, the city's original sea-facing gate.

On the Decumanus, the **Terme di Nettuno** is a must-see. This baths complex, one of 20 that originally stood in town, dates to the 2nd century and boasts some superb mosaics, including one of Neptune driving his sea-horse chariot. In the centre of the complex are the remains of an arcaded **palestra** (gym).

Next to the Terme is the **Teatro**, an amphitheatre built by Agrippa and later enlarged to hold 4000 people.

The grassy area behind the amphitheatre is the **Piazzale delle Corporazioni** (Forum of the Corporations), home to the offices of Ostia's merchant guilds. The mosaics that line the perimeter – ships, dolphins, a lighthouse and an elephant – are thought to represent the businesses housed on the square: ships and dolphins indicated shipping agencies, while the elephant probably referred to a business in the ivory trade.

The forum, Ostia's main square, is overlooked by what remains of the **Capitolium**, a temple built by Hadrian and dedicated to Jupiter, Juno and Minerva.

Nearby is another highlight: the **Thermopolium**, an ancient cafe. Check out the bar, frescoed menu, kitchen and small courtyard where customers would have relaxed next to a fountain.

Across the road are the remains of the 2nd-century **Terme del Foro**, originally the city's largest baths complex. Here, in the *forica* (public toilet), you can see 20 well-preserved latrines set sociably into a long stone bench.

Triumph of the Cross mosaic, Basilica Superiore

Basilica di San Clemente

Nowhere better illustrates the various stages of Rome's turbulent past than this fascinating, multilayered church in the shadow of the Colosseum.

Great For...

☑ Don't Miss

The temple to Mithras, deep in the bowels of the basilica.

This fascinating basilica is in fact a series of buildings laid over each other: a 12th-century basilica sits atop a 4th-century church, which in turn stands over a 2nd-century pagan temple and a 1st-century Roman house.

Basilica Superiore

The ground-floor *basilica superiore* contains some glorious works of medieval art. These include a golden 12th-century apse mosaic, the *Trionfo della Croce* (Trìumph of the Cross), showing the Madonna and St John the Baptist standing by a cross on which Christ is represented by 12 white doves. Also impressive are Masolino's 15th-century frescoes in the **Cappella di Santa Caterina**, depicting a crucifixion scene and episodes from the life of St Catherine.

EURASIA/ROBERTHARDING/GETTY IMAGES ©

ⓘ Need to Know

Map p255; www.basilicasanclemente.com; Piazza San Clemente; excavations adult/reduced €10/5; ⏱9am-12.30pm & 3-6pm Mon-Sat, 12.15-6pm Sun; ⌷Via Labicana

✗ Take a Break

Choose one of the daily specials from laid-back Il Bocconcino (p139).

★ Top Tip

Bring a sweater: the temperature drops as you descend underground.

Basilica Inferiore

Steps lead down to the 4th-century *basilica inferiore*. It was mostly destroyed by Norman invaders in 1084, but some faded 11th-century frescoes remain, illustrating the life of San Clemente.

Another level down you'll find yourself walking an ancient lane leading to a 1st-century Roman house and a dark 2nd-century **temple to Mithras** with an altar showing the god slaying a bull. Beneath it all, you can hear the eerie sound of a subterranean river flowing through a Republic-era drain.

What's Nearby?

Basilica dei SS Quattro Coronati
Basilica

(Map p255; ☎06 7047 5427; Via dei Santi Quattro 20; cloisters €2, Oratorio di San Silvestro €1;

⏱basilica 6.30am-12.45pm & 3.30-8pm, cloister 9.45-11.45am & 3.45-5.45pm Mon-Sat; ⌷Via di San Giovanni in Laterano) This brooding fortified church harbours some lovely 13th-century frescoes and a delightful hidden cloister. The frescoes, in the **Oratorio di San Silvestro**, depict the story of the Donation of Constantine, a notorious forged document with which the emperor Constantine ceded control of Rome and the Western Roman Empire to the papacy.

To access the Oratorio, ring the bell in the entrance courtyard.

Chiesa di Santo Stefano Rotondo
Church

(Map p246; www.santo-stefano-rotondo.it; Via di Santo Stefano Rotondo 7; ⏱10am-1pm & 2.30-5.30pm winter, 10am-1pm & 3.30-6.30pm summer; ⌷Via Claudia) Set in its own secluded grounds, this haunting church boasts a porticoed facade and a round, columned interior. But what really gets the heart racing is the graphic wall decor – a cycle of 16th-century frescoes depicting the tortures suffered by many early Christian martyrs.

Terme di Caracalla

The remains of the Terme di Caracalla, the emperor Caracalla's vast baths complex, are among Rome's most awe-inspiring ruins. The original 10-hectare complex comprised baths, gyms, libraries, shops and gardens.

Great For...

☑ **Don't Miss**

The white marble slab was once used in an ancient board game.

Inaugurated in AD 216, the baths remained in continuous use until 537, when the invading Visigoths cut off Rome's water supply. Excavations in the 16th and 17th centuries unearthed a number of important sculptures on the site, many of which found their way into the Farnese family's art collection.

In its heyday, the complex attracted between 6000 and 8000 people every day, while hundreds of slaves sweated underground in 9.5km of tunnels, tending to intricate plumbing systems.

The Ruins

Most of the ruins are of the central bath house. This was a huge rectangular edifice bookended by two *palestre* (gyms) and centred on a *frigidarium* (cold room), where bathers would stop after spells in the warmer *tepidarium* and dome-capped

Inside the baths complex

ⓘ Need to Know

Terme di Caracalla (☎06 3996 7700;
www.coopculture.it; Viale delle Terme di
Caracalla 52; adult/reduced €6/3; ◷9am-1hr
before sunset Tue-Sun, 9am-2pm Mon; ☐Viale
delle Terme di Caracalla)

✕ Take a Break

Pop by for an artisanal gelato or linger
over lunch at Casa Manfredi (p138).

> **★ Top Tip**
> Opera fans should check for summer
> performances at the Terme.

caldarium (hot room). As you traverse the
ruins towards the *palestra orientale,* look
out for a slab of white, pockmarked marble
on your right. This is a board from an ancient game called '*tropa*' ('the hole game').

Archaeologists have discovered an underground temple dedicated to the Persian
god Mithras.

In summer the ruins are used to stage
opera and ballet performances.

What's Nearby?

Villa Celimontana   Park

(Map p246; ◷7am-sunset; ☐Via della Navicella)
With its grassy banks and colourful flower
beds, this leafy park is a wonderful place
to escape the crowds and enjoy a summer
picnic. At its centre is a 16th-century villa
housing the Italian Geographical Society.

Basilica di Santa Sabina   Basilica

(Map p254; ☎06 57 94 01; Piazza Pietro d'Illiria
1; ◷8.15am-12.30pm & 3.30-6pm; ☐Lungote-
vere Aventino) This solemn basilica, one of
Rome's most beautiful medieval churches,
was founded by Peter of Illyria in around
AD 422. It was enlarged in the 9th century
and again in 1216, just before it was given
to the newly founded Dominican order –
note the tombstone of Muñoz de Zamora,
one of the order's founding fathers, in the
nave floor. A 20th-century restoration
returned it to its original look.

Villa del Priorato
di Malta   Historic Building

(Villa Magistrale; Map p254; Piazza dei Cavalieri
di Malta; ☐Lungotevere Aventino) Fronting an
ornate cypress-shaded piazza, the Roman
headquarters of the *Cavalieri di Malta*
(Knights of Malta) boast one of Rome's
most celebrated views. It's not immediately
apparent but look through the keyhole in
the Priorato's green door and you'll see
the dome of St Peter's Basilica perfectly
aligned at the end of a hedge-lined avenue.

Museo Nazionale delle Arti del XXI Secolo (MAXXI; p100)

Modern Architecture

Rome is best known for its classical architecture, but the city also boasts a string of striking modern buildings, many created and designed by the 21st-century's top 'starchitects'.

Great For...

ℹ Need to Know

The Auditorium and MAXXI can be accessed by tram 2 from Piazzale Flaminio.

★ **Top Tip**
Take in a gig at the Auditorium Parco della Musica (p187) to experience its perfect acoustics.

Auditorium Parco della Musica
Cultural Centre

(☎06 8024 1281; www.auditorium.com; Viale Pietro de Coubertin; guided tours adult/reduced €9/5; ⏱11am-8pm Mon-Sat, 10am-8pm Sun summer, to 6pm winter; 🚌Viale Tiziano) Designed by archistar Renzo Piano and inaugurated in 2002, Rome's flagship cultural centre is an audacious work of architecture consisting of three grey pod-like concert halls set round a 3000-seat amphitheatre.

Excavations during its construction revealed remains of an ancient Roman villa, which are now on show in the Auditorium's small **Museo Archeologico** (⏱10am-8pm summer, 11am-6pm Mon-Sat, 10am-6pm Sun winter) `FREE`.

Guided tours (organised for a minimum of 10 people) depart hourly between 11.30am and 4.30pm Saturday and Sunday, and by arrangement from Monday to Friday.

Museo Nazionale delle Arti del XXI Secolo
Gallery

(MAXXI; ☎06 320 19 54; www.fondazionemaxxi.it; Via Guido Reni 4a; adult/reduced €12/8, permanent collection free Tue-Fri & 1st Sun of month; ⏱11am-7pm Tue-Fri & Sun, to 10pm Sat; 🚌Viale Tiziano) As much as the exhibitions, the highlight of Rome's leading contemporary art gallery is the Zaha Hadid–designed building it occupies. Formerly a barracks, the curved concrete structure is striking inside and out with a multilayered geometric facade and a cavernous light-filled interior full of snaking walkways and suspended staircases.

Below left: Auditorium Parco della Musica by Renzo Piano Building Workshop, architects;
Below right: Palazzo della Civiltà Italiana

The gallery has a small permanent collection on display but more interesting are the temporary exhibitions. In recent times these have included installations by avant-garde Chinese sculptor Hang Yong Ping and an exhibition of contemporary Iranian art.

Museo d'Arte Contemporanea di Roma   Gallery

(MACRO; ☑06 06 08; www.museomacro.org; Via Nizza 138, cnr Via Cagliari; adult/reduced €11/9; ☺10.30am-7.30pm Tue-Sun; ☐Via Nizza) Along with MAXXI, this is Rome's most important contemporary art gallery. Occupying a converted Peroni brewery, it hosts tempo-rary exhibitions and displays works from its permanent collection of post-1960s Italian art.

Vying with the exhibits for your attention is the museum's sleek black-and-red interior design. The work of French architect Odile Decq, this retains much of the building's original structure while also incorporating a sophisticated steel-and-glass finish.

Museo dell'Ara Pacis   Museum

(Map p250; ☑06 06 08; www.arapacis.it; Lungotevere in Auga; adult/reduced €11/9; ☺9.30am-7.30pm Mon-Sat; Ⓜ Flaminio) The first modern construction in Rome's historic centre since WWII, Richard Meier's controversial and widely detested glass-and-marble pavilion houses the *Ara Pacis Augustae* (Altar of Peace), Augustus' great monument to peace. One of the most important works of ancient Roman sculpture, the vast marble altar – measuring 11.6m by 10.6m by 3.6m – was completed in 13 BC.

Palazzo della Civiltà Italiana   Historic Building

(Palace of Italian Civilisation; ☑06 33 45 01; www.fendi.com; Quadrato della Concordia; ☺8am-6pm Mon-Sat, 10am-7pm Sun; Ⓜ EUR Magliana) **FREE** Dubbed the Square Colosseum, the Palace of the Workers is EUR's architectural icon, a rationalist masterpiece clad in gleaming white travertine.

> ☑ **Don't Miss**
> The outlying EUR district, which is home to some impressive rationalist architecture.

MARCO CRISTOFORI/ROBERTHARDING/GETTY IMAGES ©

✕ **Take a Break**

Tucked away behind MAXXI, Neve di Latte (p140) issues scoops of near-perfect gelato.

Basilica di Santa Maria Maggiore

One of Rome's four patriarchal basilicas, this monumental church stands on the summit of the Esquilino Hill, on the site of a miraculous snowfall in the summer of AD 358.

Great For...

☑ **Don't Miss**

The luminous 13th-century apse mosaics by Jacopo Torriti.

Much altered over the centuries, the basilica is something of an architectural hybrid, with a 14th-century Romanesque belfry, an 18th-century baroque facade, a largely baroque interior, and a series of glorious 5th-century mosaics.

Exterior

The church's exterior is decorated with glimmering 13th-century mosaics, protected by Ferdinand Fuga's 1741 baroque loggia. Rising behind, the belfry tops out at 75m and is Rome's tallest.

On the piazza in front of the church, the 18.78m-high column originally stood in the Basilica of Massenzio in the Roman Forum.

Interior

The vast interior retains its original structure, despite the basilica's many overhauls.

The confessio

ℹ️ Need to Know

Map p252; ☎06 6988 6800; Piazza Santa
Maria Maggiore; basilica free, adult/reduced
museum €3/2, museum & loggia €5/4;
⊗7am-7pm, loggia guided tours 9.30am-
5.45pm; 🚇Piazza Santa Maria Maggiore

✕ Take a Break

Grab a delish, cheesy *pizzette* (small
round pizza) to take away from Trieste
Pizza (p133).

★ Top Tip

Come on 5 August to see the historic
snowfall recreated with thousands of
white petals.

Particularly spectacular are the **5th-
century mosaics** in the triumphal arch and
nave, depicting Old Testament scenes. The
central image in the apse, signed by Jacopo
Torriti, dates from the 13th century and represents the coronation of the Virgin Mary.
Beneath your feet, the nave floor is a fine
example of 12th-century Cosmati paving.

The **baldachin** over the high altar is
heavy with gilt cherubs; the altar itself is
a porphyry sarcophagus, which is said
to contain the relics of St Matthew and
other martyrs. The *Madonna col Bambino*
(Madonna and Child) panel above the altar
is believed to date from the 12th to 13th
centuries.

A simple stone plaque embedded in the
floor to the right of the altar marks the spot
where Gian Lorenzo Bernini and his father
Pietro are buried. Steps lead down to the

confessio where a statue of Pope Pius
IX kneels before a reliquary containing a
fragment of Jesus' manger.

Through the souvenir shop on the right-
hand side of the church is a **museum** with
a glittering collection of religious artefacts.
Most interesting, however, is the upper
loggia, where you'll get a close look at the
facade's iridescent 13th-century mosaics,
created by Filippo Rusuti. You'll also see
Bernini's helical staircase.

What's Nearby?

Basilica di San Pietro
in Vincoli   Basilica

(Map p246; Piazza di San Pietro in Vincoli 4a;
⊗8am-12.30pm & 3-7pm summer, to 6pm winter;
Ⓜ Cavour) Pilgrims and art lovers flock to
this 5th-century basilica for two reasons:
to marvel at Michelangelo's colossal *Moses*
(1505) sculpture and to see the chains that
supposedly bound St Peter when he was
imprisoned in the Carcere Mamertino (near
the Roman Forum).

Basilica di Santa Maria in Trastevere

The glittering Basilica di Santa Maria in Trastevere is said to be the oldest church dedicated to the Virgin Mary in Rome. Inside, its golden mosaics are a spectacle to behold.

Great for...

☑ Don't Miss

The Cappella Avila and its cleverly constructed 17th-century dome.

Dating to the early 3rd century, the basilica was commissioned by Pope Callixtus III on the site where, according to legend, a fountain of oil had miraculously sprung from the ground. The basilica has been much altered over the centuries and its current Romanesque form is the result of a 12th-century revamp. The portico came later, added by Carlo Fontana in 1702.

The Exterior

Rising above the four papal statues on Domenico Fontana's 18th-century porch, the basilica's restrained 12th-century facade is most notable for its beautiful medieval mosaic. This glittering gold banner depicts Mary feeding Jesus, surrounded by 10 women bearing lamps.

Towering above the church is a 12th-century Romanesque **bell tower**, complete

Piazza Santa Maria in Trastevere

FRANK BACH/SHUTTERSTOCK ©

❶ Need to Know

Map p254; ☑06 581 4802; Piazza Santa Maria in Trastevere; ⊙7.30am-9pm Sep-Jul, 8am-noon & 4-9pm Aug; ☑Viale di Trastevere, ☑Viale di Trastevere

✘ Take a Break

Wander east to La Gensola (p136) for a thrilling taste of Sicily.

★ Top Tip

Take some coins to drop in the light box and illuminate the mosaics.

with its very own mosaic – look in the small niche near the top.

Mosaics & Interior Design

The basilica's main drawcard is its golden 12th-century mosaics. In the **apse**, look out for the dazzling depiction of Christ and his mother flanked by various saints, and, on the far left, Pope Innocent II holding a model of the church. Beneath this is a series of six mosaics by Pietro Cavallini (c 1291) illustrating the life of the Virgin.

The interior boasts a typical 12th-century design with three naves divided by 21 **Roman columns**, some plundered from the Terme di Caracalla. On the right of the altar, near a spiralling Paschal candlestick, is an inscription, *Fons Olei,* which marks the spot where the miraculous oil fountain supposedly sprung. The spiralling

Cosmatesque floor was relaid in 1870s, a re-creation of the 13th-century original. Up above, the coffered **golden ceiling** was designed by Domenichino in 1617.

Also worth a look is the **Cappella Avila**, the last chapel on the left, with its stunning 17th-century dome. Antonio Gherardi's clever design depicts four angels holding the circular base of a large lantern whose columns rise to give the effect of a second cupola within a larger outer dome.

Piazza Santa Maria in Trastevere

Outside the basilica, **Piazza Santa Maria in Trastevere** is the neighbourhood's focal square. By day it's full of parents with strollers, chatting locals and guidebook-toting tourists; by night it's the domain of foreign students, young Romans and out-of-towners, all out for a good time. The fountain in the centre of the square is of Roman origin and was restored by Carlo Fontana in 1692.

PHOTOGOLFER/SHUTTERSTOCK ©

Galleria Doria Pamphilj

Hidden behind the grey exterior of Palazzo Doria Pamphilj, this wonderful gallery boasts one of Rome's richest private art collections, with works by Raphael, Tintoretto, Brueghel, Titian, Caravaggio, Bernini and Velázquez.

Great For...

Don't Miss

The *Ritratto di papa Innocenzo X* is generally considered the gallery's greatest masterpiece.

Palazzo Doria Pamphilj dates to the mid-15th century, but its current look was largely the work of the current owners, the Doria Pamphilj family, who acquired it in the 18th century. The Pamphilj golden age, during which the family collection was started, came during the papacy of one of their own, Innocent X (r 1644–55).

The opulent picture galleries, decorated with frescoed ceilings and gilded mirrors, are hung with floor-to-ceiling paintings. Masterpieces abound, but look out for Titian's *Salomè con la testa del Battista* (Salome with the Head of John the Baptist) and two early Caravaggios: *Riposo durante la fuga in Egitto* (Rest During the Flight into Egypt) and *Maddalene Penitente* (Penitent Magdalen). The undisputed star, though, is Velázquez' *Ritratto di papa Innocenzo X*, his portrait of an implacable Pope Innocent

ⓘ Need to Know

Map p250; ☑06 679 73 23; www.doria
pamphilj.it; Via del Corso 305; adult/reduced
€12/8; ☺9am-7pm, last admission 6pm;
🚊Via del Corso

✕ Take a Break

A short walk west, La Ciambella (p125)
is a spacious all-day eatery with tasty
traditional offerings.

★ Top Tip
Be sure to pick up the free audio guide.

X, who grumbled that the depiction was
'too real'. For a comparison, check out Gian
Lorenzo Bernini's sculptural interpretation
of the same subject.

The excellent free audio guide, narrated
by Jonathan Pamphilj, brings the place alive
with family anecdotes and background
information.

What's Nearby?

Chiesa del Gesù   Church

(Map p250; ☑06 69 7001; www.chiesadelgesu.
org; Piazza del Gesù; ☺7am-12.30pm & 4-7.45pm,
St Ignatius rooms 4-6pm Mon-Sat, 10am-noon
Sun; 🚊Largo di Torre Argentina) An imposing
example of Counter-Reformation architecture, Rome's most important Jesuit church
is a treasure trove of baroque art. Headline
works include a swirling vault fresco by
Giovanni Battista Gaulli (aka Il Baciccia), and

Andrea del Pozzo's opulent tomb for Jesuit
founder Ignatius Loyola. The Spanish saint
lived in the church from 1544 until his death
in 1556 and you can visit his **private rooms**
to the right of the main building.

The church, which was consecrated
in 1584, is fronted by an impressive and
much-copied facade by Giacomo della
Porta. But more than the masonry, the real
draw here is the church's lavish interior. The
cupola frescoes and stucco decoration were
designed by Baciccia, who also painted the
hypnotic ceiling fresco, the *Trionfo del Nome
di Gesù* (Triumph of the Name of Jesus).

Chiesa di Sant'Ignazio
di Loyola   Church

(Map p250; www.santignazio.gesuiti.it; Piazza di
Sant'Ignazio; ☺7.30am-7pm Mon-Sat, 9am-7pm
Sun; 🚊Via del Corso) Flanking a delightful
rococo piazza, this important Jesuit church
boasts a Carlo Maderno facade and two
celebrated *trompe l'œil* frescoes by Andrea
Pozzo (1642–1709). One depicts a fake
dome, whilst the other, on the nave ceiling,
shows St Ignatius Loyola being welcomed
into paradise by Christ and the Madonna.

Via Margutta

Small independent antique shops, art galleries and boutiques pepper Via Margutta, one of Rome's prettiest pedestrian cobbled lanes that's strung with ivy-laced palazzi, decorative potted plants and the odd monumental fountain.

A stone's throw from the Spanish Steps, Via Margutta is named after a 16th-century family of barbers, but has long been associated with art and artists. Characterising the area, Pietro Lombardi's recently restored fountain, the 1927 **Fontana degli Artisti**, showcases easels, palettes and artists' brushes, as well as two masks, one grinning, one frowning, demonstrating the changing moods of the artist.

Artistic notables who strode these cobblestones include the Italian futurists, who had their first meeting here in 1906; Picasso, who worked in a gallery at No 54; and Truman Capote, who stayed and wrote at No 33.

Today at No 53, you can watch *marmoraro* (marble artist) Sandro Fiorentini chip away in the enchanting La Bottega del Marmoraro (p154), a den of decorative marble

Great For...

Don't Miss

The masks of Fontana degli Artisti with their diametric expressions.

Fontana degli Artisi

ⓘ Need to Know

Map p256; Ⓜ Spagna

✕ Take a Break

Stop by vegetarian bistro Il Margutta (p128) for a great-value buffet brunch.

★ Top Tip

An engraved aphorism from Bottega del Marmoraro makes for a lovely Roman keepsake.

plaques engraved with various inscriptions: *la dolce vita, la vita e bella* etc.

In the Lime Light

Via Margutto became a celluloid star when Audrey Hepburn and Gregory Peck whispered sweet nothings to each other in Joe Bradley's apartment at No 51 in the classic movie *Roman Holiday* (1953). Of the street's more recent residents, the most famous is film director Federico Fellini, who lived at No 110 with his wife Giulietta Masina until his death in 1993.

What's Nearby?

Villa Medici   Palace

(Map p256; ☏ 06 676 13 11; www.villamedici.it; Viale Trinità dei Monti 1; 1½hr guided tour adult/reduced €12/6; ◷10am-7pm Tue-Sun; Ⓜ Spagna) This sumptuous Renaissance palace was

built for Cardinal Ricci da Montepulciano in 1540, but Ferdinando dei Medici bought it in 1576. It remained in Medici hands until 1801, when Napoleon acquired it for the French Academy. Take a tour to see the wonderful landscaped **gardens**, cardinal's painted apartments, and incredible views over Rome. Note the pieces of ancient Roman sculpture from the Ara Pacis embedded in the villa's walls.

Casa di Goethe   Museum

(Map p256; ☏ 06 3265 0412; www.casadigoethe. it; Via del Corso 18; adult/reduced €5/3; ◷10am-6pm Tue-Sun; Ⓜ Flaminio) A gathering place for German intellectuals, the Via del Corso apartment where Johann Wolfgang von Goethe enjoyed a happy Italian sojourn (despite complaining of the noisy neighbours) from 1786 to 1788 is now a lovingly maintained small museum. Exhibits include fascinating Piranesi engravings of 18th-century Rome, as well as Goethe's sketches and letters, plus some lovely sketches of him by his friend Tischbein. With advance permission, ardent fans can use the library full of first editions.

Waterfall and gardens, Villa d'Este

ITS/ADOBE/ALAMY STOCK PHOTO/GETTY IMAGES ©

Day Trip: Tivoli

A summer retreat for ancient Romans and the Renaissance rich, the hilltop town of Tivoli is home to two Unesco World Heritage Sites: sprawling Villa Adriana and the 16th-century Villa d'Este.

Great For...

☑ Don't Miss

Admire the rich mannerist frescoes of Villa d'Este before heading into the gardens.

Villa d'Este

In Tivoli's hilltop centre, the steeply terraced grounds of **Villa d'Este** (✆0774 33 29 20; www.villadestetivoli.info; Piazza Trento; adult/reduced €8/4; ⏰8.30am-1hr before sunset Tue-Sun) are a superlative example of a Renaissance garden, complete with monumental fountains, elegant tree-lined avenues and landscaped grottoes. The villa, originally a Benedictine convent, was converted into a luxury retreat by Lucrezia Borgia's son, Cardinal Ippolito d'Este, in the late 16th century. It provided inspiration for composer Franz Liszt who stayed here between 1865 and 1886 and immortalised it in his 1877 piano composition *The Fountains of the Villa d'Este*.

In the gardens, look out for the Bernini-designed **Fountain of the Organ**, which uses water pressure to play music through a

Villa Adriana

ALESSANDRO0770/GETTY IMAGES ©

> **❶ Need to Know**
>
> Information is available from the **tourist information point** (☏0774 31 35 36; Piazzale delle Nazione Unite; ⊙10am-1pm & 4-6pm Tue-Sun) near where the bus arrives.
>
> **✕ Take a Break**
>
> Enjoy a meal at family-run **Trattoria del Falcone** (☏0774 31 23 58; Via del Trevio 34; meals €30; ⊙noon-4pm & 6.30-11pm), near Villa d'Este.

> **★ Top Tip**
>
> Tivoli makes an excellent day trip from Rome, but to cover its two main sites you'll have to start early.

Must-see sights include the **canopo**, a landscaped canal overlooked by a nymphaeum (shrine to the water nymph), and the **Teatro Marittimo**, Hadrian's personal refuge. To the east, **Piazza d'Oro** makes for a memorable picture, particularly in spring when its grassy centre is cloaked in yellow wildflowers.

There are also several bath complexes, temples and barracks.

concealed organ, and the 130m-long **Avenue of the Hundred Fountains**.

Villa Adriana

The ruins of Emperor Hadrian's vast country **villa** (☏0774 38 27 33; www.villaadriana. beniculturali.it; adult/reduced €8/4; ⊙9am-1hr before sunset), 5km outside Tivoli proper, are quite magnificent, easily on a par with anything you'll see in Rome. Built between AD 118 and 138, the villa was one of the largest in the ancient world, encompassing more than 120 hectares – of which about 40 are now open to the public. You'll need several hours to explore.

Getting There & Around

Tivoli lies 30km east of Rome. It's accessible by Cotral bus (€2.20, 50 minutes, every 15 to 20 minutes) from Ponte Mammolo metro station. By car, take Via Tiburtina or the quicker Rome–L'Aquila autostrada (A24). Trains run from Rome's Stazione Tiburtina to Tivoli (€2.60, one hour, at least hourly).

The best way to see both main sites is to visit Villa d'Este first, then have lunch up in the centre, before heading down to Villa Adriana. To get to the villa from the centre, take local CAT bus 4 or 4X (€1, 10 minutes, half-hourly) from Largo Garibaldi.

Centro Storico Piazzas

Rome's historic centre boasts some of the city's most celebrated piazzas, and several lovely but lesser known squares. Each has its own character but together they encapsulate much of the city's beauty, history and drama.

Start Piazza Colonna
Distance 1.5km
Duration 3½ hours

Classic Photo of Piazza della Rotonda with the Pantheon in the background

4 It's a short walk along Via del Seminario to **Piazza della Rotonda**, where the **Pantheon** (p50) needs no introduction.

5 Piazza Navona (p62) is Rome's great showpiece square, where you can compare the two giants of Roman baroque – Gian Lorenzo Bernini and Francesco Borromini.

Corso del Rinascimento

Piazza Navona

Salita dei Crescenzi

4

5

Via degli Staderari

Via della Rotonda

Via dei Canestrari

Via Monterone

Piazza di San Pantaleo

Via dei Cappellari

Corso Vittorio Emanuele II

Via del Monserrato

Via dei Baullari

6

Lgt dei Tebaldi

Via dei Farnesi

7

FINISH

Via dei Giubbonari

Take a Break...
Those in the know head to Forno di Campo de' Fiori (p124) for some of Rome's best *pizza bianca* ('white' pizza with olive oil and salt).

7 Just beyond the Campo, the more sober **Piazza Farnese** is overshadowed by the austere facade of the Renaissance Palazzo Farnese.

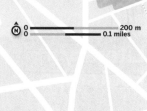

1 Piazza Colonna is dominated by the 30m-high Colonna di Marco Aurelio and flanked by Palazzo Chigi, the official residence of the Italian PM.

2 Follow Via dei Bergamaschi to **Piazza di Pietra**, a refined space overlooked by the 2nd-century Tempio di Adriano..

3 Continue down Via de' Burro to **Piazza di Sant'Ignazio Loyola**, a small piazza with a **church** (p107) boasting celebrated *trompe l'œil* frescoes.

6 On the other side of Corso Vittorio Emanuele II, **Campo de' Fiori** (p65) hosts a noisy market and boisterous drinking scene.

Literary Footsteps

This walk through the Tridente district explores the literary haunts, both real and fictional, that litter the area. Discover the cafe where Casanova drank, the hotel that inspired Cocteau and the house where Keats breathed his last.

Start Pincio Hill Gardens
Distance 1km
Duration 2 hours

2 Dan Brown's *Angels and Demons* made use of the art-rich **Basilica di Santa Maria del Popolo** (p86) in its convoluted plot.

3 Jean Cocteau stayed at the **Hotel de Russie** with Picasso, and wrote a letter home describing picking oranges from outside his window.

4 Cobbled **Via Margutta** (p108) is where Truman Capote wrote his short story *Lola*. Fellini, Picasso, Stravinsky and Puccini all lived here at some point.

Via Flaminia
Via Luisa di Savoia
Via Ferdinando di Savoia
Flaminio Ⓜ
Piazzale Flaminio
Viale del Muro Torto
Piazza del Popolo
Viale d'Annunzio
Via della Fontanella
Via del Babuino
Via del Corso
Via di San Giacomo
Via dei Greci
TRIDENTE
Via Vittoria
Via della Croce
Tiber
Via di Ripetta
Via Tomacelli
Via della F Borghese
COLONNA

Ⓝ 0 —————— 500 m
0 —————— 0.25 miles

1 Begin your walk in the panoramic **Pincio Hill Gardens** (p57), where Henry James' Daisy Miller walked with Frederick Winterborne.

VILLA BORGHESE

Viale dell' Obelisco

Viale delle Magnolie

1
START

Galoppatoio

Viale del Muro Torto

Viale Trinità dei Monti

Via Margutta

Via Alibert

CAMPO MARZIO

Via di Porta Pinciana

Ⓜ Spagna

Piazza di Spagna

Via delle Carrozze

5

Via dei Condotti

6

7
FINISH

Piazza Mignanelli

Via Sistina

Via dei Due Macelli

Via Mario de' Fiori

Classic Photo of people ascending the Spanish Steps

6 Leaving the cafe, you're almost at the **Spanish Steps** (p90), which Dickens described in his *Pictures from Italy*. Byron stayed at 25 Piazza di Spagna in 1817.

Take a Break...
Compose your own whimsical tale in the Hassler Hotel's romantic rooftop restaurant, Imàgo (p129).

7 Overlooking the Spanish Steps, the **Keats-Shelley House** (p91) is now a small museum devoted to the Romantic poets.

5 Head to Via dei Condotti, where William Thackeray stayed, and stop at **Antico Caffè Greco** (p127), a former haunt of Casanova, Goethe, Keats, Byron and Shelley.

DINING OUT

Pizza, pasta and delicious gelato

Dining Out

This is a city that lives to eat. Food feeds the Roman soul, and a social occasion would be nothing without it.

Over recent decades, Rome's dining scene has become increasingly sophisticated as cucina creativa (creative cooking) has taken off and the city's gourmet restaurants have upped their game. But the bedrock of the Roman foodscape has always been, and remains to be, the family-run trattorias that pepper the city's streets and piazzas. These simple eateries have been feeding visitors for centuries, and are still the best bet for classic, seasonal Roman fare.

In This Section

Ancient Rome......................................122

Centro Storico....................................122

Tridente, Trevi & the Quirinale 127

Vatican City, Borgo & Prati 129

Monti, Esquilino
& San Lorenzo 132

Trastevere & Gianicolo......................134

San Giovanni & Testaccio 138

Villa Borghese
& Northern Rome...............................139

Southern Rome...................................140

Price Ranges

The following price ranges refer to a meal that includes *primo* (first course), *secondo* (second course) and *dolce* (dessert), plus a glass of wine.

€ less than €25
€€ €25 to €45
€€€ more than €45

Tipping

Although service is included, leave a tip: from 5% in a pizzeria to 10% in a more upmarket place.

Villa Borghese & Northern Rome
Park cafes and smart, fashionable
restaurants (p139)

Vatican City, Borgo & Prati
Sophisticated restaurants,
delicious takeaways,
heavenly gelaterie (p129)

Tridente, Trevi & the Quirinale
Classy neighbourhood
eateries, great gelaterie
and upmarket cafes (p127)

Centro Storico
Romantic hideaways,
old-school trattorias,
top pizzerias (p122)

Monti, Esquilino & San Lorenzo
Ethnic eats, cool bars,
boho restaurants (p132)

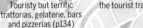

Ancient Rome
Hidden gems among
the tourist traps (p122)

Trastevere & Gianicolo
Touristy but terrific
trattorias, gelaterie, bars
and pizzerias (p134)

San Giovanni & Testaccio
Traditional Roman cuisine,
good cheap eats (p138)

Southern Rome
Trend-setting foodie venues in ex-
industrial Ostiense district (p140)

Useful Phrases

I'd like... vorrei (vo.*ray*...)
  a table un tavolo (oon *ta*.vo.lo)
  the menu il menù (eel me.*noo*)
  two beers due birre (doo.e *bee*.re)

What would you recommend? Cosami
consiglia? (*ko*.za mee kon.*see*.lya)

Can you bring me the bill, please?
Miporta il conto, per favore? (mee *por*.
taeel *kon*.to per fa.vo.re)

Classic Dishes

Cacio e pepe Pasta with *pecorino
romano* (sheep's milk cheese), black
pepper and olive oil.

Pizza bianca Unique to Rome; a plain
pizza with salt, olive oil and rosemary.

Saltimbocca alla romana A veal cutlet
jazzed up with prosciutto and sage.

Trippa alla romana Tripe cooked with
potatoes, tomato and mint; a typical
Saturday-in-Rome dish.

The Best...

Experience Rome's top restaurants and cafes

Roman

Ristorante L'Arcangelo (p131) A creative, contemporary take on Roman dishes.

Flavio al Velavevodetto (p139) Classic *cucina romana,* served in huge portions.

Da Felice (p139) In the heartland of Roman cuisine, and sticking to a traditional weekly timetable.

Palatium (p129) Roman staples and Lazio-region wines.

Creative Cuisine

Antonello Colonna Open (p134) Antonello Colonna's creative takes on Roman classics.

Pianostrada (p125) Uber-hip seasonal dining experience.

Metamorfosi (p140) Michelin-starred cuisine by wonder-chef Roy Caceres (pictured).

Casa Coppelle (p127) Creative Italian and French-inspired food in romantic surroundings.

Glass Hostaria (p137) Innovative food in a contemporary setting in Trastevere.

Pizzerias

Pizzeria Da Remo (p138) Spartan but stunning; a frenetic Roman pizzeria experience.

Emma Pizzeria (p125) Spacious surroundings and seasonal offerings.

Don (p136) Authentic fried pizzas that may have you reaching for a napkin or ten.

Pizzarium (p129) Takeaway squares of pure pizza delight.

Pizza Ostiense (p141) Friendly atmosphere and classic paper-thin pizza.

Local Gems

Pizzeria Da Remo (p138) For the full neighbourhood Roman pizza experience.

Da Felice (p139) Traditional local cooking in Testaccio, the heartland of Roman cuisine.

Da Augusto (p135; pictured) Mamma-style cooking overlooking a pretty piazza.

Alfredo e Ada (p124) No-frills surrounds, but delicious home-style cooking.

Pastry Shops

Pasticceria De Bellis (p124) Work-of-art cakes, pastries and *dolci* (sweets).

Le Levain (p136) Gallic delights from macarons to millefeuilles.

Andreotti (p141; pictured) Poem-worthy treats, from buttery tarts to golden pastries.

Grezzo (p132) A siren call to lovers of all things chocolate.

Gelaterie

Fatamorgana Corso (p128) Rome's finest artisanal flavours.

Locanda del Gelato (p136) Wine ice cream is the house speciality.

Gelateria del Teatro (p123) About 40 delicious choices, all made on-site.

Fior di Luna (p136) Perhaps the best sorbet in the world.

Gelateria Dei Gracchi (p128; pictured) A teeny taste of heaven.

Ambience

Imàgo (p129) Romantic views from the Hassler Hotel rooftop.

La Veranda (p132) Dine beneath 15th-century Pinturicchio frescoes.

Il Palazzetto (p128) A sunny terrace that overlooks the Spanish Steps.

Ristorante Roof Garden Circus (p122) Forty Seven hotel rooftop with glorious views.

★ Lonely Planet's Top Choices

Sbanco (p139) Moreish starters, creative pizzas and craft beers.

Colline Emiliane (p129) Warm service and sensational food.

L'Asino d'Oro (p133) Fantastic food, stunning value and Umbrian flavours.

Sciascia Caffè (p130) To-die-for coffee served in elegant surrounds.

La Ciambella (p125) All-day dining set over Terme di Agrippa ruins.

La Gensola (p136) Laid-back trattoria with some rip-roaring seafood.

⊗ Ancient Rome

Terrazza Caffarelli Cafe €

(Caffetteria dei Musei Capitolini; Map p246; ☑06 6919 0564; Piazzale Caffarelli 4; ⊙9.30am-7pm; 🚇Piazza Venezia) The Capitoline Museums' stylish terrace cafe is a memorable place to relax over a drink or light lunch (*panini*, salads, pastas) and swoon over magical views of the city's domes and rooftops. Although part of the museum complex, you don't need a ticket to come here as it has an independent entrance on Piazzale Caffarelli.

Terre e Domus Lazio Cuisine €€

(Map p246; ☑06 6994 0273; Via Foro Traiano 82-4; meals €30; ⊙9am-midnight Mon & Wed-Sat, 10am-midnight Sun; 🚇Via dei Fori Imperiali) This modern white-and-glass restaurant is the best option in the touristy Forum area. With minimal decor and large windows overlooking the Colonna di Traiano, it's a relaxed spot to sit down to traditional local staples, all made with ingredients sourced from the surrounding Lazio region, and a glass or two of regional wine.

Ristorante Roof Garden Circus Ristorante €€€

(Map p254; ☑06 678 78 16; www.fortyseven hotel.com; Via Petroselli 47, Hotel Forty Seven; meals €60; ⊙noon-10.30pm; 🚇Via Petroselli) The rooftop of the Forty Seven hotel sets the romantic stage for chef Giacomo Tasca's seasonal menu of classic Roman dishes and contemporary Mediterranean cuisine. With the Aventino hill rising in the background, you can tuck into stalwarts such as spaghetti *ajo e ojio* (with garlic and olive oil) or opt for something richer like fillet of beef with zucchini, peppermint and roasted peppers.

⊗ Centro Storico

Barnum Cafe Cafe €

(Map p250; ☑06 6476 0483; www.barnumcafe. com; Via del Pellegrino 87; ⊙9am-10pm Mon, to 2am Tue-Sat; 🛜; 🚇Corso Vittorio Emanuele II) A laid-back *Friends*-style cafe, evergreen Barnum is the sort of place you could quickly get used to. With its shabby-chic vintage furniture and white bare-brick walls, it's a relaxed spot for a breakfast cappuccino, a light lunch or a late afternoon drink. Come evening, a coolly dressed-down crowd sips seriously good cocktails.

Supplizio Fast Food €

(Map p250; ☑06 8987 1920; www.facebook. com/supplizioroma; Via dei Banchi Vecchi 143; supplì €3-7; ⊙noon-8pm Mon-Thu, noon-3.30pm & 6.30-10.30pm Fri & Sat; 🚇Corso Vittorio Emanuele II) Rome's favourite snack, the *supplì* (a fried croquette filled with rice, tomato sauce and mozzarella), gets a gourmet makeover at this elegant street food joint. Sit back on the vintage leather sofa and dig into a crispy classic or push the boat out and try something different, maybe a little fish number stuffed with fresh anchovies, cheese, bread and raisins.

Forno Roscioli Pizza, Bakery €

(Map p250; ☑06 686 4045; www.anticoforno roscioli.it; Via dei Chiavari 34; pizza slices from €2, snacks €2; ⊙6am-8pm Mon-Sat, 9am-7pm Sun; 🚇Via Arenula) This is one of Rome's top bakeries, which is much loved by lunching locals who crowd here for luscious sliced pizza, prize pastries and hunger-sating *supplì*. The *pizza margherita* is superb, if messy to eat, and there's also a counter serving hot pastas and vegetable side dishes.

Caffè Sant'Eustachio Cafe €

(Map p250; www.santeustachioilcaffe.it; Piazza Sant'Eustachio 82; ⊙8.30am-1am Sun-Thu, to 1.30am Fri, to 2am Sat; 🚇Corso del Rinascimento) This small, unassuming cafe, which is generally three deep at the bar, is reckoned by many to serve the best coffee in town. To make it, the bartenders sneakily beat the first drops of an espresso with several teaspoons of sugar to create a frothy paste to which they add the rest of the coffee. It's superbly smooth and guaranteed to put some zing into your sightseeing.

La Casa del Caffè
Tazza d'Oro   Cafe €

(Map p250; ☎06 678 9792; www.tazzadoro
coffeeshop.com; Via degli Orfani 84-86;
⏱7am-8pm Mon-Sat, 10.30am-7.30pm Sun;
🚇Via del Corso) A busy, stand-up affair with
burnished 1940s fittings, this is one of
Rome's best coffee houses. Its espresso
hits the mark nicely and there's a range
of delicious coffee concoctions, including
a cooling *granita di caffè*, a crushed-ice
coffee drink served with whipped cream.
There's also a small shop and, outside, a
coffee *bancomat* for those out-of-hours
caffeine emergencies.

Roscioli Caffè   Cafe €

(Map p250; ☎06 8916 5330; www.rosciolicaffe.
com; Piazza Benedetto Cairoli 16; ⏱7am-11pm
Mon-Sat, 8am-6pm Sun; 🚇Via Arenula) The
Roscioli name is a sure bet for good food
and drink in this town: the family runs one
of Rome's most celebrated delis (p127)
and a hugely popular bakery, and this
cafe doesn't disappoint either. The coffee
is wonderfully luxurious, and the artfully
crafted pastries, petits fours and *panini*
taste as good as they look.

Tiramisù Zum   Desserts €

(Map p250; ☎06 6830 7836; www.facebook.
com/zumroma; Piazza del Teatro di Pompeo 20;
desserts €2.50-6; ⏱11am-11.30pm Sun-Thu, to
1am Fri & Sat; 🚇Corso Vittorio Emanuele II) The
ideal spot for a mid-afternoon pick-me-up,
this fab dessert bar specialises in tiramisu,
that magnificent marriage of mascarpone
and liqueur-soaked ladyfinger biscuits.
Choose between the classic version with its
cocoa powdering or one of several tempting
variations – with pistachio nuts, blackber-
ries and raspberries, and Amarena cherries.

Gelateria del Teatro   Gelato €

(Map p250; ☎06 4547 4880; www.gelateriadel
teatro.it; Via dei Coronari 65; gelato €2.50-5;
⏱10.30am-8pm winter, 10am-10.30pm summer;
🚇Via Zanardelli) All the ice cream served at
this excellent gelateria is prepared on-site –
look through the window and you'll see
how. There are about 40 flavours to choose

🍴 Roman Cuisine

Like most Italian cuisines, Roman
cooking was born of careful use of local
ingredients – making use of the cheaper
cuts of meat, such as *guanciale* (pig's
cheek) and greens that could be gathered wild from the fields.

There are a few classic dishes that
are served by almost every trattoria and
restaurant in Rome. These carb-laden
comfort foods are seemingly simple,
yet notoriously difficult to prepare well.
Iconic Roman dishes include carbonara
(pasta with lardons, egg and parmesan), *alla gricia* (with pig's cheek and
onions), *amatriciana* (invented when an
enterprising chef from Amatrice added
tomatoes to *alla gricia*) and *cacio e pepe*
(with cheese and pepper).

Bucatini all'amatriciana
AGE FOTOSTOCK/ALAMY STOCK PHOTO ©

from, all made from thoughtfully sourced
ingredients such as hazelnuts from the
Langhe region of Piedmont and pistachios
from Bronte in Sicily.

Caffetteria Chiostro
del Bramante   Cafe €

(Map p250; ☎06 6880 9036; www.chiostrodel
bramante.it; Via Arco della Pace 5; meals €15-25;
⏱10am-8pm Mon-Fri, to 9pm Sat & Sun; 🛜;
🚇Corso del Rinascimento) Many of Rome's
galleries and museums have in-house cafes
but few are as beautifully located as the
Caffetteria Chiostro del Bramante on the
1st floor of Bramante's elegant Renaissance cloister. With outdoor tables overlooking the central courtyard and an all-day

🍽 Kosher Rome

If you want to eat kosher in Rome, head to Via del Portico d'Ottavia, the main strip through the Jewish Ghetto. Lined with trattorias and restaurants specialising in Roman-Jewish cuisine, it's a lively hang-out, especially on hot summer nights when diners crowd the many pavement tables. For a taste of typical ghetto cooking, try **Nonna Betta** (Map p254; ☎06 6880 6263; www. nonnabetta.it; Via del Portico d'Ottavia 16; meals €30-35; ⊙11am-11pm Wed-Mon; 🚇Via Arenula), a small tunnel of a trattoria serving traditional kosher food and local staples such as *carciofi alla guidia* (crisp fried artichokes). Further down the road, the unmarked **Cremeria Romana** (Map p250; www.cremeriaromana.com; Via del Portico d'Ottavia 1b; gelato €3; ⊙9am-6pm Mon-Fri & Sun, closed Fri dinner & Sat, longer hours summer; 🚇Via Arenula) at No 1b has a small selection of tasty kosher gelato.

Outdoor dining in Rome's Jewish quarter
WIETSE MICHIELS TRAVEL STOCK/ALAMY STOCK PHOTO ©

menu offering everything from cakes and coffee to baguettes, risottos and Caesar salads, it's a great spot for a break.

Forno di Campo de' Fiori   Pizza, Bakery €
(Map p250; www.fornocampodefiori.com; Campo de' Fiori 22; pizza slices around €3; ⊙7.30am-2.30pm & 4.45-8pm Mon-Sat, closed Sat dinner Jul & Aug; 🚇Corso Vittorio Emanuele II) This buzzing bakery on Campo de' Fiori, divided into two adjacent shops, does a roaring trade in *panini* and delicious fresh-from-

the-oven *pizza al taglio* (pizza by the slice). Aficionados swear by the *pizza bianca* ('white' pizza with olive oil, rosemary and salt), but the *panini* and *pizza rossa* ('red' pizza, with olive oil, tomato and oregano) taste plenty good too.

Pasticceria De Bellis   Pastries €
(Map p250; ☎06 686 1480; www.pasticceriade bellis.com; Piazza del Paradiso 56-57; pastries €4.50-12, burgers €6-9; ⊙9am-8pm; 🚇Corso Vittorio Emanuele II) The beautifully crafted cakes, pastries and *dolci* made at this chic *pasticceria* are miniature works of art. Curated in every detail, they look superb and taste magnificent, from traditional breakfast *cornetti* (croissants) to *cannoli,* mono-portions of cheesecake and a selection of sumptuous burgers.

Venchi   Gelato €
(Map p250; ☎06 6992 5423; www.venchi.com; Via degli Orfani 87; gelato €2.50-5; ⊙10.30am-11pm Sun-Thu, to midnight Fri & Sat summer, 10am-10pm Sun-Thu, to 11pm Fri & Sat winter; 🚇Via del Corso) Forget fancy flavours and gelato experiments, Venchi is all about the unadulterated enjoyment of chocolate. The wall shelves and counter displays feature myriad beautifully packaged delicacies, from pralines to chilli chocolate bars, as well as an assortment of decadent choc-based ice creams.

Antico Forno Urbani   Pizza, Bakery €
(Map p250; Piazza Costaguti 31; pizza slices from €1.50; ⊙7.40am-2.30pm & 5-7.45pm Mon-Fri, 8.30am-1.30pm Sat, 9.30am-1pm Sun; 🚇Via Arenula) A popular kosher bakery, this Ghetto institution makes some of the best pizza *bianca* in town, as well as freshly baked bread, biscuits and focaccias. It gets very busy but once you catch a whiff of the yeasty odours wafting off the counter, it's nearly impossible to resist the temptation for a quick pit stop.

Alfredo e Ada   Trattoria €
(Map p250; ☎06 687 8842; Via dei Banchi Nuovi 14; meals €25-30; ⊙noon-3pm & 7-10pm Tue-Sat; 🚇Corso Vittorio Emanuele II) For an authentic trattoria experience, search out this much-

loved local eatery. It's distinctly no-frills with simple wooden tables, paper napkins and homey clutter, but there's a warm, friendly atmosphere and the traditional Roman food is filling and flavoursome.

Mercato di Campo de' Fiori
Market €

(Map p250; ⏰7am-2pm Mon-Sat; ⛵Corso Vittorio Emanuele II) The most picturesque – but also the most expensive – of Rome's neighbourhood markets. Each weekday morning, local shoppers mix with tourists and visitors amid the colourful stalls of seasonal fruit and veg that take over this historic piazza.

Pianostrada
Ristorante €€

(Map p250; 🕿06 8957 2296; Via delle Zoccolette 22; meals €40; ⏰1-4pm & 7pm-midnight Tue-Fri, 10am-midnight Sat & Sun; ⛵Via Arenula) Hatched in foodie Trastevere but now across the river in a mellow white space with vintage furnishings and glorious summer courtyard, this bistro is a fashionable must. Reserve ahead, or settle for a stool at the bar and enjoy big bold views of the kitchen at work. Cuisine is refreshingly creative, seasonal, veg-packed including gourmet open sandwiches and sensational homemade focaccia as well as full-blown mains.

La Ciambella
Italian €€

(Map p250; 🕿06 683 2930; www.la-ciambella. it; Via dell'Arco della Ciambella 20; meals €35-45; ⏰bar 7.30am-midnight, wine bar & restaurant midday-11pm Tue-Sun; ⛵Largo di Torre Argentina) Central but largely undiscovered by the tourist hordes, this friendly wine-bar-cum-restaurant beats much of the neighbourhood competition. Its spacious, light-filled interior is set over the ruins of the Terme di Agrippa, visible through transparent floor panels, and its kitchen sends out some excellent food, from tartares and chickpea pancakes to slow-cooked beef and traditional Roman pastas.

Emma Pizzeria
Pizza €€

(Map p250; 🕿06 6476 0475; www.emmapizzeria. com; Via Monte della Farina 28-29; pizzas €8-18, mains €35; ⏰12.30-3pm & 7-11.30pm; ⛵Via

Arenula) Tucked in behind the Chiesa di San Carlo ai Catinari, this smart, modern pizzeria is a top spot for a cracking pizza and smooth craft beer (or a wine from its extensive list). It's a stylish setup with outdoor seating and a spacious, art-clad interior, and a menu that lists seasonal, wood-fired pizzas alongside classic Roman pastas and mains.

Armando al Pantheon
Roman €€

(Map p250; 🕿06 6880 3034; www.armandoal pantheon.it; Salita dei Crescenzi 31; meals €40; ⏰12.30-3pm Mon-Sat & 7-11pm Mon-Fri; ⛵Largo di Torre Argentina) With its cosy wooden interior and unwavering dedication to old-school Roman cuisine, Armando al Pantheon is a regular go-to for local foodies. It's been on the go for more than 50 years and has served its fair share of celebs, but it hasn't let fame go to its head and it remains as popular as ever. Reservations essential.

Osteria dell'Ingegno
Italian €€

(Map p250; 🕿06 678 06 62; www.osteriadell ingegno.com; Piazza di Pietra 45; meals €30-45; ⏰10am-1am; ⛵Via del Corso) An all-day restaurant-wine-bar with a colourful, art-filled interior, a casual, inclusive vibe, and a prime location on a charming central piazza. The daily menu hits all the right notes with a selection of seasonal pastas, creative mains and homemade desserts, while the 200-strong wine list boasts some interesting Italian labels.

Renato e Luisa
Lazio Cuisine €€

(Map p250; 🕿06 686 9660; www.renatoeluisa.it; Via dei Barbieri 25; meals €45; ⏰8pm-12.30pm Tue-Sun; ⛵Largo di Torre Argentina) Highly rated locally, this small backstreet trattoria is often packed. Chef Renato's menu features updated Roman classics that are modern and seasonal but also undeniably local, such as his signature *cacio e pepe e fiori di zucca* (pasta with pecorino cheese, black pepper and courgette flowers). Bookings recommended.

Ditirambo
Trattoria €€

(Map p250; 🕿06 687 1626; www.ristorante ditirambo.it; Piazza della Cancelleria 72; meals

Rome on a Plate

Wafer-thin base, covered in fresh bubbling toppings.

Best cooked in a blistering-hot wood-fired oven.

Often sold by weight, with prices marked per 100g.

Staples include *pizza bianca* ('white' pizza) and *pizza rossa* ('red' pizza).

Amazing washed down with a crisp lager

AFRICA STUDIO/SHUTTERSTOCK ©

Pizza by the Slice

Indulgent Dough to Go

For a snack on the run, Rome's *pizza al taglio* (pizza by the slice) places are hard to beat. Toppings are loaded atop thin, crispy, light-as-air, slow-risen bread and verge on the divine. Choose from an array at the counter; indicate how much you'd like; watch as it's cut to size (with scissors!), then head to the nearest piazza to dine al fresco.

★ Top Five for Pizza al Taglio

Pizzarium (p129) Savour Rome's best sliced pizza.

Panella (p132) Sumptuous bakery; the smell alone will lure you inside.

Forno di Campo de' Fiori (p124) Food-of-the-gods *pizza rossa* and *bianca*.

Forno Roscioli (p122) Thin and crispy, this is some of the tastiest *pizza rossa* in Rome.

Antico Forno Urbani (p124) A kosher bakery in the Ghetto with incredible *pizza bianca*.

Pizza, Trastevere district
STEFANO POLITI MARKOVINA/ALAMY STOCK PHOTO ©

€35-40; ⊗12.45-3.15pm & 7-11pm, closed Mon lunch; 🚊Corso Vittorio Emanuele II) Since opening in 1996, Ditirambo continues to win diners over with its informal trattoria vibe and seasonal, organic cuisine. Dishes cover many bases, ranging from old-school favourites to thoughtful vegetarian offerings and more exotic fare such as a *millefoglie* of sea bream and crunchy artichokes. Book ahead.

Casa Coppelle — Ristorante €€€

(Map p250; ☑06 6889 1707; www.casacoppelle. it; Piazza delle Coppelle 49; meals €65, tasting menu €85; ⊗noon-3.30pm & 6.30-11.30pm; 🚊Corso del Rinascimento) Boasting an enviable setting near the Pantheon and a plush, theatrical look – think velvet drapes, black lacquer tables and bookshelves – Casa Coppelle sets a romantic stage for high end Roman-French cuisine. Gallic trademarks like snails and onion soup feature alongside updated Roman favourites such as pasta *amatriciana* (with tomato sauce and pancetta) and *cacio e pepe* (pecorino and black pepper), here re-invented as a risotto with prawns. Book ahead.

Salumeria Roscioli — Deli, Ristorante €€€

(Map p250; ☑06 687 5287; www.salumeria roscioli.com; Via dei Giubbonari 21; meals €55; ⊗12.30-4pm & 7pm-midnight Mon-Sat; 🚊Via Arenula) The name Roscioli has long been a byword for foodie excellence in Rome, and this luxurious deli-restaurant is the place to experience it. Tables are set alongside the deli counter, laden with mouth-watering Italian and foreign delicacies, and in a small bottle-lined space behind it. The sophisticated food is top notch and there are some truly outstanding wines to go with it.

Casa Bleve — Ristorante €€€

(Map p250; ☑06 686 59 70; www.casableve. it; Via del Teatro Valle 48-49; meals €55-70; ⊗12.30-3pm & 7.30-11pm Mon-Sat; 🚊Largo di Torre Argentina) Ideal for a special occasion dinner, this palatial restaurant-wine-bar dazzles with its column-lined dining hall and stained-glass roof. Its wine list, one of

the best in town, accompanies a refined menu of creative antipasti, seasonal pastas and classic main courses.

Piperno — Ristorante €€€

(Map p254; ☑06 6880 6629; www.ristorante piperno.it; Via Monte de' Cenci 9; meals €45-55; ⊗12.45-2.20pm & 7.45-10.20pm, closed Sun dinner & Mon; 🚊Via Arenula) This historic Ghetto restaurant, complete with a formal, slightly stilted look, is a top spot to get to grips with traditional Jewish-Roman cooking and local offal dishes. Signature hits include deep-fried *filetti di baccalà* (cod fillets) and *animelle di agnello con carciofi* (lamb sweetbreads with artichokes). To finish off, try the *palle di Nonno fritte* (fried ricotta balls). Booking recommended.

⊗ Tridente, Trevi & the Quirinale

Bistro del Quirino — Italian €

(Map p252; ☑06 9887 8090; www.bistrotquirino. com; Via delle Vergini 7; brunch €10, à la carte €25; ⊗noon-3.30pm & 4pm-2am; 🚊Via del Corso) For unbeatable-value near Trevi Fountain, reserve a table at this artsy bistro adjoining Teatro Quirino. Theatre posters add bags of colour to the spacious interior where a banquet of a self-service 'brunch' buffet – fantastic salads, antipasti, hot and cold dishes – is laid out for knowing Romans to feast on.

Antico Caffè Greco — Cafe €

(Map p250; ☑06 679 17 00; Via dei Condotti 86; ⊗9am-9pm; Ⓜ Spagna) Rome's oldest cafe, open since 1760, is still working the look with the utmost elegance: waiters in black tails and bow tie, waitresses in frilly white pinnies, scarlet flock walls and age-spotted gilt mirrors. Prices reflect this amazing heritage: pay €9 for a cappuccino sitting down or join locals for the same (€2.50) standing at the bar.

Fatamorgana Corso — Gelato €

(Map p256; ☑06 3265 2238; www.gelateria fatamorgana.com; Via Laurina 10; 2/3/4/5 scoops €2.50/3.50/4.50/5; ⓧnoon-11pm; Ⓜ Flaminio) The wonderful all-natural, gluten-free gelato served at Fatamorgana is arguably Rome's best artisanal ice cream. Innovative and classic tastes of heaven abound, including flavours such as pear and caramel, all made from the finest seasonal ingredients. There are several branches around town.

Crispi   Health Food €

(Map p252; ☎06 4201 4040; Via Francesco Crispi 80; meals €9.50; ⓧ10.30am-7.30pm Mon-Fri; 🛜; Ⓜ Barberini) Homemade soups, quiches, wraps, salads, cookies and cakes jam-packed with natural goodness make for a super-powered lunch at this organic market and bistro, run by talented baker Flaminia and partner Matthew. Don't miss the creative fruit and veg juices (€6.50) and extract shots. Eat in, at bar stools around high tables between shelves of herbal teas, grains and pulses, or take away.

Gelateria Dei Gracchi   Gelateria €

(Map p256; ☎06 322 47 27; www.gelateriadei gracchi.it; Via di Ripetta 261; cones & tubs €2.50-4.50; ⓧnoon-8.10pm Sat-Wed, to midnight Thu & Fri; Ⓜ Flaminio) Handily located just off Piazza del Popolo, this outpost of the venerable Gelataria dei Gracchi by the Vatican is known for its superb ice cream made from the best ingredients. Flavours are classic.

Pepy's Bar   Cafe €

(Map p252; ☎06 4040 2364; www.pepysbar.it; Piazza Barberini 53; ⓧ7am-2am; 🛜; Ⓜ Barberini) Play the Roman: sit at a bistro table on the narrow pavement terrace and watch the fountains gush and *motorini* whizz by on Piazza Barberini at this down-to-earth, neighbourhood cafe in Trevi. It is a perfect spot for a relaxed drink any time of day, and its all-day sandwiches – made with perfectly square, crustless white bread – are almost too beautiful to eat.

Il Palazzetto   Cafe €

(Map p252; ☎06 6993 41000; Viccolo del Bottino 8; ⓧnoon-8.30pm Tue-Sun, closed in rain; Ⓜ Spagna) No terrace proffers such a fine view of the comings and goings on the Spanish Steps over an expertly shaken cocktail (€10–€13). Ride the lift up from the discreet entrance on narrow Via dei Bottino or look for steps leading to the bar from the top of the steps. Given everything is al fresco, the bar is only open in warm, dry weather.

Il Margutta   Vegetarian €€

(Map p256; ☎06 3265 0577; www.ilmargutta. bio; Via Margutta 118; lunch buffet weekdays/ weekends €15/25, meals €15-40; ⓧ8.30am-11.30pm; 🖉; Ⓜ Spagna) This chic art-gallery-bar-restaurant gets packed at lunchtime with Romans feasting on its good-value, eat-as-much-as-you-can buffet deal. Everything is organic, with an evening menu tempting with creative dishes such as tofu with marinated ginger and smoked tubers, or grilled chicory with almond cream, almond cream and candied tangerine. Among the various tasting menus is a vegan option.

Hostaria Romana   Trattoria €€

(Map p252; ☎06 474 52 84; www.hostaria romana.it; Via del Boccaccio 1; meals €40; ⓧ12.30-3pm & 7.15-11pm Mon-Sat; Ⓜ Barberini) A highly recommended address for lunch or dinner near Trevi Fountain, Hostaria Romana cooks up meaty, traditional classics like grilled goat chops, veal cutlets, roast suckling pig and T-bone steaks to a mixed Roman and tourist crowd. Busy, bustling and noisy, this is everything an Italian trattoria should be. Sign your name on the graffiti-covered walls before leaving.

Al Gran Sasso   Trattoria €€

(Map p256; ☎06 321 48 83; www.algransasso. com; Via di Ripetta 32; meals €30-35; ⓧ12.30-3.30pm & 7-11pm Sun-Fri Sep-Jul; Ⓜ Flaminio) A top lunchtime spot, this is a classic, dyed-in-the-wool trattoria that specialises in old-school country cooking. It's a relaxed place with a welcoming vibe, garish murals on the walls (strangely often a good sign) and tasty, value-for-money food. The fried dishes are excellent, or try one of the daily specials, chalked up on the board outside.

Colline Emiliane   Italian €€€

(Map p252; ✆06 481 75 38; www.collineemiliane.
com; Via degli Avignonesi 22; meals €45; ⏱12.45-
2.45pm & 7.30-10.45pm Tue-Sun, closed Sun dinner & Mon; Ⓜ Barberini) Sensational regional
cuisine from Emilia-Romagna aside, what
makes this small white-tablecloth dining
address so outstanding is its family vibe
and overwhelmingly warm service. Strong-
hold of the Latini family since the 1930s,
son Luca today runs the show together
with his mother Paola (dessert queen),
aunt Anna (watch her making fresh pasta
each morning in the glassed-off lab) and
father Massimo.

Palatium   Lazio Cusine €€€

(Map p250; ✆06 6920 2132; http://enoteca
regionalepalatium.it; Via Frattina 94; meals €45-
50; ⏱bar 11am-11pm, restaurant 12.30-3.30pm
& 7.30-10.30pm; Ⓠ Via del Corso) A rich showcase of regional bounty, this contemporary
enoteca regionale serves excellent artisanal
cheeses and salami as well as classic Roman staples such as *tonnarelli cacio e pepe*
(thick spaghetti with pecorino cheese and
black pepper). It also stocks an impressive
array of Lazio wines; try lesser-known
drops such as Aleatico.

Imàgo   Lazio €€€

(Map p252; ✆06 6993 4726; www.imagorestaurant.
com; Piazza della Trinità dei Monti 6, Hotel
Hassler; tasting menus €120-140; ⏱7-10.30pm;
Ⓜ Spagna; ✒) Even in a city of great views,
the panoramas from the Hassler Hotel's
Michelin-starred romantic rooftop restaurant are special (request the corner table),
extending over a sea of roofs to the great
dome of St Peter's Basilica. Complement-
ing the views are the bold, mod-Italian
creations of culinary whizz, chef Francesco
Apreda.

Babette   Italian €€€

(Map p256; ✆06 321 15 59; www.babette
ristorante.it; Via Margutta 1d; meals €50;
⏱1-3pm & 7-10.45pm Tue-Sun, closed Jan; ✒;
Ⓜ Spagna, Flaminio) Babette is run by two
sisters who used to produce a fashion

magazine, hence the effortlessly chic interi-
or of exposed brick walls and vintage painted signs. Cuisine is a feast of Italian dishes
with a creative French twist: *tortiglioni* with
courgette, saffron and pistachio pesto, for
example, followed by rabbit loin in juniper
sauce, then *torta Babette* (a light-as-air
lemon cheesecake).

Le Tamerici   Seafood €€€

(Map p252; ✆06 6920 0700; www.facebook.
com/letamerici; Vicolo Scavolino 79; meals
around €50; ⏱12.30-3.30pm & 7-11.30pm
Mon-Sat Sep-Jul; Ⓠ Via del Tritone) Exceptional
seafood and wine is a winning epicurean
combo at Le Tamerici, a cream-hued,
elegant escape from the Trevi Fountain
hubbub. Hidden away down an alleyway,
it impresses with its wine list, range of
digestivi and light-as-air homemade pasta
dishes laced with seafood – all served in a
twinset of intimate rooms with bleached-
wood beamed ceilings.

⊗ Vatican City, Borgo & Prati

Pizzarium   Pizza €

(Map p253; ✆06 3974 5416; Via della Meloria 43;
pizza slices €5; ⏱11am-10pm; Ⓜ Cipro-Musei
Vaticani) When a pizza joint is packed on a
wet winter's lunch, you know it's something special. Pizzarium, the takeaway of
Gabriele Bonci, Rome's acclaimed pizza
king, serves Rome's best sliced pizza, bar
none. Scissor-cut squares of soft, springy
base are topped with original combina-
tions of seasonal ingredients and served
on paper trays for immediate consump-
tion. Also worth trying are the freshly fried
supplì.

Sciascia Caffè   Cafe €

(Map p253; ✆06 321 15 80; Via Fabio Massimo
80/A; ⏱7am-8.30pm Mon-Sat, 8am-8pm Sun;
Ⓜ Ottaviano-San Pietro) There are several
contenders for the best coffee in town but
in our opinion, nothing tops the *caffè ec-
cellente* served at this polished old-school

From left: Street portrait of local baker; Babette (p129);
Mercato di Campo de' Fiori (p125)

cafe. A velvety smooth espresso served in
a delicate cup lined with melted chocolate,
it's nothing short of magnificent.

Fa-Bìo   Sandwiches €
(Map p253; ☎06 6452 5810; www.fa-bio.com;
Via Germanico 43; sandwiches €5; ⊙10.30am-
5.30pm Mon-Fri, to 4pm Sat; ☒Piazza del
Risorgimento, ⓂOttaviano-San Pietro) ☞
Sandwiches, wraps, salads and fresh
juices are all prepared with speed, skill and
fresh organic ingredients at this friendly
takeaway. Locals, Vatican tour guides and
in-the-know visitors come here to grab a
quick lunchtime bite.

Cotto Crudo   Sandwiches €
(Map p253; www.cottocrudo.it; Borgo Pio 46;
panini from €4.50; ⊙10am-6pm Tue-Sun;
☒Piazza del Risorgimento, ⓂOttaviano-San
Pietro) Amongst the tourist traps on Borgo
Pio, the main drag through what's left of
the medieval Borgo neighbourhood, this
hole-in-the-wall sandwich shop is ideal for
a Vatican pit stop. Specialising in produce
from Emilia-Romagna, it serves *panini* laden
with delectable fillings such as aged Parma

ham, *mortadella* and *culatella* (a type of
salami), as well as cheeses and vegetables.

Mo's Gelaterie   Gelato €
(Map p253; ☎06 687 43 57; Via Cola di Rienzo
174; gelato €2.50-6; ⊙11am-8pm; ☒Piazza del
Risorgimento) Chocoholics should make a
beeline for Mo's, a small gelateria nestled
between the shops on Via Cola di Rienzo.
The choice of flavours is limited but the artisanal gelato really hits the mark. The dark
chocolate is wonderful, and the banana is
packed with taste.

Il Sorpasso   Italian €€
(Map p253; ☎06 8902 4554; www.sorpasso.info;
Via Properzio 31-33; meals €20-35; ⊙7am-1am
Mon-Fri, 9am-1am Sat; ☒Piazza del Risorgimento)
A bar-restaurant hybrid sporting a vintage
cool look – vaulted stone ceilings, exposed
brick, rustic wooden tables – Il Sorpasso is
a Prati hotspot. Open throughout the day,
it caters to a fashionable crowd, serving
everything from salads and pasta specials
to *trappizini* (pyramids of stuffed pizza),
cured meats and cocktails.

Velavevodetto Ai Quiriti
Roman €€

(Map p253; ☎06 3600 0009; www.ristorante velavevodetto.it; Piazza dei Quiriti 5; meals €30-35; ⊙12.30-3pm & 7.45-11pm; ⓂLepanto) This welcoming restaurant wins you over with its unpretentious, earthy food and honest prices. The menu reads like a directory of Roman staples, and while it's all pretty good, standout choices include *fettuccine con asparagi, guanciale e pecorino* (pasta ribbons with asparagus, guanciale and pecorino cheese) and *polpette di bollito* (meat balls).

Del Frate
Wine Bar €€

(Map p253; ☎06 323 64 37; www.enotecadelfrate. it; Via degli Scipioni 122; meals €40-45; ⊙12.30-3pm & 6.30-11.45pm Mon-Sat; ⓂOttaviano-San Pietro) Locals love this upmarket wine bar–restaurant with its simple wooden tables and high-ceilinged brick-arched rooms. Dishes are designed to complement the *enoteca's* extensive wine list, so there's a formidable selection of cheeses, everything from Sicilian ricotta to Piedmontese robiola, alongside a refined menu of tartars, salads, fresh pastas and main courses.

Enoteca La Torre
Ristorante €€€

(☎06 4566 8304; www.enotecalatorreroma.com; Villa Laetitia, Lungotevere delle Armi 22; fixed-price lunch menu €60, tasting menus €95-120; ⊙12.30-2.30pm Tue-Sat & 7.30-10.30pm Mon-Sat; 🚇Lungotevere delle Armi) The art nouveau Villa Laetitia provides an aristocratic setting for this refined Michelin-starred restaurant. Since opening in 2013, it has established itself on Rome's fine-dining scene with its sophisticated brand of contemporary creative cuisine and a stellar wine list.

Ristorante L'Arcangelo
Ristorante €€€

(Map p250; ☎06 321 09 92; www.larcangelo.com; Via Giuseppe G Belli 59; meals €50; ⊙1-2.30pm Mon-Fri & 8-11pm Mon-Sat; 🚇Piazza Cavour) Styled as an informal bistro with wood panelling, leather banquettes and casual table settings, L'Arcangelo enjoys a stellar local reputation. Dishes are modern and creative yet still undeniably Roman in their use of traditional ingredients such as sweetbreads and *baccalà* (cod). A further plus is the wine list, which boasts some interesting Italian labels.

🍽 Offal on the Menu

The hallmark of an authentic Roman menu is the presence of offal. The Roman love of nose-to-tail eating arose in Testaccio around the city abattoir, and many of the area's trattorias still serve traditional offal-based dishes today. So whether you want to avoid them or try them, look out for *pajata* (veal's intestines), *trippa* (tripe), *coda alla vaccinara* (oxtail), *coratella* (heart, lung and liver), *animelle* (sweetbreads), *testarella* (head), *lingua* (tongue) and *zampe* (trotters).

Trippa alla romana soup
EZUMEIMAGES/GETTY IMAGES ©

La Veranda   Ristorante €€€

(Map p253; ☎06 687 29 73; www.laveranda.net; Borgo Santo Spirito 73; lunch €40, dinner €60-70, brunch €15-29; ⏲12.30-3pm & 7.30-11pm Tue-Sun; ▣Piazza Pia) Featured in Paolo Sorrentino's Oscar-winning film *The Great Beauty*, this fine-dining restaurant is as memorable for its setting – in the Renaissance Palazzo della Rovere – as its quality Italian cuisine. Inside, you can dine under 15th-century Pinturicchio frescoes, while in the warmer months, you can go al fresco in the garden. To enjoy the atmosphere for a snip of the regular price, stop by for Sunday brunch.

⊗ Monti, Esquilino & San Lorenzo

Panella   Bakery, Cafe €

(Map p255; ☎06 487 24 35; www.panellaroma. com; Via Merulana 54; meals €7-15; ⏲8am-11pm Mon-Thu, to midnight Fri & Sat, 8.30am-4pm

Sun; ⓂVittorio Emanuele) Pure heaven for foodies, this enticing bakery is littered with well-used baking trays loaded with freshly baked pastries loaded with confectioner's custard, wild-cherry fruit tartlets, *pizza al taglio, arancini* and focaccia – the smell alone is heavenly. Grab a bar stool between shelves of gourmet groceries inside or congratulate yourself on scoring a table on the flowery, sun-flooded terrace – one of Rome's loveliest.

La Casetta a Monti   Cafe €

(Map p246; ☎06 482 77 56; www.facebook. com/lacasettadeimonti; Via della Madonna dei Monti 62; ⏲9.30am-8pm Mon-Thu, to 10pm Fri & Sat, 8.30am-9pm Sun; 🛜; ⓂCavour) Delicious cakes, pastries and the finest chocolate salami in town is the name of the game at this uber-cute cafe, dolls-house size, run with much love and passion by Eugenio and Alessandro. Find the cafe, all fresh and sassy after a 2017 restyle, in a low-lying house with big windows and foliage-draped facade in the cobbled heart of Monti. There's breakfast, lunch, drinks and music too.

Grezzo   Pastries €

(Map p252; ☎06 48 34 43; www.grezzoitalia. it; Via Urbana 130; ice cream €3-6, desserts & smoothies €6; ⏲11am-11pm Mon-Thu & Sun, to midnight Fri & Sat; ▱; ⓂCavour) 'Raw chocolate' is the strapline of this gourmet boutique where a knowing crowd hobnobs over exquisite tiramisu miniatures, raw chocolate tarts, cheese cakes, Sicilian almond and pistachio gelato (made with fresh almond milk) and one-bite pralines. Smoothies, desserts and sweets are all raw, organic and gluten-free. Take away or squat on stools around low coffee tables crafted from corrugated cardboard and woodchip.

Mercato Centrale   Food Hall €

(Map p255; www.mercatocentrale.it/roma; Via Giolitti 36, Stazione Termini; snacks/meals from €3/10; ⏲7am-midnight; 🛜; ⓂTermini) A gourmet oasis for hungry travellers at Stazione Termini, this dazzling three-storey food hall is the latest project of Florence's savvy Umberto Montano. You'll find breads, pastries, cakes, veggie burgers, fresh pasta, truffles, pizza and a whole lot more beneath towering vaulted 1930s ceilings, as well as some of the city's most prized producers, including Gabriele Bonci (breads, focaccia and pizza), Roberto Liberati (salami), Marcella Bianchi (vegetarian).

Trieste Pizza   Pizza €

(Map p246; ☎366 8251313; www.trieste.pizza; Via Urbana 112; pizzas €2.20-3.60; ☜10am-11pm Sun-Thu, to 2am Fri & Sat; Ⓜ Cavour) A newcomer to the bohemian Monti neighbourhood, this welcoming takeaway joint serves excellent *pizzette* (small round pizzas). There are plenty to choose from, including the ever-present *margherita,* which comes with a soft, well-cooked base and a flavoursome coupling of tomato and melted mozzarella. Liquid sustenance is available in the form of bottled craft beers.

Alle Carette   Pizza €

(Map p246; ☎06 679 27 70; www.facebook.com/allecarrette; Via della Madonna dei Monti 95; pizza €5.50-8; ☜11.30am-4pm & 7pm-midnight; ⓓ; Ⓜ Cavour) Honest pizza, super thin and swiftly cooked in a wood-burning oven, is what this traditional Roman pizzeria on one of Monti's prettiest car-free streets has done well for decades. Tobacco-coloured walls give the place a vintage vibe and Roman families pile in here at weekends. Begin your local feast with some battered and deep-fried zucchini flowers or *baccalà* (salted cod).

Aromaticus   Health Food €

(Map p252; ☎06 488 13 55; www.aromaticus. it; Via Urbana 134; meals €10-15; ☜11am-3pm & 6-8.30pm; ⓢ; Ⓜ Cavour) Few addresses exude such a healthy vibe. Set within a shop selling aromatic plants and edible flowers, this inventive little cafe is the perfect place to satisfy green cravings. Its short but sweet menu features lots of creative salads, soups and gaspacho, tartare and carpaccio, juices and detox smoothies – all to stay or go.

Forno
Roscioli Pietro   Pizza, Bakery €

(Map p255; ☎06 446 71 46; www.facebook.com/fornorosciolipietro; Via Buonarroti 46-48; pizza slices €3.50; ☜7am-8pm Mon-Sat; Ⓜ Vittorio Emanuele) The off-the-beaten-track branch of this splendid deli-bakery-pizzeria has utterly delicious *pizza al taglio,* pasta dishes and other goodies that make it ideal for a swift lunch or stocking up for a picnic. It's on a road leading off Piazza Vittorio Emanuele II.

Necci dal 1924   Cafe €

(☎06 9760 1552; www.necci1924.com; Via Fanfulla da Lodi 68; ☜8am-2am; ⓢ ⓓ; ⓠ Via Prenestina) An all-round hybrid in edgy Pigneto, iconic Necci opened as a gelateria in 1924 and later became a favourite of film director Pier Paolo Pasolini. These days, it has English chef and owner Ben Hirst at its helm, who caters to a buoyant hipster crowd with its laid-back vibe, retro interior and food served all day. Huge kudos for the fabulous summertime terrace.

L'Asino d'Oro   Italian €€

(Map p252; ☎06 4891 3832; www.facebook. com/asinodoro; Via del Boschetto 73; weekday lunch menu €16, meals €45; ☜12.30-2.30pm & 7.30-11pm Tue-Sat; Ⓜ Cavour) This fabulous restaurant was transplanted from Orvieto, and its Umbrian origins resonate in Lucio Sforza's exceptional cooking. Unfussy yet innovative dishes feature bags of flavourful contrasts, like lamb meatballs with pear and blue cheese. Save room for the equally amazing desserts. Intimate, informal and classy, this is one of Rome's best deals – its lunch menu is a steal.

Temakinho   Sushi €€

(Map p246; ☎06 4201 6656; www.temakinho. com; Via dei Serpenti 16; meals €40; ☜12.30-3.30pm & 7pm-midnight; Ⓜ Cavour) In a city where food is still mostly resolutely (though deliciously) Italian, this Brazilian-Japanese hybrid serving up sushi and ceviche makes for a sensationally refreshing change. As well as delicious, strong caipirinhas, which combine Brazilian *cachaça,* sugar, lime and fresh fruit, there are 'sakehinhas' made with sake. It's very popular; book ahead.

Da Valentino — Trattoria €€

(Map p252; ☎06 488 06 43; Via del Boschetto 37; meals €30; ☺12.30-2.45pm & 8-11pm Mon-Sat; ☒Via Nazionale) The 1930s sign outside says 'Birra Peroni' and its enchanting vintage interior feels little changed. Come to this mythical dining address for delicious bruschetta, grilled meats, the purest of hamburgers and *scamorza,* a type of Italian cheese that is grilled and melted atop myriad different ingredients: tomato and rocket, artichokes, wafer-thin slices of aromatic *lardo di colonnata* (pork fat) from Tuscany and porcini mushrooms. No coffee.

Tram Tram — Osteria €€

(Map p255; ☎06 49 04 16; www.tramtram.it; Via dei Reti 44; meals €35-45; ☺12.30-3.30pm & 7.30-11.30pm Tue-Sun; ☒Via Tiburtina, ☒Via dei Reti) This wildly popular, old-style trattoria with lace curtains takes its name from the trams that rattle by outside. It's a family-run affair with a kitchen that unusually mixes classical Roman dishes with seafood from Puglia in Italy's hot south. Taste sensation *tiella riso, patata* and *cozze* (baked rice dish with rice, potatoes and mussels) is not to be missed. Book well ahead.

Trattoria Monti — Trattoria €€

(Map p255; ☎06 446 65 73; Via di San Vito 13a; meals €45; ☺1-2.45pm & 8-10.45pm Tue-Sat, 1-2.45pm Sun; ⓜVittorio Emanuele) The Camerucci family runs this elegant brick-arched trattoria proffering top-notch traditional cooking from the Marches region. There are wonderful *fritti* (fried things), delicate pastas and ingredients such as *pecorino di fossa* (sheep's milk cheese aged in caves), goose, swordfish and truffles. Try the egg-yolk *tortelli* pasta. Desserts are delectable, including apple pie with *zabaglione* (egg and marsala custard). Book ahead.

Doozo — Japanese €€

(Map p252; ☎06 481 56 55; www.doozo.it; Via Palermo 51; meals €15-30; ☺12.30-3pm & 7.30-11pm Tue-Sat, 7.30-10.30pm Sun; ☒Via Nazionale) Doozo (meaning 'welcome') is a spacious, Zen restaurant, bookshop and art gallery that serves traditional Japanese staples including tofu, sushi, sashimi, miso soup and tempura fries. The ambience is elegant and serene and the icing on the cake is a glorious courtyard garden, which, in summer, is a hidden oasis of peace, tranquillity and much-welcomed shade.

Antonello Colonna Open — Italian €€€

(Map p252; ☎06 4782 2641; www.antonellocolonna.it; Via Milano 9a; lunch/brunch €16/30, meals €16-100; ☺12.30-3.30pm & 8-11pm Tue-Sat, 12.30-3.30pm Sun; ☀; ☒Via Nazionale) Spectacularly set at the back of Palazzo delle Esposizioni, super-chef Antonello Colonna's Michelin-starred restaurant lounges dramatically under a dazzling all-glass roof. Cuisine is new Roman – innovative takes on traditional dishes, cooked with wit and flair – and the all-you-can-eat lunch buffet and weekend brunch are unbeatable value. On sunny days, dine al fresco on the rooftop terrace.

Said — Italian €€€

(Map p255; ☎06 446 92 04; www.said.it; Via Tiburtina 135; meals €50; ☺6pm-12.30am Mon, 10am-12.30am Tue-Fri, to 1.30am Sat, to midnight Sun; ☎; ☒Via Tiburtina, ☒Via dei Reti) Housed in an early 1900s chocolate factory, this hybrid cafe-bar, restaurant and boutique is San Lorenzo's coolest hipster haunt. Its Japanese pink-tea pralines, indulged in with a coffee or bought wrapped to take home, are glorious, and dining here is urban chic, with battered sofas, industrial antiques and creative cuisine. Lunch and dinner reservations, served from 12.30pm and 8pm, are recommended.

❸ Trastevere & Gianicolo

Da Augusto — Trattoria €

(Map p254; ☎06 580 37 98; Piazza de' Renzi 15; meals €25; ☺12.30-3pm & 8-11pm; ☒Viale di Trastevere, ☒Viale di Trastevere) Bag one of Augusto's rickety tables outside and tuck into some truly fabulous mamma-style cooking on one of Trastevere's prettiest piazza terraces. Hearty portions of all the Roman classics are dished up here as well as lots of rabbit, veal, hare and *pajata* (calf intestines). Winter dining is around vintage formica tables in a bare-bones interior, unchanged for decades. Be prepared to queue. Cash only.

La Prosciutteria   Tuscan €

(Map p254; ☑06 6456 2839; www.laprosciutteria. com/roma-trastevere; Via della Scala 71; chopping board €5 per person; ☺11am-11.30pm; ☐Piazza Trilussa) For a gratifying taste of Tuscany in Rome, consider lunch or a decadent *aperitivo* at this Florentine *prosciutteria* (salami shop). Made-to-measure *taglieri* (wooden chopping boards) come loaded with different cold cuts, cheeses, fruit and veg and are best devoured over a glass of Brunello di Montalcino or simple Chianti Classico. Bread comes in peppermint-green tin saucepans and dozens of hams and salami dangle overhead.

Bar San Calisto   Cafe €

(Map p254; Piazza San Calisto 3-5; ☺6am-2am Mon-Sat; ☐Viale di Trastevere, ☐Viale di Trastevere) Those in the know head to 'Sanca' for its basic, stuck-in-time atmosphere and cheap prices (beer from €1.50). It attracts everyone from intellectuals to keeping-it-real Romans, alcoholics and foreign students. It's famous for its chocolate – come for hot chocolate with cream in winter, and chocolate gelato in summer. Try the *sambuca con la mosca* ('with flies' – raw coffee beans). Expect occasional late-night jam sessions.

Da Enzo   Trattoria €€

(Map p254; ☑06 581 22 60; www.daenzoal29. com; Via dei Vascellari 29; meals €30; ☺12.30-3pm & 7-11pm Mon-Sat; ☐Viale di Trastevere, ☐Viale di Trastevere) Vintage buttermilk walls, red checked tablecloths and a traditional menu featuring all the Roman classics: what makes this staunchly traditional trattoria exceptional is its careful sourcing of local, quality products, many from nearby farms in Lazio. The seasonal,

⑩ Grattachecca

It's summertime, the living is easy, and Romans like nothing better in the sultry evening heat than to amble down to the river and partake of some *grattachecca* (crushed ice covered in fruit and syrup). It's the ideal way to cool down, and there are kiosks along the riverbank to satisfy this Roman favourite; try **Sora Mirella Caffè** (Map p254; Lungotevere degli Anguillara; grattachecca €3-6; ☺11am-3am May-Sep; ☐Lungotevere degli Anguillara), next to Ponte Cestio.

Grattachecca stand
VITANTONIO CAPORUSSO/ALAMY STOCK PHOTO ©

deep-fried Jewish artichokes and the *pasta cacio e pepe* in particular are among the best in Rome.

Fatamorgana Trastevere   Gelateria €

(Map p254; ☑06 580 36 15; www.gelateria fatamorgana.com; Via Roma Libera 11, Piazza San Cosimato; 2/3 scoops €2.50/3.50; ☺12.30pm-midnight summer, to 10.30pm winter; ☐Viale di Trastevere, ☐Viale di Trastevere) One of several Fatamorgana branches across Rome, this is one of the finest among the city's gourmet gelatarie. Quality natural ingredients are used to produce creative flavour combos such as pineapple and ginger or pear and gorgonzola. Gluten-free.

Don   Pizza €

(Map p254; www.donpizzafritta.com; Via di San Francesco a Ripa 103; pizzas €4-6.50; ☺noon-3pm & 7pm-midnight Tue-Sun; ☐Viale di Trastevere, ☐Viale di Trastevere) A small corner of

Naples in Trastevere, Don serves authentic fried pizzas. These golden half-moons of comforting doughiness and melted cheese are delicious and joyfully messy to eat – be careful not to burn your mouth on the first bite! Pizzas come in two sizes (*sorriso* and *Napoli d'Oro*) and feature fillers such as San Marzano tomatoes, sausage and *mozzarella di bufala*.

Fior di Luna   Gelateria €

(Map p254; ☑ 06 6456 1314; http://fiordiluna. com; Via della Lungaretta 96; gelato from €1.70; ☺ 11.30am-11.30pm Easter-Oct, to 9pm Tue-Sun Nov-Easter; ☐ Viale di Trastevere, ☐ Viale di Trastevere) For many Romans this busy little hub makes the best handmade gelato and sorbet in the world. Produced in small batches using natural, seasonal ingredients – a few flavours are even made from donkeys' milk. Favourites include walnut and honey, blueberry yoghurt, kiwi (complete with seeds) and pistachio.

Le Levain   Bakery €

(Map p254; ☑ 06 6456 2880; www.lelevain roma.it; Via Luigi Santini 22-23; meals €5.50-10; ☺ 8am-8.30pm Tue-Sat, 9am-7.30pm Sun; ☐ Viale di Trastevere, ☐ Viale di Trastevere) Many a foreigner living in Rome swears by this *pâtisserie au beurre fin* for their daily dose of rich and creamy butter, albeit it in the guise of authentic croissants, *pains au chocolat* and other French pastries. Traditional French cakes – colourful macarons, flaky millefeuilles, miniature *tartes aux pommes* (apple tarts) – are equally authentic.

Locanda del Gelato   Gelato €

(Map p254; www.locandadelgelato.it; Via di San Francesco a Ripa 71; tubs & cones €2-4.50; ☺ noon-midnight, shorter hours in winter; ☐ Viale di Trastevere, ☐ Viale di Trastevere) This artisanal gelateria has quickly risen to the top of the ice-cream charts since it opened in April 2016. It serves classic flavours alongside more adventurous creations such as *prosecco* and pear. The house specialty is *gelato al vino* (wine ice cream). Alternatively, there are crêpes and great smoothies.

Da Olindo   Trattoria €

(Map p254; ☑ 06 581 88 35; Vicolo della Scala 8; meals €25; ☺ noon-2.30pm & 7.30-11pm Mon-Sat; ☐ Piazza Trilussa) This is your classic family affair – the menu is short, the cuisine is robust, the portions are huge, and the atmosphere is lively. Expect *baccalà con patate* (salted cod stewed with potatoes) on Friday and *trippa* (tripe) on Saturday, but other dishes – such as *coniglio all cacciatore* (rabbit, hunter-style) or *polpette al sugo* (meatballs in sauce) – whichever day you like.

Mercato di Piazza San Cosimato   Market €

(Map p254; Piazza San Cosimato; ☺ 7am-2pm Mon-Sat; ☐ Viale di Trastevere, ☐ Viale di Trastevere) Trastevere's neighbourhood open-air market is a top spot to stock up on globe and violet artichokes, *Romanesco broccoli* (Roman cauliflower), dandelion greens and other seasonal foodstuffs, as has been the case for at least a century. Bring your own bag or basket.

La Gensola   Sicilian €€

(Map p254; ☑ 06 581 63 12; Piazza della Gensola 15; meals €45; ☺ 12.30-3pm & 7.30-11.30pm, closed Sun summer; ☐ Viale di Trastevere, ☐ Viale di Trastevere) Enjoy delicious traditional cuisine with an emphasis on seafood at this upmarket trattoria which can feel a tad overpriced. Begin the feast with a half-dozen oysters or wafer-thin slices of raw tuna, amberjack or seabass carpaccio, followed perhaps by a heap of *spaghellini* with fingernail-sized clams or seared anchovies with chicory. Meat lovers, tuck into Roman classics such as *coda alla vaccinara* (oxtail stew) or *trippa* (tripe).

Roma Sparita   Trattoria €€

(Map p254; ☑ 06 580 07 57; www.romasparita. com; Piazza di Santa Cecilia 1; meals €30; ☺ 12.30-2.30pm & 7.30-11.30pm Tue-Sat, 12.30-2.30pm Sun, closed last 2 weeks Aug; ☐ Viale di Trastevere, ☐ Viale di Trastevere) With its traditional country-style interior – all white-washed beams, terracotta tiled floor and pretty pastel colour palette – and summertime terrace overlooking one of Trastevere's most peaceful car-free piazzas, Roma Sparita is something of a find. The cuisine is Roman, with house speciality *pasta cacio e pepo* served in an edible bowl made of crisp, golden Parmesan. Don't hold back.

Buff Cheese €€

(Map p254; ✆06 581 96 67; www.ilbuff.it; Via di San Francesco a Ripa 141; meals €30-35; ⏱noon-midnight; 🚊Viale di Trastevere, 🚊Viale di Trastevere) Buff stands for buffalo, as in buffalo burgers and buffalo mozzarella, two of the specialties served at this cheese-themed eatery. A youthful, laid-back place with a casual vibe and modern rustic decor, it serves a wide-ranging menu of flavoursome dishes made with produce from its farm in Calabria.

Trattoria degli Amici Trattoria €€

(Map p254; ✆06 580 60 33; www.trattoriadegli amici.org; Piazza Sant'Egidio 6; meals €30-35; ⏱12.30-3pm & 7.30-11.30pm; 🚊Viale di Trastevere, 🚊Viale di Trastevere) Boasting a prime location on a pretty piazza, this cheerful trattoria is staffed by volunteers and people with disabilities who welcome guests with a warmth not always apparent in this touristy neck of the woods. Grab a square-side table and dig into fried starters and fresh, well-prepared Italian classics.

Paris in Trastevere Ristorante €€€

(di Dario Cappellanti; Map p254; ✆06 581 53 78; www.ristoranteparis.it; Piazza San Calisto 7a; meals €45-55; ⏱12.30-3pm & 7.30-11pm Tue-Sun; 🚊Viale di Trastevere, 🚊Viale di Trastevere) An old-school restaurant set in a 17th-century building with outdoor tables on a buzzing piazza, Paris – named for its founder, not the French capital – is the best place outside the Ghetto to sample Roman-Jewish cuisine. Signature dishes include *gran fritto vegetale con baccalà* (deep-fried vegetables with salted cod) and *carciofi alla giudia* (fried artichoke).

Glass Hostaria Italian €€€

(Map p254; ✆06 5833 5903; www.glass-restaurant.it; Vicolo del Cinque 58; menus €85-140, meals €90; ⏱7.30-11.30pm Tue-Sun; 🚊Piazza Trilussa) Trastevere's foremost

Piazza Santa Maria in Trastevere (p105)

foodie address, Michelin-starred Glass cooks up innovative cuisine in a contemporary, sophisticated space with mezzanine. Law graduate-turned-chef Cristina Bowerman creates inventive, delicate dishes that combine seasonal ingredients with traditional elements to delight and surprise the palate – best experienced with her tasting menu. There's also a vegetarian menu available.

 San Giovanni & Testaccio

Cafè Cafè   Bistro €

(Map p246; ✆06 700 87 43; www.cafecafe bistrot.it; Via dei Santi Quattro 44; meals €15-20; ◔9.30am-8.50pm; ⎔Via di San Giovanni in Laterano) Cosy, relaxed and welcoming, this cafe-bistro is a far cry from the usual impersonal eateries in the Colosseum area. With its rustic wooden tables, butternut walls and wine bottles, it's a charming spot to charge your batteries over an egg and bacon breakfast, a light lunch, or afternoon tea and homemade cake.

Trapizzino   Fast Food €

(✆06 4341 9624; www.trapizzino.it; Via Branca 88; trapizzini from €3.50; ◔noon-1am Tue-Sun; ⎔Via Marmorata) The original of what is now a growing countrywide chain, this is the birthplace of the *trapizzino,* a kind of hybrid sandwich made by stuffing a cone of doughy focaccia with fillers like *polpette al sugo* (meatballs in tomato sauce) or *pollo alla cacciatore* (stewed chicken). They're messy to eat but quite delicious.

Mordi e Vai   Street Food €

(www.mordievai.it; Box 15, Nuovo Mercato di Testaccio; panini €3.50-5; ◔8am-3pm Mon-Sat; ⎔Via Galvani) Chef Sergio Esposito's critically acclaimed and much frequented market stall – 'Bite and Go' in English – is all about the unadulterated joy of traditional Roman street food. That means *panini* such as his signature *allesso di scottona,* filled with tender slow-cooked beef, and plastic plates of no-nonsense meat-and-veg dishes.

Cups   Street Food €

(Box 44, Nuovo Mercato di Testaccio; dishes €5-8; ◔8am-4pm Mon-Sat; ⎔Via Galvini) This gourmet food stall at Testaccio market is the latest venture of local celebrity chef Cristina Bowerman. It takes its name from the carton cups used to serve dishes such as meatballs in tomato sauce and *brodo di pho,* a scorching take on the traditional Vietnamese soup dish. You can also order *panini,* focaccias, pastries and artisanal gelato.

Casa Manfredi   Cafe €

(✆06 9760 5892; Viale Aventino 93; ◔7am-9pm; ⎔Viale Aventino, ⎔Viale Aventino) Very 'in' when we visited, Casa Manfredi is a good-looking cafe in the wealthy Aventine neighbourhood. Join well-dressed locals for a quick coffee in the gleaming glass and chandelier interior, a light al fresco lunch or chic evening *aperitivo.* It also does a tasty line in artisanal gelato.

Pizzeria Da Remo   Pizza €

(✆06 574 62 70; Piazza Santa Maria Liberatrice 44; meals €15; ◔7pm-1am Mon-Sat; ⎔Via Marmorata) For an authentic Roman experience, join the noisy crowds here, one of the city's best-known and most popular pizzerias. It's a spartan-looking place, but the fried starters and thin-crust Roman pizzas are the business, and there's a cheerful, boisterous vibe. Expect to queue after 8.30pm.

Linari   Cafe €

(✆06 578 23 58; Via Nicola Zabaglia 9; ◔7am-9.30pm Wed-Mon; ⎔Via Marmorata) An authentic local hang-out, this cafe-*pasticceria* has the busy clatter of a good bar, with excellent pastries, splendid coffee and plenty of bar-side banter. There are a few outside tables, ideal for a cheap lunch, but you'll have to outfox the neighbourhood ladies to get one.

Sbanco   Pizza €€

(✆06 78 93 18; Via Siria 1; pizzas €7.50-12.50; ◔7.30pm-midnight; ⎔Piazza Zama) With its informal warehouse vibe and buzzing atmosphere, Sbanco is one of the capital's hottest pizzerias. Since opening in 2016, it has quickly made a name for itself with its creative, wood-fired pizzas and sumptuous fried starters – try the carbonara *supplì*. To top things off, it serves some deliciously drinkable craft beer.

Flavio al Velavevodetto   Roman €€
(✆06 574 41 94; www.ristorantevelavevodetto. it; Via di Monte Testaccio 97-99; meals €30-35; ⏰12.30-3pm & 7.45-11pm; 🚇Via Galvani) Housed in a rustic Pompeian-red villa set into the side of Monte Testaccio, an artificial hill of smashed Roman amphorae, this casual eatery is celebrated locally for its earthy, no-nonsense *cucina romana* (Roman cuisine). Expect antipasti of cheeses, cured meats and fried titbits, huge helpings of homemade pastas, and uncomplicated meat dishes.

Da Felice   Roman €€
(✆06 574 68 00; www.feliceatestaccio.it; Via Mastro Giorgio 29; meals €30-40; ⏰noon-3pm & 7.30-11pm; 🚇Via Marmorata) Much loved by local foodies and well-dressed diners, this historic stalwart is famous for its unwavering dedication to Roman culinary traditions. In contrast to the light-touch modern decor, the menu is pure old school with a classic weekly timetable: *pasta e fagioli* (pasta and beans) on Tuesdays, *bollito di manzo* (boiled beef) on Thursdays, fish on Fridays. Reservations essential.

Il Bocconcino   Lazio Cuisine €€
(Map p246; ✆06 7707 9175; www.ilbocconcino. com; Via Ostilia 23; meals €30-35; ⏰12.30-3.30pm & 7.30-11.30pm Thu-Tue; 🚇Via Labicana) One of the better options in the touristy pocket near the Colosseum, this easy-going trattoria stands out for its authentic regional cooking and use of locally sourced seasonal ingredients. Daily specials are chalked up on blackboards or there's a regular menu of classic Roman pastas, grilled meats, fish, and imaginative desserts.

Aroma   Ristorante €€€
(Map p246; ✆06 9761 5109; www.aromarestaurant.it; Via Labicana 125; meals €120-150; ⏰12.30-3pm & 7.30-11.30pm; 🚇Via Labicana) One for a special occasion, the rooftop

★ **Top Five for Vegetarians**

Il Margutta (p128)

Imàgo (p129)

Verde Pistacchio (p141)

Ditirambo (p125)

Grezzo (p132)

restaurant of the Palazzo Manfredi hotel offers once-in-a-lifetime views of the Colosseum and Michelin-starred food that rises to the occasion. Overseeing the kitchen is chef Giuseppe Di Iorio, whose seasonal menus reflect his passion for luxurious, forward-thinking Mediterranean cuisine.

Checchino dal 1887   Roman €€€
(✆06 574 63 18; www.checchino-dal-1887. com; Via di Monte Testaccio 30; meals €40-65; ⏰12.30-3pm & 8pm-midnight, closed Sun dinner & Mon; 🚇Via Galvani) A pig's whisker from the city's former slaughterhouse, this old-school restaurant, complete with dated wood-panelled interior, is a long-standing champion of the *quinto quarto* (fifth quarter – or insides of the animal). Signature dishes include *coda all vaccinara* (oxtail stew) and *rigatoni alla pajata* (pasta with a sauce of tomato and veal intestines).

⊗ Villa Borghese & Northern Rome

Pasticceria Gruè   Pastries €
(✆06 841 22 20; Viale Regina Margherita 95; pastries from €1.50; ⏰7am-9pm Sun-Fri; 🚇Viale Regina Margherita) One of many eateries on Viale Regina Margherita, this sleek *pasticceria*-cafe is a local hotspot – suits and sharply dressed office workers lunch here on delicate *panini* and daily pastas while the evening sees the aperitif crowd move in. But its real calling cards are the exquisitely designed pastries and chocolates that stare out from beneath the counter.

🍽 Hidden Gelato Gems

The northern neck of Rome harbours some outstanding gelaterie. They're not the easiest to find, though, and unless you know where to look you're unlikely to stumble on them. A typical case in point is **Neve di Latte** (🗘06 320 84 85; Via Poletti 6; gelato €2.50-5; ⊙noon-11pm Sun-Thu, to midnight Fri & Sat; 🚊Viale Tiziano), an innocuous looking place near MAXXI that serves some of the best classical ice creams in town. The pistachio, made with nuts from the Sicilian town of Bronte, is outstanding, as is the creme caramel.

LISAY/GETTY IMAGES ©

Caffè delle Arti   Cafe, Ristorante €€

(Map p256; 🗘06 3265 1236; www.caffedelle artiroma.com; Via Gramsci 73; meals €40-45; ⊙8am-5pm Mon, 8am-midnight Tue-Sun; 🚊Piazza Thorvaldsen) The cafe-restaurant of La Galleria Nazionale (p57) is situated in neoclassical splendour in a tranquil corner of Villa Borghese. An elegant venue, it's at its best on warm sunny days when you can sit on the terrace and enjoy the romantic setting over a lunch salad, cocktail or al fresco dinner of classic Italian cuisine.

Metamorfosi   Ristorante €€€

(🗘06 807 68 39; www.metamorfosiroma.it; Via Giovanni Antonelli 30; tasting menus €100-130; ⊙12.30-2.30pm & 8-10.30pm, closed Sat lunch & Sun; 🚊Via Giovanni Antonelli) This Michelin-starred Parioli restaurant is one of Rome's top dining tickets offering international fusion cuisine and a contemporary look that marries linear clean-cut lines with warm earthy tones. Chef Roy Carceres' cooking is eclectic, often featuring playful updates of traditional Roman dishes, such as his signature Uovo 65° carbonara antipasto, a deconstruction of Rome's classic pasta dish.

Molto   Ristorante €€€

(🗘06 808 29 00; www.moltoitaliano.it; Viale dei Parioli 122; meals €50-60; ⊙12.30-3pm & 7.30-11pm; 🚊Viale Parioli) Fashionable and quietly chic, Molto is a Parioli favourite. The discreet entrance gives onto an elegant, modern interior and open-air terrace, while the menu offers everything from cured meat and cheese starters to traditional Roman pastas and succulent roast meats. Saturday features a burger menu and there's brunch on Sunday (€40).

⊗ Southern Rome

Eataly   Italian €

(www.eataly.net; Piazzale XII Ottobre 1492; meals €10-50; ⊙shops 9am-midnight, restaurants typically noon-3.30pm & 7-11pm; 🛜; Ⓜ Piramide) Be prepared for some serious taste bud titillation in this state-of-the-art food emporium of gargantuan proportions. Four shop floors showcase every conceivable Italian food product (dried and fresh), while multiple themed food stalls and restaurants offer plenty of opportunity to taste or feast on Italian cuisine.

Doppiozeroo   Italian €

(🗘06 5730 1961; www.doppiozeroo.com; Via Ostiense 68; meals €15; ⊙7am-2am; 🚊Via Ostiense, Ⓜ Piramide) This easygoing bar was once a bakery, hence the name ('double zero' is a type of flour). But today the sleek, modern interior attracts hungry, trendy Romans who pile in here for its cheap, canteen-style lunches, famously lavish *aperitivo* (6pm to 9pm) and abundant weekend brunch (12.30pm to 3.30pm).

Verde Pistacchio Vegetarian, Vegan €

(✆06 4547 5965; www.facebook.com/verde
pistacchioroma; Via Ostiense 181; lunch menu
€14; ⊘10am-3.30pm & 5.30pm-midnight Mon-
Thu, 10am-3.30pm & 5.30pm-2am Fri, 6pm-2am
Sat, 6pm-midnight Sun; 🛱; ꟼVia Ostiense,
ⓂGarbatella) Camilla, Raffaele and Francesco are the trio of friends behind Green
Pistachio, a stylish bistro and cafe with a
minimalist, vintage interior and streetside
tables in the sun in summer. The kitchen
cooks up fantastic vegetarian and vegan
cuisine, and the lunchtime deal is a steal.
Lunch here before or after visiting Rome's
second-largest church, a stone's throw
away on the same street.

Pizza Ostiense Pizza €

(✆06 5730 5081; www.pizzeriaostiense.com; Via
Ostiense 56; pizzas from €5.50; ⊘6.30pm-1am,
closed Tue winter; ꟼVia Ostiense, ⓂPiramide)
Run by folk formerly of the much-lauded
classic Roman pizzeria Remo in Testaccio,
Pizza Ostiense offers similarly paper-thin,
crispy bases and delicious fresh toppings
and scrumptious *fritti* (fried things) in unfussy surroundings. There's a friendly vibe.

Andreotti Pastries €

(✆06 575 07 73; www.andreottiroma.it; Via Ostiense 54; pastries from €1.20; ⊘7.30am-10pm;
ꟼVia Ostiense, ⓂPiramide) Film director and
Ostiense local Ferzan Ozpetek is such a fan
of the pastries crafted at this 1934 *pasticceria* that he's known to cast them in his films.
They're all stars, from the buttery *crostate*
(tarts) to the piles of golden *sfogliatelle
romane* (ricotta-filled pastries). Hanging
out over a coffee on the sunny pavement
terrace is a warm-weather delight.

Porto Fluviale Italian €€

(✆06 574 31 99; www.portofluviale.com; Via del
Porto Fluviale 22; meals €25; ⊘10.30am-2am
Sun-Thu, to 3am Fri & Sat; 🛱; ⓂPiramide) A hip,
buzzing restaurant-bar in the industrial-chic
vein, Porto Fluviale attracts a mixed crowd –
lots of families included – with its spacious
lounge-style interior and good-value kitchen

that turns out everything from pasta, pizza
and *cicchetti* (tapas-style appetisers) to
burgers and meal-sized salads, all available
in half-portions too. Streetside seating is
limited to an attractive handful of turquoise
bistro tables.

L'Archeologia
Ristorante Italian €€€

(✆06 788 04 94; www.larcheologia.it; Via Appia
Antica 139; meals €50; ⊘12.30-3pm & 8-11pm;
ꟼVia Appia Antica) At home in an old horse
exchange on the Appian Way, this 19th-
century inn exudes vintage charm. Dining
is elegant, with white-tablecloth-covered
tables beneath age-old beams or in front of
the fireplace. In summer, dining is alfresco
and fragrant with the blooms of a magnificent 300-year-old wisteria. Cuisine is traditional Roman, and the wine list, exemplary.
Reservations recommended.

Qui Nun Se More Mai Italian €€

(✆06 780 39 22; www.facebook.com/qvinunse
moremai; Via Appia Antica 198; meals around
€40; ⊘noon-3pm & 7.30-11.45pm Tue-Sat,
noon-3pm Sun; ꟼVia Appia Antica) This small,
charismatic restaurant has an open fire for
grilling, plus a small terrace for when the
weather's good. The menu offers Roman
classics such as pasta *amatriciana,* carbonara, *alla gricia* and *cacio e pepe* – just the
thing to set you up for the road ahead.

Seacook Seafood €€€

(✆06 5730 1512; www.seacook.it; Via del
Porto Fluviale 7d-e; meals €60; ⊘noon-3pm
& 7pm-midnight; 🛱; ⓂPiramide) For stylish
seafood dining set in a chic aquatic ambience, look no further than this glorious
Scandinavian-styled space in Ostiense
with sea-blue bar-stool seating, potted
plants in white ceramic jugs and bamboo
lampshades. *'Cuochi e Pescatori'* (Cooks
and Fishermen) is the strapline and fish
is caught fresh from seafaring Salento in
southern Italy. Kick off your fishy feast with
the fish carpaccio of the day with papaya
and lime.

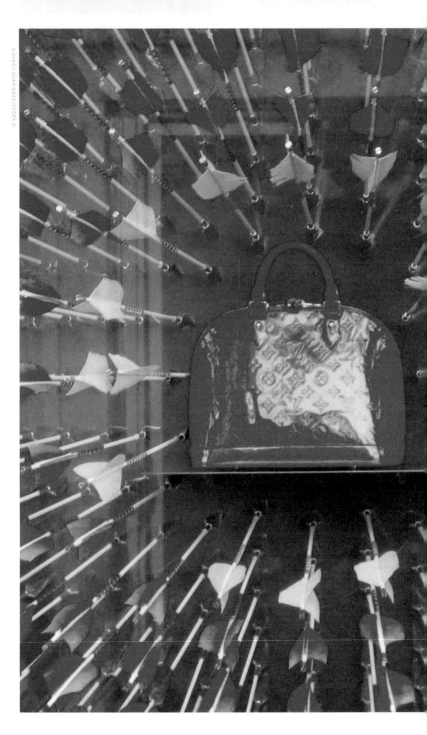

TREASURE HUNT

Begin your shopping adventure

Treasure Hunt

Rome boasts the usual flagship chain stores and glitzy designer outlets, but what makes shopping here so special is the legion of small, independent outfits: historic delis, dusty furniture workshops, small-label fashion boutiques and tiny artists' studios. Adding to the fun are much-frequented neighbourhood markets, selling everything from secondhand jeans to bumper produce from local farms.

Italy's reputation for quality is deserved and Rome is a top place for designer clothes, shoes and leather goods. Foodies will find no end of heavenly comestibles to enjoy, and homewares-lovers will discover enticing kitchenware and gorgeous objets d'art.

In This Section

Centro Storico.....................................148

Tridente, Trevi & the Quirinale 153

Vatican City, Borgo & Prati 156

Monti, Esquilino
& San Lorenzo 157

Trastevere & Gianicolo.......................159

San Giovanni & Testaccio 161

Villa Borghese
& Northern Rome................................161

Useful Phrases

I'd like to buy... Vorrei comprare...(vo. ray kom.*pra*.re)

I'm just looking. Sto solo guardando. (sto *so*.lo gwar.*dan*.do)

Can I look at it? Posso dareun'occhia-ta? (po.so *da*.re oo.no.*kya*.ta)

How much is this? Quanto costaques-to? (*kwan*.to *kos*.ta *kwe*.sto)

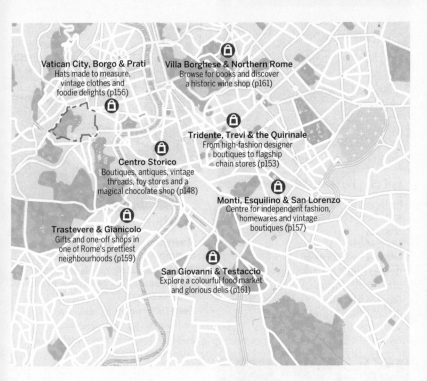

Vatican City, Borgo & Prati
Hats made to measure,
vintage clothes and
foodie delights (p156)

Villa Borghese & Northern Rome
Browse for books and discover
a historic wine shop (p161)

Tridente, Trevi & the Quirinale
From high-fashion designer
boutiques to flagship
chain stores (p153)

Centro Storico
Boutiques, antiques, vintage
threads, toy stores and a
magical chocolate shop (p148)

Monti, Esquilino & San Lorenzo
Centre for independent fashion,
homewares and vintage
boutiques (p157)

Trastevere & Gianicolo
Gifts and one-off shops in
one of Rome's prettiest
neighbourhoods (p159)

San Giovanni & Testaccio
Explore a colourful food market
and glorious delis (p161)

Opening Hours

Larger stores & city-centre shops
9am to 7.30pm (or 10am to 8pm) Monday to Saturday; some close Monday morning.

Smaller shops 9am to 1pm and 3.30pm to 7.30pm (or 4pm to 8pm) Monday to Saturday.

Sale Seasons

To grab a bargain, time your visit to coincide with the *saldi* (sales), which often offer savings of between 20% and 50%. Winter sales run from the first Saturday in January to mid-February, and summer sales from the first Saturday in July to early September.

The Best...

Experience Rome's best shopping

Gifts

Re(f)use (p153) Clever jewellery and bags made from upcycled materials.

Fabriano (p155) Leather-bound diaries, funky notebooks and products embossed with street maps of Rome.

Officina della Carta (p160) Beautiful hand-decorated notebooks, paper and cards.

Federico Buccellati (p154) Delightfully delicate nature-inspired jewellery pieces.

Clothing

Manila Grace (p153) Local label with unique, flamboyant designs.

Tina Sondergaard (p159) Have a retro-inspired dress adjusted to fit perfectly at this Monti boutique.

Gente (p153; pictured) Emporium-style boutique with big-name designers.

SBU (p149) High-end denim displayed on 19th-century shelving.

Homewares & Design

Artisanal Cornucopia (p153) Exclusive handmade pieces by Italian designers.

Mercato Monti Urban Market (p158) Vintage homewares cram this weekend market.

c.u.c.i.n.a (p154) Gastronomic gadgets to enhance your culinary life.

Leone Limentani (p153) Kitchenware and more at great prices.

Food & Wine

Volpetti (p161; pictured) Bulging with delicious delicacies, and notably helpful staff.

Les Vignerons (p160) Superb collection of natural wines and craft beers.

Salumeria Roscioli (p148) The name is a byword for foodie excellence.

La Bottega del Cioccolato (p158) Chocolates. Marvellous, irresistible chocolates.

Bookshops

Feltrinelli International (p157) An excellent range of the latest releases.

Almost Corner Bookshop (p160; pictured) A crammed haven full of rip-roaring reads.

Open Door Bookshop (p160) A trove of secondhand books in different languages.

Libreria l'Argonauta (p161) Lovely travel bookshop.

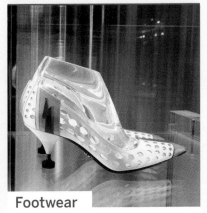

Footwear

Benheart (p159) Handmade shoes in a super-chic boutique.

Borini (p150) An unfussy shop filled with the latest women's footwear fashions.

Fausto Santini (p154) Butter-soft leather offerings from Rome's acclaimed shoe designer.

Giacomo Santini (p159) Pick up an exquisite Fausto-designed bargain at this outlet store.

Handicrafts

Ibiz – Artigianato in Cuoio (p148) Colourful leather wallets, bags and sandals.

La Bottega del Marmoraro (p154; pictured) Commission a marble inscription to remind you of Rome.

Le Artigiane (p149) Handmade clothes, jewellery, ceramics and design objects.

Pelletteria Nives (p154) Bespoke leather bags.

★ **Lonely Planet's Top Choices**

Confetteria Moriondo & Gariglio (p148) A magical-seeming chocolate shop.

Rechicle (p156) Iconic vintage fashions waiting to be found.

Pelletteria Nives (p154) Leather artisans make bags, wallets and more to your specifications.

Rachele (p148) Brightly coloured, handmade kids' clothing.

Il Sellaio (p156) Lovely hand-stitched bags and accessories.

🔒 Centro Storico

Confetteria Moriondo & Gariglio
Chocolate

(Map p250; 📞06 699 08 56; Via del Piè di Marmo 21-22; ⏰9am-7.30pm Mon-Sat; 🚇Via del Corso) Roman poet Trilussa was so smitten with this historic chocolate shop – established by the Torinese confectioners to the royal house of Savoy – that he was moved to mention it in verse. And we agree, it's a gem. Decorated like an elegant tearoom with crimson walls, tables and glass cabinets, it specialises in delicious handmade chocolates, many prepared according to original 19th-century recipes.

Ibiz – Artigianato in Cuoio
Fashion & Accessories

(Map p250; 📞06 6830 7297; www.ibizroma.it; Via dei Chiavari 39; ⏰9.30am-7.30pm Mon-Sat; 🚇Corso Vittorio Emanuele II) In her diminutive family workshop, Elisa Nepi and her team craft exquisite, soft-as-butter leather wallets, bags, belts and sandals, in simple but classy designs and myriad colours. You can

pick up a belt for about €35, while for a bag you should bank on at least €110.

Rachele
Children's Clothing

(Map p250; 📞329 6481004; www.facebook.com/racheleart; Vicolo del Bollo 6; ⏰10.30am-2pm & 3.30-7.30pm Tue-Sat; 🚇Corso Vittorio Emanuele II) If the kids' (under 12s) wardrobe needs an update you would do well to look up Rachele in her delightful shop just off Via del Pellegrino. With everything from hats and mitts to romper suits and jackets, all brightly coloured and all handmade, this sort of shop is a dying breed.

Salumeria Roscioli
Food & Drinks

(Map p250; 📞06 687 52 87; www.salumeriaroscioli.com; Via dei Giubbonari 21; ⏰8.30am-8.30pm Mon-Sat; 🚇Via Arenula) The rich scents of cured meats, cheeses, conserves, olive oil and balsamic vinegar intermingle at this top-class deli, one of Rome's finest. Alongside iconic Italian products, you'll also find a vast choice of wines and a range of French cheeses, Spanish hams and Scottish salmon.

SBU

REDA &CO SRL/ALAMY STOCK PHOTOS ©

Bartolucci — Toys

(Map p250; www.bartolucci.com; Via dei Pastini 98; ⊙10am-10.30pm; ⊠Via del Corso) It's difficult to resist going into this magical toyshop where everything is carved out of wood. By the main entrance, a Pinocchio pedals his bike robotically, perhaps dreaming of the full-size motorbike parked nearby, while inside there are all manner of ticking clocks, rocking horses, planes and more Pinocchios than you're likely to see in your whole life.

namasTèy — Tea

(Map p250; ☎06 6813 5660; www.namastey.it; Via della Palombella 26; ⊙10.30am-7.30pm Tue-Sat, 11.30am-7.30pm Sun, closed Aug; ⊠Largo di Torre Argentina) After a visit to this charming shop, you'll be reminded of it every time you have a tea. Set up like an apothecary with ceiling-high shelves and rows of jars, it stocks blends from across the globe, as well as everything you could ever need for your home tea ritual – teapots, cups, infusers and filters. It also sells coffee and bite-size snacks.

I Colori di Dentro — Art

(Map p250; ☎06 683 24 94; www.mgluffarelli. com; Via dei Banchi Vecchi 29; ⊙11am-6.45pm Mon-Sat; ⊠Corso Vittorio Emanuele II) Take home some Mediterranean sunshine. Artist Maria Grazia Luffarelli's paintings are a riotous celebration of Italian colours, with sunny yellow landscapes, blooming flowers, Roman cityscapes and comfortable-looking cats. You can buy original watercolours or prints, as well as postcards, T-shirts, notebooks and calendars.

SBU — Clothing

(Map p250; ☎06 6880 2547; www.sbu.it; Via di San Pantaleo 68-69; ⊙10am-7.30pm Mon-Sat; ⊠Corso Vittorio Emanuele II) The flagship store of hip jeans label SBU, aka Strategic Business Unit, occupies a 19th-century workshop near Piazza Navona, complete with cast-iron columns and wooden racks. Alongside jeans, superbly cut from top-end Japanese denim, you can also pick up casual shirts, jackets, hats, sweaters and T-shirts.

 Tax Free for Tourists

Non-EU residents who spend more than €175 at shops with a 'Tax Free for Tourists' sticker (www.taxrefund.it) are entitled to a tax refund. Complete a form and get it stamped by customs as you leave Italy.

Gucci shop window
RICHARD I'ANSON/GETTY IMAGES ©

Le Artigiane — Arts & Crafts

(Map p250; ☎06 6830 9347; www.leartigiane. it; Via di Torre Argentina 72; ⊙10am-7.30pm; ⊠Largo di Torre Argentina) A space for local artisans to showcase their wares, this eclectic shop is part of an ongoing project to sustain and promote Italy's artisanal traditions. It's a browser's dream with an eclectic range of handmade clothes, costume jewellery, ceramics, design objects and lamps.

Luna & L'Altra — Fashion & Accessories

(Map p250; ☎06 6880 4995; www.lunaelaltra. com; Piazza Pasquino 76; ⊙3.30-7.30pm Mon, 10am-7.30pm Tue-Sat; ⊠Corso Vittorio Emanuele II) An address for those with their finger on the pulse, this all-white fashion boutique is one of a number of independent stores on and around Via del Governo Vecchio. In its austere, gallery-like interior, clothes by designers Comme des Garçons, Issey Miyake and Yohji Yamamoto are exhibited in reverential style.

Mondello Ottica — Fashion & Accessories

(Map p250; ☎06 686 19 55; www.mondelloottica. it; Via del Pellegrino 98; ⊙10am-1.30pm & 4-7.30pm Tue-Sat; ⊠Corso Vittorio Emanuele II)

 High Fashion

Big-name designer boutiques gleam in the grid of streets between Piazza di Spagna and Via del Corso. The great Italian and international names are represented here, as well as many lesser-known designers, selling clothes, shoes, accessories and dreams. The immaculately clad high-fashion spine is Via dei Condotti, and there's also plenty of high fashion in Via Borgognona, Via Frattina, Via della Vite and Via del Babuino.

Downsizing a euro or two, Via Nazionale, Via del Corso, Via dei Giubbonari and Via Cola di Rienzo are good for midrange clothing stores, with some enticing small boutiques set among the chains.

GREG ELMS/GETTY IMAGES ©

Eyewear becomes art at this modish optician's on Via del Pellegrino. Known for its avant-garde window displays, often styled by contemporary artists, Mondello Ottica sells boldly coloured frames by leading designers such as Belgian brand Theo.

Borini Shoes
(Map p250; ✆06 687 56 70; Via dei Pettinari 86-87; ☺10am-7.30pm Mon-Sat; ◻Via Arenula) Don't be fooled by the workaday look of the store – those in the know head to this shop for the latest footwear fashions. Women's styles, ranging from ballet flats to heeled sandals, are displayed in functional glass cabinets, alongside a small selection of men's boots and leather lace-ups.

Le Tartarughe Fashion & Accessories
(Map p250; ✆06 679 22 40; www.letartarughe. eu; Via del Piè di Marmo 17; ☺10am-7.30pm Tue-Sat, 4-7.30pm Mon; ◻Via del Corso) Fashionable, versatile and elegant, Susanna Liso's catchy seasonal designs adorn this relaxed, white-walled boutique. Her clothes, often blended from raw silks, cashmere and fine merino wool, provide vibrant modern updates on classic styles. You'll also find a fine line in novel accessories.

**Atelier Patrizia
Pieroni** Fashion & Accessories
(Arsenale Gallery; Map p250; ✆06 6880 2424; www.patriziapieroni.it; Via del Pellegrino 172; ☺3.30-7.30pm Mon, 10am-7.30pm Tue-Sat; ◻Corso Vittorio Emanuele II) The atelier of celebrated Roman designer Patrizia Pieroni is a watchword for original, high-end women's fashion. The virgin white interior creates a clean, contemporary showcase for Patrizia's latest colourful creations, and exhibitions and cultural events are often hosted here.

Casali Art
(Map p250; ✆06 687 37 05; Via dei Coronari 115; ☺10am-1pm & 3-7.30pm Mon-Fri, 10am-1pm Sat; ◻Via Zanardelli) On Via dei Coronari, a street renowned for its antique shops, Casali deals in original and reproduction etchings and prints, many delicately hand-coloured. The shop is small but the choice isn't, ranging from 16th-century botanical manuscripts to postcard prints of Rome.

De Sanctis Ceramics
(Map p250; ✆06 6880 6810; www.desanctis 1890.com; Piazza di Pietra 24; ☺10.30am-1.30pm & 3-7.30pm Mon & Wed-Sat, 3.30-7.30pm Tue, 11am-5.30pm Sun Apr-Dec; ◻Via del Corso) In business since 1890, De Sanctis is full of impressive Sicilian and Tuscan ceramics, with sunbursts of colour decorating crockery, kitchenware, house numbers, *Cave Canem* ('Beware of the dog' in Latin) tiles and objets d'art. Items too heavy for your suitcase can be shipped worldwide.

Aldo Fefè Arts & Crafts
(Map p250; ☏06 6880 3585; Via della Stelletta 20b; ◷8am-7.30pm Mon-Sat; ☐Corso del Rinascimento) In his small workshop, master craftsman Aldo Fefè continues to bind books and produce beautifully hand-painted notebooks, albums, boxes and photo albums (from €18). You can also buy Florentine wrapping paper and calligraphic pens here.

Nardecchia Art
(Map p250; ☏06 686 93 18; Via del Monserrato 106; ◷10am-1pm & 4-7.30pm, closed Mon morning & Sun; ☐Lungotevere dei Tebaldi) Famed for its antique prints, historic Nardecchia sells everything from 18th-century etchings by Giovanni Battista Piranesi to more affordable 19th-century panoramas of Rome. Expect to pay at least €150 for a small framed print.

Alberta Gloves Fashion & Accessories
(Map p250; ☏06 679 73 18; Corso Vittorio Emanuele II 18; ◷10am-7pm Mon-Sat; ☐Largo di Torre Argentina) From elbow-length silk evening gloves to tan-coloured driving mitts, this tiny family-run shop has a hand-made glove for every conceivable occasion. Silk scarves and woolly hats too. Reckon on about €40 to €45 for a classic leather pair.

Tempi Moderni Jewellery, Vintage
(Map p250; Via del Governo Vecchio 108; ◷10.30am-1pm & 4.30-7.30pm Mon-Sat; ☐Corso Vittorio Emanuele II) Klimt prints sit side by side with pop art paintings and cartoon ties at this kooky curiosity shop. It's packed with vintage costume jewellery, Bakelite pieces from the 1930s and '40s, art nouveau and art deco trinkets, 19th-century resin brooches, and pieces by couturiers such as Chanel, Dior and Balenciaga.

Feltrinelli Books
(Map p250; www.lafeltrinelli.it; Largo di Torre Argentina 5a; ◷9am-9pm Mon-Fri, to 10pm Sat, 10am-9pm Sun; ☐Largo di Torre Argentina) Italy's most famous bookseller (and publisher) has shops across the capital. This one has a wide range of books (in Italian) on art, photography, cinema and history, as well as an extensive selection of literature and travel guides in various languages,

Dolce & Gabbana

Top Five Rome Souvenirs

Italian Wine

For a medium-bodied Barbera or a full-bodied Barolo, and to discover the difference, try Les Vignerons (p160), Enoteca Costantini (p157) or Bulzoni (p161).

Marble Carving

In Vino Veritas. *Carpe Diem*. *Nulla nuova, buona nuova*. Choose your fave Italian saying and set it in stone, literally, at La Bottega del Marmoraro (p154).

Leather Gloves

Could there be anything more Italian than pulling on a pair of leather driving gloves? Alberta Gloves (p151) or Sermoneta (p154) will get you sorted.

Perfume

Evoke the romantic aroma of Italy every day with a unique 'made in Rome' scent from Flumen Profumi (p155), Officina Profumo Farmaceutica di Santa Maria Novella (p155) or Olfattorio (p155).

One-Off Fashions

Rome is known for its sense of style. Stop by a *centro storico* or Monti boutique to find that perfect item.

including English. You'll also find CDs, DVDs and a range of stationery products.

Leone Limentani   Homewares

(Map p254; ☑06 6830 7000; www.limentani. com; Via del Portico d'Ottavia 47; ☺9am-1pm & 3.30-7.30pm Mon-Fri, 10am-7.30pm Sat; ☐Via Arenula) An institution in the Jewish Ghetto, and supposedly one of Rome's oldest shops, this well-stocked basement store sells everything you might need to decorate a house, from kitchenware and tableware to porcelain, furniture, lighting and objets d'art, many by top international brands.

AS Roma Store   Sports & Outdoors

(Map p250; ☑06 6978 1232; www.asromastore. com; Piazza Colonna 360; ☺10am-8pm; ☐Via del Corso) An official club store of AS Roma, one of Rome's two top-flight football teams. There's an extensive array of Roma-branded kit, including shirts, caps, T-shirts, scarves, hoodies, key rings and a whole lot more. You can also buy match tickets for Roma's home games at the Stadio Olimpico (p194).

⊙ Tridente, Trevi & the Quirinale

Artisanal Cornucopia   Design

(Map p256; ☑342 8714597; www.artisanal cornucopia.com; Via dell'Oca 38a; ☺10am-7pm; ☐Flaminio) One of several stylish independent boutiques on Via dell'Oca, this chic concept store showcases exclusive handmade pieces by Italian designers: think a trunk full of Anthony Peto hats, bold sculpture-like lamps by Roman designer Vincenzo Del Pizzo, and delicate gold necklaces and other jewellery crafted by Giulia Barela. It also sells artisan bags, shoes, candles, homewares and other lovely handmade objects.

Re(f)use   Design

(Map p250; ☑06 6813 6975; www.carmina campus.com; Via della Fontanelle di Borghese 40; ☺11am-7pm; ☐Via del Corso) Fascinating to browse, this clever boutique showcases

unique Carmina Campus pieces – primarily bags and jewellery – made from upcycled objects and recycled fabrics. The brand is the love child of Rome-born designer Ilaria Venturini Fendi (of *the* Fendi family), a passionate advocate of ethical fashion, who crafts contemporary bracelets from beer and soft drink cans, and bold bags from recycled materials.

Gente   Fashion & Accessories

(Map p256; ☑06 320 76 71; www.genteroma. com; Via del Babuino 77; ☺10.30am-7.30pm Mon-Thu, to 8pm Fri & Sat, 11.30am-7.30pm Sun; ☐Spagna) This multi-label boutique was the first in Rome to bring all the big-name luxury designers – Italian, French and otherwise – under one roof and its vast emporium-styled space remains an essential stop for every serious fashionista. Labels include Dolce & Gabbana, Prada, Alexander McQueen, Sergio Rossi and Missoni.

Manila Grace   Fashion & Accessories

(Map p250; ☑06 679 78 36; www.manilagrace. com; Via Frattina 60; ☺10am-7.30pm; ☐Spagna) An essential homegrown label for dedicated followers of fashion, Manila Grace mixes bold prints, patterns and fabrics to create a strikingly unique, assertive style for women who like to stand out in a crowd. Think a pair of red stiletto shoes with a fuchsia-pink pom pom on the toe, a striped jacket or a glittering gold bag with traditional tan-leather trim. Alessia Santi is the talented designer behind the brand.

Galleria Alberto Sordi   Shopping Centre

(Map p250; ☑06 6919 0769; www.galleria albertosordi.it; Piazza Colonna, Galleria di Piazza Colonna; ☺8.30am-9pm Mon-Sat, 9.30am-9pm Sun; ☐Via del Corso) This elegant stained-glass arcade appeared in Alberto Sordi's 1973 classic, *Polvere di stelle* (Stardust), and has since been renamed for Rome's favourite actor, who died in 2003. It's a serene place to browse stores such as Zara and Feltrinelli, and there's an airy cafe ideal for a quick coffee break.

La Bottega del Marmoraro   Art

(Map p256; 📞06 320 76 60; Via Margutta 53b; ⊗8am-7.30pm Mon-Sat; Ⓜ Flaminio) Watch *marmoraro* (marble artist) Sandro Fiorentini chip away in this enchanting Aladdin's cave filled, floor to ceiling, with his decorative marble plaques engraved with various inscriptions: *la dolce vita*, *la vita e bella* (life is beautiful) etc. Plaques start at €10 and Sandro will engrave any inscription you like (from €15). On winter days, warm your hands with Sandro in front of the open log fire.

Fendi   Fashion & Accessories

(Map p250; 📞06 33 45 01; www.fendi.com; Largo Carlo Goldoni 420, Palazzo Fendi; ⊗10am-7.30pm Mon-Sat, 10.30am-7.30pm Sun; Ⓜ Spagna) With traverstine walls, stunning contemporary art and sweeping red-marble staircase, the flagship store of Rome's iconic fashion house inside 18th-century Palazzo Fendi is dazzling. Born in Rome in 1925 as a leather and fur workshop on Via del Plebiscit, this luxurious temple to Roman fashion is as much concept store as *maison* selling ready-to-wear clothing for men and women (including its signature leather and fur pieces).

Fausto Santini   Shoes

(Map p250; 📞06 678 41 14; www.faustosantini. com; Via Frattina 120; ⊗11am-7.30pm Mon-Sat, to 7pm Sun; Ⓜ Spagna) Rome's best-known shoe designer, Fausto Santini, is famous for his beguilingly simple, architectural shoe designs, with beautiful boots and shoes made from butter-soft leather. Colours are beautiful, and the quality, impeccable. Seek out the end-of-line discount shop (p159) if the shoes here are out of your price range.

Federico Buccellati   Jewellery

(Map p250; 📞06 679 03 29; www.buccellati.com; Via dei Condotti 31; ⊗3-7pm Mon, 10am-1.30pm & 3-7pm Tue-Fri, 10am-1.30pm & 2-7pm Sat; Ⓜ Sagna) Run today by the third generation of one of Italy's most prestigious silver- and goldsmiths, this historical shop opened in 1926. Everything is handcrafted and often delicately engraved with decorative flowers, leaves and nature-inspired motifs.

Don't miss the Silver Salon on the 1st floor showcasing some original silverware and jewellery pieces by grandfather Mario.

Tod's   Shoes

(Map p250; 📞06 6821 0066; www.tods.com; Via della Fontanella di Borghese 56a; ⊗10.30am-7.30pm Mon-Sat, 11am-2pm & 3-7.30pm Sun; 🚌 Via del Corso) The trademark of this luxury Italian brand, known more recently as the generous benefactor behind the much-needed clean-up of the northern and southern facades of the Colosseum, is its rubber-studded loafers – perfect weekend footwear for kicking back at your country estate.

Pelletteria Nives   Fashion & Accessories

(Map p250; 📞333 3370831; Via delle Carrozze 16, 2nd fl; ⊗9am-7pm Mon-Sat; Ⓜ Spagna) Take the rickety lift to this workshop, choose from the softest leathers, and you will shortly be the proud owner of a handmade, designer-style bag, wallet, belt or briefcase – take a design with you. Bags cost €150 to €350 and take around a week to make.

Sermoneta   Fashion & Accessories

(Map p252; 📞06 679 19 60; www.sermoneta gloves.com; Piazza di Spagna 61; ⊗9.30am-8pm Mon-Sat, 10am-7pm Sun; Ⓜ Spagna) Buying leather gloves in Rome is a rite of passage for some, and its most famous glove-seller opposite the Spanish Steps is the place to go. Choose from a kaleidoscopic range of quality leather and suede gloves lined with silk and cashmere. An expert assistant will size up your hand in a glance. Just don't expect them to crack a smile.

c.u.c.i.n.a.   Homewares

(Map p250; 📞06 679 12 75; www.cucinastore. com; Via Mario de' Fiori 65; ⊗3.30-7.30pm Mon, 10am-7.30pm Tue-Fri, 10.30am-7.30pm Sat; Ⓜ Spagna) Make your own *cucina* (kitchen) look the part with the designer ware from this famous kitchenware shop, with everything from classic *caffettiere* (Italian coffee makers) to cutlery and myriad devices you'll decide you simply must have.

Fabriano — Arts & Crafts

(Map p256; ☎06 3260 0361; www.fabriano
boutique.com; Via del Babuino 173; ⊙10am-
8pm; Ⓜ Flaminio, Spagna) Fabriano makes
stationery sexy, with deeply desirable
leather-bound diaries, funky notebooks
and products embossed with street maps
of Rome. It's perfect for picking up a gift,
with other items including beautifully made
leather key rings and quirky paper jewellery
by local designers.

Salumeria Focacci — Food

(Map p250; ☎06 679 12 28; www.salumeria
focacci.it; Via della Croce 43; ⊙8am-8pm Mon-
Sat; Ⓜ Spagna) One of several smashing delis
along this pretty street, Salumeria Focacci is
the place to buy cheese, cold cuts, smoked
fish, caviar, pasta, olive oil and wine.

La Rinascente — Department Store

(Map p250; ☎06 678 42 09; www.rinascente.it;
Piazza Colonna, Galleria Alberto Sordi; ⊙10am-
9pm; ☐ Via del Corso) La Rinascente is a
stately, upmarket department store, with a
particularly buzzing cosmetics department,
all amid art nouveau interiors.

Furla — Fashion & Accessories

(Map p252; ☎06 679 71 59; www.furla.com;
Piazza di Spagna 22; ⊙10am-7.30pm; Ⓜ Spagna)
Simple, good-quality bags in soft leather
and in a brilliant array of colours is why the
handbagging hordes keep flocking to Furla,
where all sorts of accessories, from sun-
glasses to shoes, are available. There are
many other branches dotted across Rome.

Vertecchi Art — Art

(Map p250; ☎06 332 28 21; www.vertecchi.
com; Via della Croce 70; ⊙10am-8pm Mon-Sat,
11am-8pm Sun; Ⓜ Spagna) This paperware and
art shop has beautiful printed paper, cards
and envelopes that will inspire you to bring
back the art of letter writing, plus an amazing
choice of notebooks and art stuff.

Mercato delle Stampe — Market

(Print Market; Map p250; Piazza Borghese;
⊙10am-7pm, closed Aug; ☐ Piazza Augusto
Imperatore) The Mercato delle Stampe is
well worth a look if you're a fan of vintage

 Perfume Perfection

Try unique 'made in Rome' scents at
Flumen Profumi (Map p250; ☎06 6830
7635; www.flumenprofumi.com; Via della
Fontanella di Borghese 41; ⊙11am-2pm &
3.30-8pm Mon-Sat, 11am-2pm & 3-7.30pm
Sun; ☐ Via del Corso) on Tridente's smart-
est shopping strip. Natural perfumes
are oil-based, contain four to eight base
notes and evoke *la dolce vita*. Incantro
fuses pomegranate with white flowers,
while Ritrovarsi Ancora features fig, fig
leaf and fig wood bark.

Roma-Store (Map p254; ☎06 581 87 89;
www.romastoreprofumi.it; Via della Lungaretta 63; ⊙10am-8pm; ☐ Viale di Trastevere,
☐ Viale di Trastevere) is an enchanting perfume shop crammed full of deliciously
enticing bottles of scent, including lots
of small, lesser-known brands that will
have perfume-lovers practically fainting
with joy.

The Roman branch of one of Italy's
oldest pharmacies, **Officina Profumo
Farmaceutica di Santa Maria Novella**
(Map p250; ☎06 687 96 08; www.smnovella.
com; Corso del Rinascimento 47; ⊙10am-
7.30pm Mon-Sat; ☐ Corso del Rinascimento)
stocks natural perfumes and cosmetics
as well as herbal infusions and teas.

Olfattorio (Map p256; ☎06 361 23
25; www.baraparfums.it; Via di Ripetta 34;
⊙10.30am-7.30pm Mon-Sat, 11am-7pm Sun;
Ⓜ Flaminio) is like an *enoteca*, but with
perfume instead of drinks: scents are
concocted with names such as Artisan
Parfumeur, Diptyque and Coudray.

Officina Profumo Farmaceutica di Santa Maria Novella

books and old prints. Squirrel through the permanent stalls and among the tired posters and dusty back editions, and you might turn up some interesting music scores, architectural engravings or chromolithographs of Rome.

Fratelli Fabbi   Food

(Map p250; ☑06 679 06 12; www.fabbi.it; Via della Croce 27-28; ⊗8am-8pm Mon-Sat; ⓂSpagna) This small but flavour-packed delicatessen is a good place to pick up all sorts of Italian delicacies – fine cured meats, buffalo mozzarella from Campania, *parmigiano reggiano,* olive oil, *porchetta* from Ariccia, as well as Iranian caviar.

⊙ Vatican City, Borgo & Prati

Il Sellaio   Fashion & Accessories

(Map p253; ☑06 321 17 19; www.serafinipelletteria.it; Via Caio Mario 14; ⊗9.30am-7.30pm Mon-Fri, 9.30am-1pm & 3.30-7.30pm Sat; ⓂOttaviano-San Pietro) During the 1960s Ferruccio Serafini was one of Rome's most sought-after

artisans, making handmade leather shoes and bags for the likes of JFK, Liz Taylor and Marlon Brando. Nowadays, his daughter Francesca runs the family shop where you can pick up beautiful hand-stitched bags, belts and accessories. You can also have your own designs made to order.

Rechicle   Vintage

(Map p253; ☑06 3265 2469; Piazza dell' Unità 21; ⊗10.30am-2pm & 3.30-7.30pm Mon-Sat; ☐Via Cola di Rienzo) Lovers of vintage fashions should make a beeline for this fab boutique. Furnished with antique family furniture and restored cabinets, it's full of wonderful finds such as Roger Vivier comma heels (with their original box), iconic Chanel jackets, Hermès bags, Balenciaga coats and much more besides.

Antica Manifattura Cappelli   Hats

(Map p253; ☑06 3972 5679; www.antica-cappelleria.it; Via degli Scipioni 46; ⊗9am-7pm Mon-Sat; ⓂOttaviano-San Pietro) A throwback to a more elegant age, the atelier-boutique of milliner Patrizia Fabri offers a wide range of beautifully crafted hats. Choose from the off-the-peg line of straw Panamas, vintage

cloches, felt berets and tweed deerstalkers, or have one made to measure. Prices range from about €70 to €300 and ordered hats can be delivered within the day.

Enoteca Costantini
Wine

(Map p250; ☎06 320 35 75; www.pierocostantini. it; Piazza Cavour 16; ☺9am-1pm Tue-Sat, 4.30-8pm Mon-Sat; ☒Piazza Cavour) If you're after a hard-to-find grappa or something special for your wine collection, this excellent *enoteca* is the place to try. Opened in 1972, Piero Costantini's superbly stocked shop is a point of reference for aficionados with its 800-sq-m basement cellar and a colossal collection of Italian and world wines, champagnes and more than 1000 spirits from across the globe.

Castroni
Food & Drinks

(Map p253; ☎06 687 43 83; www.castronicoladi rienzo.com; Via Cola di Rienzo 196; ☺8am-8pm Mon-Sat, 9.30am-8pm Sun; ☒Via Cola di Rienzo) Founded in 1932, this historic food shop is an Aladdin's cave of gourmet treats. Towering, ceiling-high shelves groan under the weight of Italian wines and regional specialities, foreign delicacies, and all manner

of sweets and chocolates. Adding to the atmosphere are the coffee odours that waft up from the in-store bar.

ⓐ Monti, Esquilino & San Lorenzo

Feltrinelli International
Books

(Map p252; ☎06 482 78 78; www.lafeltrinelli. it; Via VE Orlando 84-86; ☺9am-8pm Mon-Sat, 10.30am-1.30pm & 4-8pm Sun; ☒Repubblica) The international branch of Italy's ubiquitous bookseller has a splendid collection of books in English, Italian, Spanish, French, German and Portuguese. You'll find everything from recent bestsellers to dictionaries, travel guides, DVDs and an excellent assortment of maps.

Fabio Piccioni
Jewellery

(Map p246; ☎339 4627261; Via del Boschetto 148; ☺2-8pm Mon, 10.30am-1pm & 2-8pm Tue-Sun; ☒Cavour) A sparkling treasure trove of decadent, one-of-a-kind costume jewellery. Artisan Fabio Piccioni recycles old trinkets to create remarkable art deco–inspired pieces.

★ Top Five Markets

Nuovo Mercato di Testaccio (p161)

Nuovo Mercato Esquilino (p158)

Porta Portese Market (p160)

Mercato Monti Urban Market (p158)

Via Sannio (p161)

From left: Porta Portese Market; Children's activities, Nuovo Mercato di Testaccio; Artichokes

 Unique Boutiques & Vintage Finds

Bohemian Via del Governo Vecchio is the best destination for cutting-edge designer boutiques and vintage clothing; it runs from a small square just off Piazza Navona towards the river. You'll also find one-off boutiques along Via del Pellegrino and around Campo de' Fiori. Via del Boschetto, Via Urbana and Via dei Serpenti in the Monti area feature unique clothing boutiques, including a couple where you can get your clothes adjusted to fit, as well as jewellery makers. Monti is also a centre for vintage clothes shops, and home to a weekend vintage market, **Mercato Monti Urban Market**.

REINER ELSEN/ALAMY STOCK PHOTO©

Transmission
Music

(Map p255; ☎06 4470 4370; www.transmission roma.com; Via Salentini 27; ☺10am-2pm & 3-6pm Mon-Sat; ☒Via Tiburtina) One of a handful of shops serving Rome's record collectors, this San Lorenzo store is vinyl nirvana. Its eclectic collection of LPs, CDs, 7-inch singles, DVDs and Blu-rays covers the whole musical gamut, ranging from classical music and 1950s oldies to jazz, reggae, punk, new wave and modern dance.

Mercato Monti Urban Market
Market

(Map p246; www.mercatomonti.com; Via Leonina 46; ☺10am-8pm Fri-Sun Sep-Jun; Ⓜ Cavour) Vintage clothes, accessories, one-off pieces by local designers: this market in the hip hood of Monti is well worth a rummage.

Podere Vecciano
Food

(Map p246; ☎06 4891 3812; www.podere vecciano.com; Via dei Serpenti 33; ☺10am-8pm; Ⓜ Cavour) Selling produce from its Tuscan farm, this shop is a great place to pick up presents, such as different varieties of pesto, honey and marmalade, selected wines, olive-oil-based cosmetics and beautiful olive wood chopping boards. There's even an olive tree growing in the middle of the shop.

Abito
Fashion & Accessories

(Map p252; ☎06 488 10 17; www.legallinelle.it; Via Panisperna 61; ☺11am-8pm Mon-Sat, 3-8pm Sun; Ⓜ Cavour) Wilma Silvestre, founder of local label Le Gallinelle, designs elegant clothes with a difference. Here at her Monti boutique you can browse her chic, laid-back styles and buy off the rack.

Nuovo Mercato Esquilino
Market

(Map p255; Via Filippo Turati 160; ☺5am-3pm Mon-Thu, to 5pm Fri & Sat; Ⓜ Vittorio Emanuele) Lap up the real Rome at this buzzing covered food market where budget-conscious Romans and students shop for fresh fruit, veg, exotic herbs, spices and more.

La Bottega del Cioccolato
Food

(Map p246; ☎06 482 14 73; www.labottegadel cioccolato.it; Via Leonina 82; ☺9.30am-7.30pm; Ⓜ Cavour) Run by the younger generation of a long line of *chocolatiers*, this is an exotic world of scarlet walls and old-fashioned glass cabinets set into black wood, with irresistible smells wafting in from the kitchen and rows of lovingly homemade chocolates on display. Hot chocolate and cups of milk chocolate, hazelnut or eggnog mousse to take away too.

Tina Sondergaard
Fashion & Accessories

(Map p252; ☎334 3850799; Via del Boschetto 1d; ☺3-7.30pm Mon, 10.30am-1pm & 1.30pm-7.30pm Tue-Sat, closed Aug; Ⓜ Cavour) Sublimely cut and whimsically retro-esque, Tina Sondergaard's handmade threads for women are a hit with fashion cognoscenti, including Italian rock star Carmen Consoli and the city's theatre and TV crowd. You can have adjustments made (included in the price); dresses cost around €150.

Giacomo Santini — Shoes

(Map p252; 📞06 488 09 34; Via Cavour 106; ⏱10am-1pm & 3.30-7.30pm Tue-Fri, 10am-1pm & 3-7.30pm Sat; Ⓜ Cavour) This Fausto Santini outlet, named after the Roman accessory designer's father Giacomo, sells last season's and discounted Fausto Santini boots, shoes and bags. Expect to pay €90 to €190 – a snip of the regular retail price – for a pair of his signature architectural designs in leather any colour of the rainbow. Sizes can be limited.

🅕 Trastevere & Gianicolo

Benheart — Fashion & Accessories

(Map p254; 📞06 5832 0801; www.benheart.it; Via del Moro 47; ⏱11am-11pm; 🚊Piazza Triussa) From the colourful resin floor papered with children's drawings to the vintage typewriter, dial-up telephone and old-fashioned tools decorating the interior, everything about this artisanal leather boutique is achingly cool.

Benheart, a young Florentine designer, is one of Italy's savviest talents and his fashionable handmade shoes (from €190) and jackets for men and women are glorious.

Antica Caciara Trasteverina — Food

(Map p254; 📞06 581 28 15; www.anticacaciara. it; Via San Francesco a Ripa 140; ⏱7am-2pm & 4-8pm Mon-Sat; 🚊Viale di Trastevere, 🚊Viale di Trastevere) The fresh ricotta is a prized possession at this century-old deli, and it's all usually snapped up by lunchtime. If you're too late, take solace in the to-die-for *ricotta infornata* (oven-baked ricotta), 35kg wheels of famous, black-waxed *pecorino romano* DOP (€16.50 per kilo), and aromatic garlands of *guanciale* (pig's jowl) begging to be chopped up, pan-fried and thrown into the perfect carbonara.

Biscottificio Innocenti — Food

(Map p254; 📞06 580 39 26; www.facebook. com/biscottificioInnocenti; Via delle Luce 21; ⏱8am-8pm Mon-Sat, 9.30am-2pm Sun; 🚊Viale di Trastevere, 🚊Viale di Trastevere) For homemade biscuits, bite-sized meringues and

Volpetti (p161)

 Local Artisans

Rome's shopping scene has a surpris-
ing number of artists and artisans who
create their goods on the spot in hidden
workshops. There are several places in
Tridente where you can have a bag, wallet or belt made to your specifications;
Pelletteria Nives (p154) is an excellent
example. At other shops you can commission lamps or embroidery.

Handcrafted leather bag
ISTOCK/GETTY IMAGES ©

tiny fruit tarts, there is no finer address in
Rome than this vintage *biscottificio* with
ceramic-tiled interior, fly-net door curtain
and a set of old-fashioned scales on the
counter to weigh out biscuits (€16 to €24
per kilo). The shop has been run with much
love and passion for several decades by the
ever-dedicated Stefania.

Les Vignerons
Wine

(Map p254; ☑06 6477 1439; www.lesvignerons.it;
Via Mameli 61; ⊙4-9pm Mon, 11am-9pm Tue-Thu,
11am-9.30pm Fri & Sat; 🚋Viale di Trastevere,
🚋Viale di Trastevere) If you're looking for
some interesting wines to take home,
search out this lovely Trastevere wine
shop. It boasts one of the capital's best
collections of natural wines, mainly from
small Italian and French producers, as well
as a comprehensive selection of spirits and
international craft beers.

Porta Portese Market
Market

(Map p254; Piazza Porta Portese; ⊙6am-2pm
Sun; 🚋Viale di Trastevere, 🚋Viale di Trastevere)
To see another side of Rome, head to this

mammoth flea market. With thousands of
stalls selling everything from rare books
and fell-off-a-lorry bikes to Peruvian shawls
and MP3 players, it's crazily busy and a lot
of fun. Keep your valuables safe and wear
your haggling hat.

Almost Corner Bookshop
Books

(Map p254; ☑06 583 69 42; Via del Moro 45;
⊙10am-8pm Mon-Sat, 11am-8pm Sun; 🚋Piazza
Trilussa) This is how a bookshop should
look: a crammed haven full of rip-roaring
reads, with every millimetre of wall space
containing English-language fiction and
nonfiction (including children's) and travel
guides. Heaven to browse.

Scala Quattordici
Clothing

(Map p254; ☑06 588 35 80; Villa della Scala
13; ⊙10am-1.30pm & 4-8pm Tue-Sat, 4-8pm
Mon; 🚋Piazza Trilussa) Make yourself over à
la Audrey Hepburn with these classically
tailored clothes in beautiful fabrics – either
made-to-measure or off-the-peg. Pricey (a
frock will set you back €600 plus) but oh
so worth it.

Officina della Carta
Gifts & Souvenirs

(Map p254; ☑06 589 55 57; Via Benedetta 26b;
⊙10.30am-7.30pm Mon-Sat; 🚋Piazza Trilussa) A
perfect present pit stop, this tiny workshop produces attractive hand-painted
paper-bound boxes, photo albums, recipe
books, notepads, photo frames and diaries.

Open Door Bookshop
Books

(Map p254; ☑06 589 64 78; www.books-in-italy.
com; Via della Lungaretta 23; ⊙10.30am-7.30pm
Mon-Sat; 🚋Viale di Trastevere, 🚋Viale di
Trastevere) A lovely crammed secondhand
bookshop, this is a great place to browse
and happen on a classic, with novels and
nonfiction in English, Italian, French and
Spanish.

La Cravatta
su Misura
Fashion & Accessories

(Map p254; ☑06 8901 6941; www.cravattasu
misura.it; Via di Santa Cecilia 12; ⊙10am-7pm
Mon-Sat, closed Aug; 🚋Viale di Trastevere,
🚋Viale di Trastevere) With ties draped over
the wooden furniture, this inviting shop

resembles the study of an absent-minded professor. But don't be fooled: these guys know their ties. Only the finest Italian silks and English wools are used in neckwear made to customers' specifications. At a push, a tie can be ready in a few hours. Expect to pay upwards of €49.

🜨 San Giovanni & Testaccio

Volpetti
Food & Drinks

(www.volpetti.com; Via Marmorata 47; ⊙8.30am-2pm & 4.30-8.15pm Mon-Wed, 8.30am-8.15pm Thu-Sat; 🚇Via Marmorata) This super-stocked deli, considered by many the best in town, is a treasure trove of gourmet delicacies. Helpful staff will guide you through the extensive selection of smelly cheeses, homemade pastas, olive oils, vinegars, cured meats, veggie pies, wines and grappas. It also serves excellent sliced pizza.

Nuovo Mercato di Testaccio
Market

(entrances Via Galvani, Via Beniamino Franklin, Via Volta, Via Manuzio, Via Ghiberti; ⊙7am-3.30pm Mon-Sat; 🚇Via Marmorata) A trip to Testaccio's neighbourhood market is always fun. Occupying a modern, purpose-built site, it hums with morning activity as locals go about their daily shopping, picking, prodding and sniffing the brightly coloured produce and browsing displays of shoes and clothes. You'll also find several stalls serving fantastic street food.

Soul Food
Music

(Map p255; 🕿06 7045 2025; www.haterecords.com; Via di San Giovanni in Laterano 192; ⊙10.30am-1.30pm & 3.30-7.30pm Tue-Sat; 🚇Via di San Giovanni in Laterano) Run by Hate Records, Soul Food is a laid-back record store with an eclectic collection of vinyl that runs the musical gamut, from '60s garage and rockabilly to punk, indie, new wave, folk, funk and soul. You'll also find retro T-shirts, fanzines and other groupie clobber.

Via Sannio
Market

(Map p255; ⊙9am-4.30pm Mon-Sat; Ⓜ San Giovanni) This historic clothes market sits in the shadow of the Aurelian Walls near San Giovanni metro station. Not a big place, it's awash with wardrobe staples, including heaps of cheap sweaters, new and vintage jeans, leather jackets and military garb. Note that some vendors can be quite in your face.

🜨 Villa Borghese & Northern Rome

Libreria l'Argonauta
Books

(🕿06 854 34 43; www.librerialargonauta.com; Via Reggio Emilia 89; ⊙10am-8pm Mon-Fri, 10am-1pm & 4-8pm Sat winter, 10am-8pm Mon-Fri summer; 🚇Via Nizza) Near the MACRO modern art museum, this travel bookshop is a lovely place to browse. With its serene atmosphere and shelves of travel literature, guides, maps and photo tomes, it can easily spark daydreams of far-off places. It also hosts regular talks and cultural events.

Bulzoni
Wine

(🕿06 807 04 94; www.enotecabulzoni.it; Viale dei Parioli 36; ⊙8.30am-2pm, 4.30-8.30pm Mon-Sat; 🚇Viale Parioli) This historic *enoteca* has been supplying Parioli's wine buffs since 1929. It has a formidable collection of Italian regional wines, as well as European and New World labels, and a carefully curated selection of champagnes, liqueurs, craft beers, olive oils and gourmet delicacies.

Bagheera
Fashion & Accessories

(🕿06 807 00 46; www.bagheeraboutique.com; Piazza Euclide 30; ⊙9.30am-1pm Tue-Sat & 3.30-7.30pm Mon-Sat; 🚇Piazza Euclide) This modish Parioli boutique has long been a local go-to for the latest fashions. Alongside sandals and vampish high heels, you'll find a range of jeans, dresses, bags and accessories by big-name international designers such as Chloé, Givenchy and Alexander Wang.

BAR OPEN

Afternoon beers, evening wines and
midnight cocktails

Bar Open

The best way to enjoy the nightlife is to wander from restaurant to bar, happily getting lost down picturesque cobbled streets. No other city has better backdrops for a drink: savour a Campari while overlooking the Roman Forum or artisanal beer while watching the light bounce off baroque fountains.

Most locals spend evenings checking each other out, partaking in gelato, and not drinking too much. Romans tend to dress up to go out, especially in the smarter clubs and bars in the centro storico *(historic centre) and Testaccio. Over in Pigneto and San Lorenzo, however, or at the* centri sociali *(social centres), the style is much more alternative.*

In This Section

Ancient Rome.....................................168

Centro Storico...................................168

Tridente, Trevi & the Quirinale 170

Vatican City, Borgo & Prati 170

Monti, Esquilino
& San Lorenzo 171

Trastevere & Gianicolo.......................175

San Giovanni & Testaccio 177

Villa Borghese
& Northern Rome................................178

Southern Rome...................................179

Opening Hours

Cafes 7.30am to 8pm

Traditional bars 7.30am to 1am or 2am

Bars, pubs and enoteche (wine bars)
Lunchtime or 6pm to 2am

Nightclubs 10pm to 4am

Villa Borghese & Northern Rome
From cool bars to hip
alternative venues (p178)

Vatican City, Borgo & Prati
Low-key scene with a sprinkling
of quiet wine bars (p170)

Tridente, Trevi & the Quirinale
Historic haunts and swanky, good-
looking cocktail bars (p170)

Centro Storico
Bars and a few clubs, a mix of
touristy and sophisticated (p168)

Monti, Esquilino & San Lorenzo
Boho bars, attractive *enoteche*
and grungy underground
clubs (p171)

Ancient Rome
A couple of popular retreats
near the Roman ruins (p168)

Trastevere & Gianicolo
Buzzing area riddled with
bars, pubs and cafes (p175)

San Giovanni & Testaccio
Night owls swarm to Testaccio's
strip of poptastic clubs (p177)

Southern Rome
Serious clubbing territory with
cool venues in Ostiense's ex-
industrial warehouses (p179)

Costs

Prices can be lower in the early evening, when there are often happy hours and *aperitivo* specials.

Glass of wine From €3
Pint of beer From €5
Cocktails From €10

Tipping

Tipping in bars is not necessary, although many people leave small change (say €0.20) if standing at the bar.

Key Phrases

Aperitivo A buffet of snacks to accompany evening drinks, usually from around 6pm till 9pm.

Bella figura Loosely translated as 'looking good'; dress to impress when heading out in Rome.

Enoteche Wine bars were originally known for their rough local wine poured straight from the barrel; nowadays they tend to be a tad more sophisticated.

The Best...

Experience Rome's finest drinking establishments

Aperitivo

Mescita Ferrara (p177) Delicious nibbles in this tiny *enoteca* adjoining La Ferrara restaurant.

Vinile (p179) Ostiense club with an 8pm banquet to fuel the evening.

Momart (p178) Students and local professionals love the expansive array of pizza and other snacks.

Freni e Frizioni (p176) Perennially cool bar with a lavish nightly buffet of snacks.

Enoteche

Il Tiaso (p171) A hip, living-room vibe, plentiful wines and live music.

Fafiuché (p173) A charming space with wine and artisanal beers.

La Barrique (p175) Inviting Monti address serving great wines and accompanying meals.

Ai Tre Scalini (p171; pictured) Buzzing *enoteca* that feels as convivial as a pub.

For a Lazy Drink

Stravinskij Bar (p170) The elegant bar of Hotel de Russie.

Yeah! Pigneto (p173) Boho bar with plenty of places to sit and chat.

Circus (p169) Laid-back ambience, free wi-fi and a varied crowd.

Streat San Lorenzo (p173) Beanbags, cocktails and an eclectic interior.

For Beer

Ma Che Siete Venuti a Fà (p177) Pint-sized bar crammed with real-ale choices.

Open Baladin (p168) More than 40 beers on tap and up to 100 bottled brews.

Bir & Fud (p176) Craft beer on tap and pizzas to match.

BrewDog Roma (p168) Scottish brewery with up to 20 draught options.

L'Oasi della Birra (p178) An oasis catering to beery thirsts.

To See & Be Seen

Etablì (p169) Chic bar near Campo de' Fiori, filled with vintage French furniture.

Salotto 42 (p169; pictured) A sitting-room-style bar facing the old Roman Stock Exchange.

Co.So (p172) Pigneto's hippest haunt.

Rec 23 (p178) Sharp New York style and locally inspired cocktails.

Alternative Options

Lanificio 159 (p178) Cool underground venue hosting live gigs and club nights.

Big Star (p177) Backstreet Trastevere bar, with regular DJs and a laid-back crowd.

Yeah! Pigneto (p173) Cool bar hosting live gigs and DJs in Rome's most boho district.

Locanda Atlantide (p175) Grunge and punk galore in this huge student-filled space.

Gay Bars & Clubs

Coming Out (p178; pictured) Friendly bar open all day, with drag shows and karaoke later on.

My Bar (p178) A mixed crowd by day that gets more gay by night.

Vicious Club (p173) Gay-friendly spot with a fashion-forward vibe.

★ Lonely Planet's Top Choices

Zuma Bar (p170) City views from the rooftop terrace of Palazzo Fendi.

Co.So (p172) Buzzy Pigneto hot spot, serving up out-there cocktails on bubble-wrap coasters.

Il Tiaso (p171) A charming space, a charming host, affordable wines by the glass and occasional live music.

Yellow Bar (p172) Young, effervescent vibe and themed parties à gogo.

Il Goccetto (p169) An old-school *vino e olio* (wine and oil) shop and neighbourhood bar.

🏛 Ancient Rome

0,75 Bar

(Map p246; 📞06 687 57 06; www.075roma.com; Via dei Cerchi 65; 🕙11am-2am; 🛜; 🚇Via dei Cerchi) This welcoming bar overlooking the Circo Massimo is good for a lingering evening drink, an *aperitivo* or casual meal (mains €6 to €16.50). It's a friendly place with a laid-back vibe, an international crowd, attractive wood-beam look, and cool tunes.

Cavour 313 Wine Bar

(Map p246; 📞06 678 54 96; www.cavour313.it; Via Cavour 313; 🕙12.30-3.15pm daily & 6pm-11.30pm Mon-Thu, 6pm-midnight Fri & Sat, 7-11pm Sun, closed Aug; 🚇Cavour) Close to the Forum, Cavour 313 is a historic wine bar, a snug, wood-panelled retreat frequented by everyone from tourists to actors and politicians. It serves a selection of salads, cold cuts and cheeses (€9 to €12), but the headline act here is the wine. And with more than 1000 labels to choose from, you're sure to find something to please your palate.

BrewDog Roma Craft Beer

(Map p246; 📞392 9308655; www.brewdog.com/bars/worldwide/roma; Via delle Terme di Tito 80; 🕙noon-1am Sun-Thu, to 2am Fri & Sat; 🚇Colosseo) This new bar by Scottish brewery BrewDog has proved a hit with Rome's craft-beer lovers since opening in the shadow of the Colosseum in late 2015. With a stripped-down grey and brick look and up to 20 brews on tap, it's a fine spot to kick back after a day on the sights.

🏛 Centro Storico

Open Baladin Bar

(Map p250; 📞06 683 8989; www.openbaladinroma.it; Via degli Specchi 6; 🕙noon-2am; 🛜; 🚇Via Arenula) For some years, this cool, modern pub near Campo de' Fiori has been a leading light in Rome's craft beer scene, and it's still a top place for a pint with more than 40 beers on tap and up to 100 bottled brews, many from Italian artisanal microbreweries. There's also a decent food menu with *panini,* gourmet burgers and daily specials.

Open Baladin

Jerry Thomas Project   Cocktail Bar

(Map p250; ☏370 1146287; www.thejerrythomas
project.it; Vicolo Cellini 30; ☺10pm-4am Tue-Sat;
🚇Corso Vittorio Emanuele II) A self-styled
speakeasy with a 1920s look and a pass-
word to get in – check the website and call
to book – this hidden bar has led the way in
Rome's recent love affair with cocktails. Its
master mixologists know their stuff and the
retro decor gives the place a real Prohibition-
era feel. Note there's a €5 'membership' fee.

Etablì   Wine Bar, Cafe

(Map p250; ☏06 9761 6694; www.etabli.it; Vicolo
delle Vacche 9a; ☺cafe 7.30am-6pm, wine bar
6pm-1am; 🛜; 🚇Corso del Rinascimento) Housed
in a 16th-century *palazzo* (mansion), Etablì
is a rustic-chic lounge-bar-restaurant where
you can drop by for a morning coffee, have
a light lunch or chat over an *aperitivo*. It's
laid-back and good-looking, with original
French-inspired country decor – leather
armchairs, rough wooden tables and a fireplace. It also serves full restaurant dinners
(€45) and hosts occasional live music.

Circus   Bar

(Map p250; ☏06 9761 9258; www.circusroma.
it; Via della Vetrina 15; ☺10am-2am; 🛜; 🚇Corso
del Rinascimento) A great little bar tucked
around the corner from Piazza Navona. It's
a laid-back place – think sofas, TV switched
on, newspapers to read – popular with a
young international crowd who come here
to catch up with friends and hang out over
a leisurely drink. The atmosphere heats up
in the evening, when cocktails and shots
take over from tea and cappuccino.

Salotto 42   Bar

(Map p250; ☏06 678 5804; www.salotto42.
space; Piazza di Pietra 42; ☺10.30am-2am; 🚇Via
del Corso) On a picturesque piazza, facing
the columns of the Temple of Hadrian, this
is a glamorous lounge bar, complete with
subdued lighting, vintage 1950s armchairs,
Murano lamps and heavyweight design
books. Come for the daily lunch buffet or to
hang out with the 'see and be seen' crowd
over one of its signature cocktails.

An Evening in the Centro Storico

Nightlife in the *centro storico* (historic
centre) is focused on two main areas:
the lanes around Piazza Navona, where
a number of elegant bars cater to
hip, beautiful people; and the rowdier
area around Campo de' Fiori, where
the crowd is younger and the drinking
heavier. The latter is where people con-
gregate after football games and where
foreign students head out on the booze.

L'Angolo Divino   Wine Bar

(Map p250; ☏06 686 4413; www.angolodivino.
it; Via dei Balestrari 12; ☺10.30am-3pm Tue-Sat,
plus 5pm-1am daily; 🚇Corso Vittorio Emanuele
II) This warm wine bar near Campo de' Fiori
is an oasis of genteel calm, with a carefully
curated wine list (mostly Italian but a few
French and New World labels), regional Italian cheeses and cured meats, and a small
daily menu of hot and cold dishes.

Il Goccetto   Wine Bar

(Map p250; www.facebook.com/Ilgoccetto;
Via dei Banchi Vecchi 14; ☺11.30am-2.30pm
Tue-Sat, plus 6.30pm-midnight Mon-Sat, closed
mid-Aug; 🚇Corso Vittorio Emanuele II) This
authentic *vino e olio* (wine and oil) shop has
everything you could want in a neighbourhood wine bar: a colourful cast of regulars,
a cosy interior, a selection of cheeses and
cold cuts, and an 800-strong wine list.

Gin Corner   Cocktail Bar

(Map p250; ☏06 6880 2452; www.facebook.
com/thegincorner; Via Pallacorda 2, Hotel Adriano; ☺6pm-midnight; 🚇Via di Monte Brianzo)
Forget fine wines and craft beers, this
chic bar in the Hotel Adriano is all about
the undistilled enjoyment of gin. Here the
making of a simple gin and tonic is raised
to an art form – the menu lists more than
10 varieties – and martinis are beautifully
executed. You can also get cocktails made
from other spirits if gin isn't your thing.

🕑 Tridente, Trevi & the Quirinale

Zuma Bar — Cocktail Bar

(Map p250; 📞06 9926 6622; www.zumarestaurant.com; Via della Fontanella di Borghese 48, Palazzo Fendi; ⊗6pm-1am Sun-Thu, to 2am Fri & Sat; 🛜; 🚇Via del Corso) Dress up for a drink on the rooftop terrace of Palazzo Fendi of fashionhouse fame – few cocktail bars in Rome are as sleek and hip as this. City rooftop views are predictably fabulous; cocktails mix exciting flavours like shiso with juniper berries, elderflower and *prosecco;* and DJ sets spin Zuma playlists at weekends.

Stravinskij Bar — Bar

(Map p256; 📞06 3288 8874; Via del Babuino 9, Hotel de Russie; ⊗9am-1am; 🚇Flaminio) Can't afford to stay at the celeb-magnet Hotel de Russie? Then splash out on a drink at its swish bar. There are sofas inside, but best is a drink in the courtyard, with tables overlooked by terraced gardens. Impossibly romantic in the best *dolce vita* style, it's perfect for a pricey cocktail or beer accompanied by appropriately posh bar snacks.

Canova — Bar

(Map p256; 📞06 361 22 31; http://lnx.canovapiazzadelpopolo.it; Piazza del Popolo 16; ⊗7.30am-12.30am; 🚇Flaminio) While left-wing authors Italo Calvino and Alberto Moravia used to drink at **Rosati** (📞06 322 58 59; www.barrosati.com; Piazza del Popolo 5; ⊗7.30am-11.30pm) on the other side of the square, their right-wing counterparts came to Canova, in the biz since 1890. Piazza views from the buzzing street terrace (heated in winter) remain as good as ever, and come 6pm, there's a generous *aperitivi* spread to nibble on with a sundowner.

🕑 Vatican City, Borgo & Prati

Be.re — Craft Beer

(Map p253; 📞06 9442 1854; www.be-re.eu; Piazza del Risorgimento, cnr Via Vespasiano; ⊗10am-2am; 🚇Piazza del Risorgimento) Rome's craft-beer fans keenly applauded the opening of this contemporary bar in late 2016. With its copper beer taps, exposed brick decor and high vaulted ceilings, it's a

From left: Americano cocktail; Stravinskij Bar courtyard; Trastevere nightlife

good-looking spot for an evening of Italian beers and cask ales. And should hunger strike, there's a branch of hit takeaway Trappizino right next door.

Passaguai
Wine Bar

(Map p253; ☎06 8745 1358; www.passaguai. it; Via Leto 1; ☺10am-2am Mon-Fri, 6pm-2am Sat & Sun; ☎; ☐Piazza del Risorgimento) A basement bar with tables in a cosy stone-clad interior and on a quiet side street, Passaguai feels pleasingly off-the-radar. It's a great spot for a post-sightseeing cocktail or glass of wine – there's an excellent choice of both – accompanied by cheese and cold cuts, or even a full meal from the small menu.

Makasar Bistrot
Wine Bar, Teahouse

(Map p253; ☎06 687 46 02; www.makasar.it; Via Plauto 33; ☺noon-midnight Mon-Thu, to 2am Fri & Sat, 5pm-midnight Sun; ☐Piazza del Risorgimento) Recharge your batteries with a quiet drink at this bookish bistro. Pick your tipple from the 250-variety tea menu or opt for an Italian wine and sit back in the softly lit earthenware-hued interior. For something

to eat, there's a small menu of salads, bruschetta, baguettes and hot dishes.

❸ Monti, Esquilino & San Lorenzo

Il Tiaso
Bar

(☎06 4547 4625; www.iltiaso.com; Via Ascoli Piceno 25; ☺6pm-2am; ☎; ☐Circonvallazione Casilina) Think living room with zebra-print chairs, walls of indie art, Lou Reed biographies wedged between wine bottles, and 30-something owner Gabriele playing his latest New York Dolls album to neo-beatnik chicks, corduroy-clad professors and the odd neighbourhood dog. Expect well-priced wine, an intimate chilled vibe, regular live music and lovely pavement terrace.

Ai Tre Scalini
Wine Bar

(Map p246; ☎06 4890 7495; www.aitrescalini. org; Via Panisperna 251; meals €25; ☺12.30pm-1am; ⓂCavour) A firm favourite since 1895, the 'Three Steps' is always packed, with crowds spilling out of the violet door and into the street. Enjoy a heart-warming array of

Craft Beer & Lazio Wine

In recent years beer drinking has really taken off in Italy, and especially in Rome, with specialised bars and restaurants now offering microbrewed beers. Local favourites include **Birradamare** (www.birradamare.it) in Fiumicino, **Porto Fluviale** (p141) in Ostiense, and **Birra del Borgo** in Rieti (on the border between Lazio and Abruzzo), which opened local beer haunts **Bir & Fud** (p176) and **Open Baladin** (p168). Local beers even reflect the seasonality that's so important in Rome – look, for example, for winter beers made from chestnuts.

Lazio wines may not be household names yet, but it's well worth trying some local wines while you're here. Although whites dominate Lazio's production – 95% of the region's Denominazione di Origine Controllata (DOC; the second of Italy's four quality classifications) wines are white – there are a few notable reds as well. To sample Lazio wines, **Palatium** (p129) and **Terre e Domus** (p122) are the best places to go.

cheeses, salami and dishes such as *polpette al sugo* (meatballs with sauce), washed down with a superb choice of wine or beer.

Gatsby Café   Bar, Cafe

(Map p255; ☑06 6933 9626; Piazza Vittorio Emanuele II 106; cocktails €7-10; ☺8am-midnight Mon-Thu, to 2am Fri & Sat; Ⓜ Termini) There's good reason why the friendly bar staff here all wear flat caps, feather-trimmed trilbies and other traditional gents hats: this fabulous 1950s-styled space with salvaged vintage furniture and flashes of funky geometric wallpapering was originally a milliner's shop called Galleria Venturini. Brilliant rhubarb or elderflower *spritz,* craft cocktails, gourmet *panini* (€5) and *taglieri* (salami and cheese platters) make it a top *aperitivo* spot.

Il Sorì   Wine Bar

(Map p255; ☑393 4318661; www.ilsori.it; Via dei Volsci 51; ☺7.30pm-2am Mon-Sat; ☐ Via Tiburtina) Every last salami slice and chunk of cheese has been carefully selected from Italy's finest artisanal and small producers at this gourmet wine bar and bottega, an unexpected pearl of a stop for dedicated foodies in student-driven San Lorenzo. Interesting and unusual wine tastings, theme nights, 'meet the producer' soirées and other events cap off what is already a memorable drinking (and dining) experience.

Spirito   Cocktail Bar

(☑327 2983900; www.club-spirito.com; Via Fanfulla da Lodi 53; ☺7.30pm-3am Wed-Mon; ☐ Via Prenestina) A fashionable address only for those in the know, Spirito is spirited away behind a simple white door at the back of a sandwich shop in edgy Pigneto. New Yorker in style, this is a Prohibition speakeasy with expertly mixed craft cocktails (around €10), gourmet food, live music and shows, roulette at the bar and a fun-loving crowd.

Yellow Bar   Bar

(☑06 446 35 54; www.the-yellow.com; Via Palestro 40; ☺24hr; ☎; Ⓜ Castro Pretorio) With its vintage zinc bar, high vaulted ceiling and amusing house rules chalked on the blackboard, this is a definite notch up from your bog-standard pub. Across the street from the hostel of the same name, around-the-clock Yellow is packed with young, fun, international travellers. DJs spin tunes from 10pm until 4am, there are live bands at weekends and themed parties galore. Breakfast and all-day food is also served.

Co.So   Cocktail Bar

(☑06 4543 5428; Via Braccio da Montone 80; ☺7pm-3am Mon-Sat; ☐ Via Prenestina) The chicest bar in Pigneto, tiny Co.So (meaning 'Cocktails & Social') is run by Massimo D'Addezio (a former master mixologist at Hotel de Russie) and is hipster to the hilt. Think Carbonara Sour cocktails (with pork-fat-infused vodka), bubblewrap coasters, and popcorn and M&M bar snacks. Check its Facebook page for the latest happenings.

Streat San Lorenzo
Lounge, Bar

(Map p255; ☏06 6401 3486; www.facebook. com/streatSL; Piazza dei Campani 6-8; ⊗11am-2am; 🛜; 🚊Via dei Reti) The sort of place where you can really kick back and relax, this lounge bar is an enticing all-rounder for meals, late-night cocktails or afternoon lounging over drinks. Vintage curiosities – an old Polaroid camera, printing blocks, copper tea pots – add visual interest and mixed-bag seating covers everything from bar stools and beanbags to a saggy leather sofa. Yes, punters can tinkle on the piano.

Vicious Club
Club

(Map p255; ☏345 845 65 91; www.viciousclub. com; Via Achille Grandi 7a; ⊗10pm-late Mon-Sat; 🚊Piazza di Porta Maggiore) This hugely trendy, gay-friendly club and cocktail bar near Termini station is the hottest kid on the block (not to mention a little wild around the edges) on Rome's fairly conservative clubbing scene. Expect an underground vibe, unfamiliar to Romans, with its black interior covered almost entirely in mirrors, sultry twinset of DJ booths and smoking room.

Yeah! Pigneto
Bar

(☏06 6480 1456; www.yeahpigneto.com; Via Giovanni de Agostini 41; ⊗7.30pm-2am; 🚊Via Casilina) We say si! to Yeah! Pigneto, a relaxed boho-feeling bar with a mismatched vintage look, DJs playing jazz and the walls covered in collages and classic album covers. It's a good place for lingering over drinks and food. Regular weekend gigs.

Fafiuché
Wine Bar

(Map p246; ☏06 699 09 68; www.fafiuche.it; Via della Madonna dei Monti 28; ⊗5.30pm-1am Mon-Sat; Ⓜ Cavour) Fafiuché roughly translates as 'playful' or 'unusual' in Piedmontese dialect, and this narrow, bottle-lined bar more than lives up to that. Come here to *'liberate la gola'* (literally 'clear your throat' but something more akin to 'free your taste buds') with fine wine, artisanal beers and tasty dishes originating from all over Italy. A lavish *aperitivo* buffet (6pm to 9pm) is served.

Zest Bar
Bar

(Radisson Blu es. Hotel; Map p255; ☏06 4448 4384; Via Filippo Turati 171; ⊗9am-1am; 🛜; Ⓜ Vittorio Emanuele) In need of a cocktail in

Evening drinks streetside in Trastevere

Rome in a Glass

1 slice of orange

medium tumbler or highball

ice

90ml fresh orange juice

30ml Campari

A Garibaldi Aperitivo

How to make a Garibaldi

○ Plenty of ice is key. Fill up the glass!

○ Pour in the Campari and juice and stir briefly. Garnish with the orange slice. *Salute!*

Story Behind the Cocktail

Invented at the beginning of the 20th century, the Garibaldi takes its name from Giuseppe Garibaldi, an Italian general who fought to liberate Sicily and bring it into the Kingdom of Italy. The drink's two components – Campari (from Italy's north) and oranges (from Sicily) – represent this unification of the Beautiful Country. To top it off, the drink's rosy hue is also reminiscent of the red shirts of Garibaldi's victorious soldiers.

★ Top Five Bars for Cocktails

Freni e Frizioni (p176)

Co.So (p172)

Jerry Thomas Project (p169)

Gatsby Café (p172)

0,75 (p168)

Portrait of Giuseppe Garibaldi
DE AGOSTINI PICTURE LIBRARY/GETTY IMAGES ©

the Termini district? Pop up to the 7th-floor bar at the slinkily designed Radisson Blu es. Hotel. Chairs are by Jasper Morrison, views are through plate-glass, and there's a sexy outdoor rooftop pool to gaze at, open May to September.

Vini e Olii   Bar
(Via del Pigneto 18; ☺11am-2pm & 6pm-midnight Mon-Sat; 🚊Circonvallazione Casilina) Forget the other bars with their scattered outside tables and styled interiors that line Pigneto's main pedestrianised drag. If you want authenticity, this traditional 'wine and oil' shop is the place, with its cheap beer and wine and menu of antipasti and *porchetta* (pork roasted in herbs). Outside seating only.

Ice Club   Bar
(Map p246; ☎06 9784 5581; www.iceclubroma.it; Via della Madonna dei Monti 18; ☺5pm-1am Mon-Thu & Sun, to 2am Fri & Sat; Ⓜ Cavour) Novelty value is what the Ice Club is all about. Pay €15 (you get a free vodka cocktail served in a glass made of ice), don a (completely unflattering) hospital-blue thermal cloak and mittens, and enter the bar, in which everything is made of ice (temperature: −5°C). Most people won't chill here for too long.

Gente di San Lorenzo   Bar
(Map p255; ☎06 445 44 25; Via degli Aurunci 42; ☺7am-2am; 🤖; 🚊Via dei Reti) San Lorenzo's signature bar is a chilled place to hang with students over a drink, snack or meal. The interior is airy, with warm wooden floors, brick arches and a couple of sofas, but the real action happens outside on the pavement terrace where there are prime people-watching views of Piazza dell'Immacolata and its throngs of students lazing beneath orange trees on balmy nights.

Al Vino al Vino   Wine Bar
(Map p246; ☎06 48 58 03; Via dei Serpenti 19; ☺10.30am-2.30pm & 6pm-12.30am; Ⓜ Cavour) Mixing lovely ceramic-topped bistro tables with bottle-lined walls and the odd contemporary painting, this rustic *enoteca* (wine bar) is an attractive spot to linger over a

fine collection of wine, including several *passiti* (sweet wines). The other speciality is *distillati* – grappa, whisky and so on.

La Barrique   Wine Bar
(Map p252; ☎06 4782 5953; Via del Boschetto 41b; ☺1-3pm & 7.30-11.30pm Mon-Fri, 7.30-11.30pm Sat & Sun; Ⓜ Cavour) This traditional *enoteca,* with old-fashioned wooden furniture and whitewashed walls, is a classy yet casual place to linger over excellent French, Italian and German wines. A choice of creative pastas and mains provide a great accompaniment, or stick to enticing tasting platters of artisanal cheeses and cold cuts to honour your *vino.*

Locanda Atlantide   Club
(Map p255; ☎06 9604 5875; www.facebook.com/locanda.atlantide; Via dei Lucani 22b; cover varies; ☺9.30pm-late Oct-Jun; 🚊Scalo San Lorenzo) Come and tickle Rome's grungy underbelly. Descend through a door in a graffiti-covered wall into this cavernous basement dive, packed to the rafters with studenty, alternative crowds and featuring everything from prog-folk to techno and psychedelic trance.

Libreria Caffè Bohemien   Bar
(Map p246; ☎339 7224622; www.caffebohemien.it; Via degli Zingari 33-36; ☺2pm-1am Sun, Mon, Wed & Thu, to 2am Fri & Sat; Ⓜ Cavour) This hybrid wine bar, tearoom and bookshop with fantastic paint-peeling front door lives up to its name; it feels like something you might stumble on in Left Bank Paris. It's small, with mismatched vintage furniture and an eclectic crowd drinking wine by the glass, aperitifs, tea and coffee.

🍸 Trastevere & Gianicolo

Pimm's Good   Bar
(Map p254; ☎06 9727 7979; www.facebook.com/pimmsgood; Via di Santa Dorotea 8; ☺10am-2am; 🤖; 🚊Piazza Trilussa) 'Anyone for Pimm's' is the catchline of this eternally popular bar with part red-brick ceiling that does indeed serve Pimm's – the classic way or in a variety of cocktails (€10). The party-loving

Al fresco drinking by the Tiber

guys behind the bar are serious mixologists and well-crafted cocktails is their thing. Look for the buzzing street-corner pavement terrace – lit up in winter with flaming outdoor heaters.

Keyhole — Cocktail Bar

(Map p254; Via Arco di San Calisto 17; ⊙10pm-2am; ⊠Viale di Trastevere, ⊠Viale di Trastevere) The latest in a growing trend of achingly hip, underground speakeasies in Rome, Keyhole ticks all the boxes: no identifiable name or signage outside the bar; a black door smothered in keys; and Prohibition-era decor including leather Chesterfield sofas, dim lighting and an electric craft cocktail menu. Not sure what to order? Ask the talented mixologists to create your own bespoke cocktail (around €10).

Il Baretto — Bar

(Map p254; ☎06 589 60 55; www.ilbarettoroma. com; Via Garibaldi 27; ⊙7am-2am Mon-Sat; ⊠Via Garibaldi) Venture a little way up the Gianicolo, up a steep flight of steps from Trastevere – go on, it's worth it. Because there you'll discover this cocktail bar where the basslines are meaty, the bar staff hip, and the interior a mix of vintage and pop art.

Freni e Frizioni — Bar

(Map p254; ☎06 4549 7499; www.freniefrizioni. com; Via del Politeama 4-6; ⊙7pm-2am; ⊠Piazza Trilussa) This perennially cool Trastevere bar is housed in an old mechanic's workshop – hence its name ('brakes and clutches') and tatty facade. It draws a young *spritz*-loving crowd that swells onto the small piazza outside to sip superbly mixed cocktails (€10) and seasonal punches, and fill up on its lavish early-evening *aperitivo* buffet (7pm to 10pm). Table reservations are essential on Friday and Saturday evenings.

Bir & Fud — Craft Beer

(Map p254; ☎06 589 40 16; www.birandfud.it; Via Benedetta 23; ⊙noon-2am; ⊠Piazza Trilussa) On a narrow street lined with raucous drinking holes, this brick-vaulted bar-pizzeria wins plaudits for its outstanding collection of craft *bir* (beer), many on tap, and equally tasty *fud* (food) for when late-night munchies strike. Its Neapolitan-style wood-fired pizzas are particularly excellent.

Ma Che Siete Venuti a Fà Pub

(Map p254; ☑06 6456 2046; www.football-pub.
com; Via Benedetta 25; ⊙11am-2am; ☑Piazza
Trilussa) Named after a football chant, which
translates politely as 'What did you come
here for?', this small Trastevere pub is a
beer-buff's paradise, stocking around 15 international craft beers on tap and even more
by the bottle. Expect some rowdy drinking.

Mescita Ferrara Wine Bar

(Map p254; ☑06 5833 3920; www.enotecaferrara.
it; Piazza Trilussa 41; ⊙6pm-2am; ☑Piazza
Trilussa) This tiny bar inside the entrance
to upmarket restaurant Enoteca Ferrara
serves delectable *aperitivo* and has a wide
range of wines by the glass – perfect for an
intimate tête-à-tête.

Ombre Rosse Bar

(Map p254; ☑06 588 41 55; www.ombrerossein
trastevere.it; Piazza Sant'Egidio 12; ⊙10am-2am;
☑Piazza Trilussa) A seminal Trastevere
hangout. Grab a table on the lovely piazza
terrace and watch the world go by amid
a mixed Roman and tourist clientele. The
drinks and food menu covers the whole
gambit of tastes and budgets, and there's
live music (jazz, blues, world) most nights.

Hýbris Bar

(Map p254; ☑06 9437 6374; www.hybrisartgallery.
com; Via della Lungaretta 164; 🛜; ☑Viale di
Trastevere, 🚊Viale di Trastevere) This cafe-bar
on pedestrian, shop-strewn Via della Lungaretta is an artsy spot for early-evening drinks
between marble busts and art works.
Vintage typewriters, a piano and armchairs
add a generous dose of trendy old-world
ambience, and the marble balustrade bar
gets top marks for design. Live jazz and
blues, DJ sets and art exhibitions too.

Big Star Bar

(Map p254; ☑380 3405948; www.facebook.
com/bigstar.rome; Via Mameli 25; ⊙7.30pm-
2am; ☑Viale di Trastevere, 🚊Viale di Trastevere)
Off the beaten Trastevere track, away from
the main action, this is a rip-roaring rock
'n' roll backstreet bar with music, beers,
cocktails, hipster DJs and an international
crowd. It exudes a definite alternative vibe.

🍷 San Giovanni & Testaccio

Bibenda Wine Concept Wine Bar

(Map p246; ☑06 7720 6673; www.wineconcept.
it; Via Capo d'Africa 21; ⊙noon-3pm & 6pm-
midnight Mon-Thu, to 2am Fri & Sat, closed
Sat lunch & Sun; ☑Via Labicana) Wine buffs
looking to excite their palate should search
out this smart modern *enoteca*. Boasting a
white, light-filled interior, it has an extensive
list of Italian regional labels and European
vintages, as well as a small daily food menu.
Wines are available to drink by the glass or
buy by the bottle.

Rec 23 Bar

(☑06 8746 2147; www.rec23.com; Piazza
dell'Emporio 2; ⊙6.30pm-2am daily & 12.30-
3.30pm Sat & Sun; ☑Via Marmorata) All exposed brick and mismatched furniture, this

---

 Gay & Lesbian Rome

There is only a smattering of dedicated
gay and lesbian clubs and bars in Rome,
though many nightclubs host regular
gay and lesbian nights. For local information, pick up a copy of the monthly
magazine *AUT*, published by **Circolo
Mario Mieli** (www.mariomieli.org) or
look online at **AZ Gay** (www.azgay.it).
Lesbians can find out more about the
local scene at Coordinamento **Lesbiche
Italiano** (www.clrbp.it).

The bottom end of Via di San Giovanni
di Laterano, the sloping street that runs
from the Basilica di San Giovanni in
Laterano to near the Colosseum, is a favourite haunt of Rome's gay community.
In the evening bars such as **Coming Out**
(p178) and **My Bar** (p178) burst into life,
attracting crowds of mainly gay men.

Most gay venues (bars, clubs and
saunas) require you to have an **Arcigay**
(☑06 6450 1102; www.arcigayroma.it; Via
Nicola Zabaglia 14) membership card.
These cost €15/8 per year/three
months and are available from any
venue that requires one.

large, New York–inspired venue caters to all moods, serving *aperitivo*, restaurant meals, and a weekend brunch. Arrive thirsty to take on a Bud Spencer, one from the ample list of cocktails, or get to grips with the selection of Scottish whiskies and Latin American rums. Thursday's blues aperitif is a popular weekly appointment.

Coming Out   Bar
(Map p246; ☑️06 700 98 71; www.comingout. it; Via di San Giovanni in Laterano 8; ⏱️7.30am-2am; 🚇Via Labicana) On warm evenings, with lively crowds on the street and the Colosseum as a backdrop, there are few finer places to sip a drink than this friendly gay bar. It's open all day, but is at its best in the evening when the atmosphere hots up, the cocktails kick in and the drag shows and karaoke nights get under way.

L'Oasi della Birra   Bar
(☑️06 574 61 22; Piazza Testaccio 41; ⏱️4pm-12.30am; 🚇Via Marmorata) Housed in the Palombi Enoteca, a longstanding bottle shop on Piazza Testaccio, this is exactly what it says it is – an Oasis of Beer. With hundreds of labels, from Teutonic heavyweights to British bitters and Belgian brews, as well as wines, cheeses and cold cuts, it's ideally set up for an evening's quaffing, either in the cramped cellar or piazza-side terrace.

Centri Sociali

Rome has a surprisingly alternative underbelly, centred on left-wing *centri sociali:* grungy squatter arts centres that host live music and contemporary arts events. They offer Rome's most unusual, cheap and alternative nightlife options. These include **Esc Atelier** (Map p255; www.escatelier.net; Via dei Volsci 159; ⏱️hours vary; 🚇Via Tiburtina, 🚇Via dei Reti) and clubby **Brancaleone** (☑️339 5074012; www.brancaleone.it; Via Levanna 11; ⏱️hours vary, typically 10pm-late; 🚇Via Nomentana).

Il Pentagrappolo   Wine Bar
(Map p255; ☑️06 709 63 01; Via Celimontana 21b; ⏱️noon-3pm & 6pm-1am Mon-Thu, 6pm-2am Fri-Sun; Ⓜ️Colosseo) This vaulted, softly lit wine bar is the perfect antidote to sightseeing overload. Join the mellow crowd for an evening of wine, piano music and jazz courtesy of the frequent live gigs. There's also a full menu served at lunch and dinner.

My Bar   Bar
(Map p246; Via di San Giovanni in Laterano 12; ⏱️9am-2am; 🚇Via Labicana) A fixture on Rome's so-called Gay Street, this cafe near the Colosseum serves mainly tourists during the day and a largely gay crowd in the evenings. DJs, themed parties and cocktails fuel the fun and ensure a casual, lighthearted atmosphere.

🍷 Villa Borghese & Northern Rome

Momart   Cafe
(☑️06 8639 1656; www.momartcafe.it; Viale XXI Aprile 19; ⏱️noon-2am, to 3am Sat & Sun; 🚇Viale XXI Aprile) A modish restaurant-cafe in the university district near Via Nomentana, Momart serves one of Rome's most bountiful *apericena* spreads. A mixed crowd of students and local professionals flocks here to fill up on the ample buffet and kick back over cocktails on the pavement terrace.

Lanificio 159   Club
(☑️06 4178 0081; www.lanificio.com; Via Pietralata 159a; ⏱️club nights 11pm-4.30am Fri-Sun; 🚇Via Pietralata) Occupying an ex-wool factory in Rome's northeastern suburbs, this cool underground venue hosts live gigs and hot clubbing action, led by top Roman crews and international DJs. The club is part of a larger complex which stages more reserved events such as Sunday markets, exhibitions and aperitifs.

Chioschetto di Ponte Milvio   Bar
(Piazzale Ponte Milvio; ⏱️6pm-2am summer, 5pm-2am Thu-Sat, 9am-11pm Sun winter; 🚇Ponte Milvio) A local landmark, this green kiosk

next to the Ponte Milvio is perennially popular with the young crowd from Rome's wealthy northern suburbs. It might look like a shack – it is a shack – but the mojitos are top-notch and it does an excellent thirst-quenching *grattachecca* (shaved ice flavoured with fruit syrup).

Southern Rome

Circolo Illuminati Club, Bar

(327 761 52 86; www.circolodegliilluminati. it; Via Libetta 1a; ⊗midnight-late; Ⓜ Garbatella) Tech house, hip-hop and chill music revs up clubbers at this wildly popular Ostiense club on the international DJ club circuit. The vibe is very much underground, and its courtyard garden with potted plants and olive trees is a gorgeous space in which to kick off the evening beneath the stars.

Goa Club

(327 06 574 82 77; www.goaclub.com; Via Libetta 13; ⊗11.30pm-4.30am Thu-Sat; Ⓜ Garbatella) At home in a former motorbike repair shop down a dead-end alley in industrial-style Ostiense, Goa is Rome's serious super-club with an exotic India-inspired decor and international DJs mixing house and techno. Expect a fashion-forward crowd, podium dancers, thumping dance floor, sofas to lounge on and heavies on the door.

Vinile Club

(327 06 5728 8666; www.vinileroma.it; Via Libetta 19; ⊗8pm-2am Tue & Wed, to 3am Thu, to 4am Fri & Sat, 12.30-3pm & 8pm-2am Sun; Ⓜ Garbatella) On weekends a mixed bag of Romans of all ages hit the dance floor at Vinyl, a buzzing bar and club cooking up food, music and party happenings on the southern fringe of Ostiense. Inside its huge cavernous interior with part-vegetal, part-frescoed ceiling the night kicks off with an *aperitivo* banquet from 8pm; DJ sets start at 11.30pm. On Sunday students pile in here for the unbeatable-value brunch.

🍷 Out in Ostiense

The ex-industrial area of Ostiense is fertile clubbing land, with its many ware-houses, workshops and factories given a new lease of life as pockets of nightlife nirvana. This is where Rome's serious clubbers lose countless hours worship-ping at the shrines of electro, nu-house, nu-funk and all sorts of other eclectica.

Clubs tend to get busy after midnight, or even after 2am. Often admission is free, but drinks are pricey; cocktails can cost from €10 to €20. You can drink much more cheaply in the studenty clubs of San Lorenzo, Pigneto and the *centri sociali* (social centres).

LISEGAGNE/GETTY IMAGES ©

Neo Club Club

(327 338 949 25 26; www.piovra.it; Via degli Argo-nauti 18; ⊗11.30pm-6am Fri & Sat; Ⓜ Garbatella) This small, dark two-level club has an underground feel and it's one of the funki-est choices in the zone, featuring a dance-tastic mish-mash of breakbeat, techno and old-school house.

Rashōmon Bar & Club Club

(www.facebook.com/rashomonclub; Via degli Ar-gonauti 16; ⊗10pm-4am Tue-Sat Oct-May; Ⓜ Gar-batella) Rashōmon is sweaty, not posey, and the place to head when you want to dance until dawn. Shake it to a music lover's feast of the sound of the underground, especially house, techno and electronica.

SHOWTIME

Opera, jazz, theatre and more

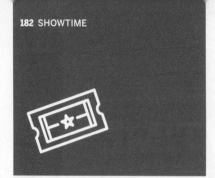

Showtime

Watching the world go by in Rome is often entertainment enough, but there's plenty more to having a good time than just people-watching. The city's music scene is a hive of activity, with gigs and concerts of all musical genres drawing knowledgeable and enthusiastic audiences. Theatres put on everything from Shakespearean drama to avant-garde dance; cinemas screen art-house flicks; and arts festivals turn the city into a stage, particularly in summer when al fresco performances play out against backdrops of spectacular Roman ruins. Whether you're an opera buff or a rapper, a cinephile or a theatre-goer, you're sure to find something to suit your taste.

In This Section

Centro Storico....................................184

Tridente, Trevi & the Quirinale 184

Vatican City, Borgo & Prati 184

Monti, Esquilino
& San Lorenzo 186

Trastevere & Gianicolo.......................186

San Giovanni & Testaccio 187

Villa Borghese
& Northern Rome................................187

Southern Rome...................................188

Tickets

Tickets for concerts, live music and theatrical performances are widely available across the city. Prices range enormously depending on the venue and artists. Hotels can often reserve tickets for guests, or you can contact the venue or organisation directly – check listings publications for booking details. You can also try the following:

Hellò Ticket (www.helloticket.it)

Orbis (Map p252; ☑06 482 74 03; Piazza dell'Esquilino 37; ◷9.30am-1pm & 4-7pm Mon-Sat; ☒Via Cavour)

Rebecca Bianchi dances at the Auditorium Conciliazione (p184)

The Best...

Jazz & Blues

Alexanderplatz (p184) Rome's foremost jazz club.

Charity Café (p186) Regular live gigs in an intimate space.

Big Mama (p186) An atmospheric option for jazz, blues, funk and soul.

Gregory's Jazz Club (p184) Smooth venue popular with local musicians.

Fonclea (p184) Pub regularly hosting live jazz; moves riverside in summer.

Classical Venues

Auditorium Parco della Musica (p187) Multiple concert halls and great acoustics.

Teatro dell'Opera di Roma (p186) Gilt venue hosting Rome's opera and dance companies.

Terme di Caracalla (p187) Wonderful outdoor setting for opera and ballet.

Auditorium Conciliazione (p184) Classical and contemporary concerts, theatre productions and cabarets.

✪ Centro Storico

Teatro Argentina   Theatre

(Map p250; ☏06 68400 0311; www.teatrodi
roma.net; Largo di Torre Argentina 52; tickets
€12-32; ◻Largo di Torre Argentina) Founded
in 1732, Rome's top theatre is one of the
two official homes of the Teatro di Roma –
the other is the Teatro India (p189) in the
southern suburbs. Rossini's *Barber of
Seville* premiered here in 1816 and it today
stages a wide-ranging program of drama
(mostly in Italian), high-profile dance performances and classical music concerts.

Isola del Cinema   Outdoor Cinema

(Map p254; www.isoladelcinema.com; Isola Tiberina; tickets €6) From mid-June to September, the Isola Tiberina sets the stage for a
season of outdoor cinema, featuring Italian
and international films, some shown in their
original language.

✪ Tridente, Trevi & the Quirinale

Gregory's Jazz Club   Jazz

(Map p252; ☏06 679 63 86; www.gregorys
jazz.com; Via Gregoriana 54d; obligatory drink
€15-20; ◷8pm-2am Tue-Sun; ⓜBarberini,
Spagna) If Gregory's were a tone of voice,
it would be husky: unwind over a whisky
in the downstairs bar, then unwind some
more on squashy sofas upstairs to some
slinky live jazz and swing, with quality local
performers who also like to hang out at
this club.

Teatro Quirino   Theatre

(Map p252; ☏06 679 45 85; www.teatroquirino.
it; Via delle Vergini 7; ◻Via del Corso) Within
splashing distance of Trevi Fountain, this
grand 19th-century theatre produces the
odd new work and a stream of well-known
classics – expect to see works (in Italian)
by Arthur Miller, Tennessee Williams,
Shakespeare, Seneca and Luigi Pirandello.

Teatro Sistina   Theatre

(Map p252; ☏06 420 07 11; www.ilsistina.it;
Via Sistina 129; ⓜBarberini) Theatre spec-
taculars, musicals, concerts and comic
star performances are the staples of the
Sistina's ever-conservative, ever-popular
repertoire.

✪ Vatican City, Borgo & Prati

Alexanderplatz   Jazz

(Map p253; ☏06 8377 5604; www.facebook.
com/alexander.platz.37/; Via Ostia 9; ◷8.30pm-
1.30am; ⓜOttaviano-San Pietro) Intimate,
underground, and hard to find – look for
the black door – Rome's most celebrated
jazz club draws top Italian and international performers and a respectful cosmopolitan crowd. Book a table for the best stage
views or to dine here, although note that
it's the music that's the star act not the
food.

Fonclea   Live Music

(Map p253; ☏06 689 63 02; www.fonclea.it; Via
Crescenzio 82a; ◷6pm-2am Sep-May, concerts
9.30pm; ◻Piazza del Risorgimento) Fonclea is
a great little pub venue, with nightly gigs
by bands playing everything from jazz
and soul to pop, rock and doo-wop. Get in
the mood with a drink during happy hour
(6pm to 8.30pm daily). In summer, the
pub ups sticks and moves to a site by the
Tiber.

Auditorium Conciliazione   Live Performance

(Map p253; ☏06 6813 4748; www.auditorium
conciliazione.it; Via della Conciliazione 4;
◻Piazza Pia) On the main approach road
to St Peter's Basilica, this large auditorium plays host to a wide range of events
– classical and contemporary concerts,
cabarets, dance spectacles, theatre productions, film screenings, exhibitions and
conferences.

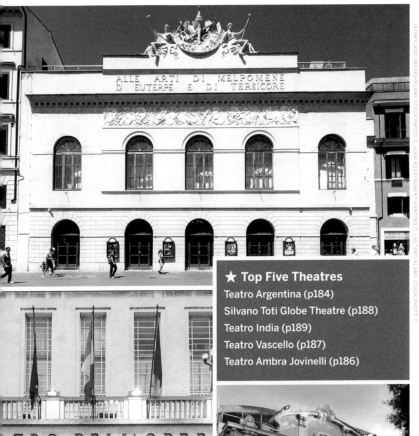

ALLE ARTI DI MELPOMENE
D'EUTERPE E DI TERSICORE

★ **Top Five Theatres**

Teatro Argentina (p184)

Silvano Toti Globe Theatre (p188)

Teatro India (p189)

Teatro Vascello (p187)

Teatro Ambra Jovinelli (p186)

Clockwise from top: Teatro Argentina; Teatro Ambra Jovinelli; Teatro dell'Opera di Roma (p186)

❂ Monti, Esquilino & San Lorenzo

Teatro dell'Opera di Roma
Opera, Ballet

(Map p252; ☑06 48 16 01; www.operaroma.it; Piazza Beniamino Gigli 1; ☺box office 10am-6pm Mon-Sat, 9am-1.30pm Sun; Ⓜ Repubblica) Rome's premier opera house boasts a plush gilt interior, a Fascist 1920s exterior and an impressive history: it premiered Puccini's *Tosca,* and Maria Callas once sang here. Opera and ballet performances are staged between September and June.

Nuovo Cinema Palazzo
Arts Centre

(Map p255; www.nuovocinemapalazzo.it; Piazza dei Sanniti 9a; ☺hours vary; ☐Via Tiburtina) Students, artists and activists are breathing new life into San Lorenzo's former Palace Cinema with a bevy of exciting creative happenings: think film screenings, theatre performances, DJ sets, concerts, live music, break dance classes and a host of other artsy events. In warm weather, the action spills outside onto the street terrace, overlooked by a B&W stencil mural by Rome street artists Sten & Lex.

Blackmarket
Live Music

(Map p252; www.blackmarketartgallery.it/monti; Via Panisperna 101; ☺7.30pm-2am; Ⓜ Cavour) A bit outside the main Monti hub, this charming bar filled with eclectic vintage furniture is a small but rambling place, great for sitting back on mismatched armchairs for a leisurely, convivial drink. It hosts regular acoustic indie and folk gigs, which feel a bit like having a band in your living room.

Charity Café
Live Music

(Map p252; ☑06 4782 5881; www.charitycafe.it; Via Panisperna 68; ☺7pm-2am Tue-Sun; Ⓜ Cavour) Think narrow space, spindly tables, dim lighting and laid-back vibe: this is a place to snuggle down and listen to some slinky live jazz and blues. Civilised, relaxed, untouristy and very Monti. Gigs usually take place from 10pm, with live music and *aperitivo.*

Teatro Ambra Jovinelli
Theatre

(Map p255; ☑06 8308 2884; www.ambrajovinelli. org; Via G Pepe 43-47; Ⓜ Vittorio Emanuele) A home away from home for many Italian comics, the Ambra Jovinelli is a historic venue for alternative comedians and satirists. Its program is still geared towards comedians today, although it also stages the odd drama, musical and contemporary work.

Wishlist
Live Music

(Map p255; ☑349 749 4659; www.facebook.com/ wishlistclub; Via dei Volsci 126b; admission €5; ☺Wed, Fri & Sat; ☐Via Tiburtina, ☐Via dei Reti) A black door marks the entrance to this eternally popular music club, in a low-lying building on one of San Lorenzo's grungiest streets. Gigs cover all sounds, kicking off at 9.30pm or 10pm.

❂ Trastevere & Gianicolo

Lettere Caffè
Live Music

(Map p254; ☑340 004 41 54; www.letterecaffe. org; Vicolo di San Francesco a Ripa 100-101; ☺6pm-2am, closed mid-Aug–mid-Sep; ☐Viale di Trastevere, ☐Viale di Trastevere) Like books? Poetry? Blues and jazz? Then you'll love this place, a clutter of bar stools and books, where there are regular live gigs, poetry slams, comedy and gay nights, plus DJ sets playing electronic, indie and new wave. *Aperitivo,* with tempting vegetarian buffet, is served between 7pm and 9pm.

Nuovo Sacher
Cinema

(Map p254; ☑06 581 81 16; www.sacherfilm.eu; Largo Ascianghi 1; ☐Viale di Trastevere, ☐Viale di Trastevere) Owned by cult Roman film director Nanni Moretti, this small cinema with classic red velvet seats is the place to catch the latest European art-house offering. There are regular screenings of Italian and international films, many in their original language.

Big Mama
Blues

(Map p254; ☑06 581 25 51; www.bigmama.it; Vicolo di San Francesco a Ripa 18; ☺9pm-1.30am, shows 10.30pm, closed Jun-Sep; ☐Viale di Trastevere, ☐Viale di Trastevere) Head to this cramped Trastevere basement for a mellow night of Eternal City blues. A longstanding venue, it also stages jazz, funk, soul and R&B acts, as well as popular cover bands.

Teatro Vascello   Theatre
(☎06 588 10 21; www.teatrovascello.it; Via Giacinto Carini 72, Monteverde; ☒Via Giacinto Carini) Left-field in vibe and location, this independent fringe theatre in off-the-beaten-tourist-track Monteverde stages interesting, cutting-edge new work, including avant-garde dance, multimedia events and works by emerging playwrights.

✪ San Giovanni & Testaccio

Terme di Caracalla   Opera
(www.operaroma.it; Viale delle Terme di Caracalla 52; tickets €20-150; ☒Viale delle Terme di Caracalla) The hulking ruins of this vast 3rd-century baths complex set the memorable stage for the Teatro dell'Opera's summer season of music, opera and ballet, as well as shows by big-name Italian performers.

ConteStaccio   Live Music
(☎06 5728 9712; www.contestaccio.com; Via di Monte Testaccio 65b; ⊗8pm-4am Thu-Sun; ☒Via Galvani) With an under-the-stars terrace and buzzing vibe, ConteStaccio is one of the top venues on the Testaccio clubbing strip. It's something of a multi-purpose outfit with a cocktail bar, pizzeria and restaurant, but is best known for its free live music. Gigs by emerging groups set the tone, spanning indie, rock, acoustic, funk and electronic.

Villaggio Globale   Live Music
(www.facebook.com/pages/Villaggio-Globale/161652650554595; Lungotevere Testaccio 1; ⊗gigs 10pm-late; ☒Via Marmorata) For a taste of the underground, head to this historic *centro sociale* (an ex-squat turned cultural centre) occupying the city's graffiti-sprayed former slaughterhouse. It stages gigs, often dancehall, reggae, and ska, as well as a wide range of cultural events.

 Opera & Dance

Rome's opera house, the Teatro dell'Opera di Roma (p186), is a magnificent, grandiose venue, lined in gilt and red, but productions can be a bit hit and miss. It's also home to Rome's official Corps de Ballet and has a ballet season running in tandem with its opera performances. Both ballet and opera move outdoors for the summer season at the ancient Roman Terme di Caracalla, which is an even more spectacular setting.

You can see opera in various other outdoor locations; check listings or at the tourist information kiosks for details.

Rome's Auditorium Parco della Musica hosts classical and contemporary dance performances, as well as the Equilibrio Festival della Nuova Danza in February. The Auditorium Conciliazione (p184) is another option to catch contemporary dance companies. Invito alla Danza is a contemporary dance festival held in July, and encompasses tango, jazz dance, contemporary and more.

Teatro dell'Opera di Roma
JASON KNOTT/ALAMY STOCK PHOTO ©

✪ Villa Borghese & Northern Rome

**Auditorium Parco
della Musica**   Concert Venue
(☎06 8024 1281; www.auditorium.com; Viale Pietro de Coubertin; ☒Viale Tiziano) The hub of Rome's thriving cultural scene, the Auditorium is the capital's premier concert venue. Its three concert halls offer superb acoustics, and together with a 3000-seat open-air arena, stage everything from classical music concerts to jazz gigs, public lectures and film screenings.

The Auditorium is also home to Rome's world-class **Orchestra dell'Accademia Nazionale di Santa Cecilia** (www.santacecilia.it).

Teatro Olimpico   Theatre
(☎06 326 59 91; www.teatroolimpico.it; Piazza Gentile da Fabriano 17; 🚇Piazza Mancini, 🚊Piazza Mancini) The Teatro Olimpico hosts a varied programme of opera, dance, one-man shows, musicals and comedies, as well as classical music concerts by the Accademia Filarmonica Romana.

Casa del Cinema   Cinema
(Map p256; ☎06 06 08; www.casadelcinema.it; Largo Marcello Mastroianni 1, Villa Borghese; 🚊Via Pinciana) In Villa Borghese, the Casa del Cinema comprises three projection halls, an exhibition space, and a 200-seat outdoor theatre. It screens everything from documentaries to shorts, indie flicks and art-house classics (sometimes in their original language), and hosts a regular programme of retrospectives and film-related events.

Silvano Toti Globe Theatre Theatre
(Map p256; ☎06 06 08; www.globetheatreroma.com; Largo Aqua Felix, Villa Borghese; tickets €10-28; 🚊Piazzale Brasile) Like London's Globe Theatre but with better weather, Villa Borghese's open-air Elizabethan theatre serves up Shakespeare (performances mostly in Italian) from July through to early October.

✪ Southern Rome

Caffè Letterario   Live Music
(☎06 5730 2842; www.caffeletterarioroma.it; Via Ostiense 95; ⏱10am-2am Tue-Sat, 4pm-2am Sun; 🚊Via Ostiense, Ⓜ Piramide) Caffè Letterario is an intellectual hangout housed in the funky converted, post-industrial space of a former garage. It combines designer looks, a bookshop, gallery, co-working space, performance area and lounge bar. There are regular gigs from 10pm to midnight, ranging from soul and jazz to Indian dance.

XS Live   Live Music
(☎06 5730 5102; www.xsliveroma.com; Via Libetta 13; ⏱10.30pm-late Thu-Sun; Ⓜ Garbatella) A rocking live music and club venue, hosting regular gigs and club nights ranging from Oasis tributes to reggae and dance-hall parties.

Outdoor concert at Terme di Caracalla (p96)

La Casa del Jazz — Jazz

(🎵06 70 47 31; www.casajazz.it; Viale di Porta Ardeatina 55; ⊘hours vary; 🚌Viale di Porta Ardeatina) In the middle of a 2500-sq-metre park in the southern suburbs, the Jazz House resides in a three-storey 1920s villa that once belonged to the boss of the *banda del Magliana,* a powerful local mafia outfit. When he was caught, Rome Council converted it into a jazz complex with a 150-seat auditorium, rehearsal rooms, cafe and restaurant. Gig admission varies; some events are free.

Teatro India — Theatre

(🎵06 68400 0311; www.teatrodiroma.net; Lungotevere Vittorio Gassman 1; Ⓜ Stazione Trastevere) Inaugurated in 1999 in the post-industrial landscape of Rome's southern suburbs, the India is the younger sister of Teatro Argentina. It's a stark modern space in a converted industrial building, a fitting setting for its cutting-edge program, with a calendar of international and Italian works.

Palalottomatica — Live Music

(🎵06 54 09 01; www.palalottomatica.it; Piazzale dello Sport 1; Ⓜ EUR Palasport) Originally built for the 1960 Olympics, this multipurpose

 Miracle Players

In summer, the **Miracle Players** (🎵06 7039 3427; www.miracleplayers.org) theatre group performs classic drama or historical comedy next to the Roman Forum and other open-air locations, making glorious use of Rome's archaeological scenery. Performances are in English and usually free.

Roman Forum (p78)
MATTEO COLOMBO/GETTY IMAGES ©

venue hosts top rock stars and Italian swooners as well as staging musicals, theatrical performances and big-bash spectacles.

ACTIVE ROME

From football to cooking courses

Active Rome

The Romans have long been passionate about sport and enjoy a good performance, ever since crowds flocked to the ancient Colosseum to support their favourite gladiators and to the Circo Massimo to cheer on chariot riders. Rome's modern-day Colosseum is the Stadio Olimpico, where footballing rivalries are played out in front of thousands of fans. Rome also hosts the Italian Open tennis tournament and various Six Nations rugby tournament matches.

If you prefer your pursuits more hands-on, choose from a range of courses to take and tours to head out on.

In This Section

Spectator Sports 194
Tours 194
Courses 197
Spas 197

What to Watch

Football is the big sport in Rome, with the season running from September to May. Rugby fans can watch matches on weekends in February and March, and tennis fans enjoy world-class games at the Italian Open in May.

Boat tour along the Tiber

The Best...

Sporting Venues

Foro Italico (p194) Magnificent Fascist-era sports complex.

Stadio Olimpico (p194) Rome's 70,000-seat football stadium, part of the Fascist-era Foro Italico.

Piazza di Siena (p56) Lovely race-course in the heart of the Villa Borghese park.

Palalottomatica (p189) Circular stadium close to EUR in Southern Rome.

Walking Tours

Eating Italy Food Tours (p195) Foodie tours of Testaccio and Trastevere, with requisite grazing along the way.

Through Eternity Cultural Association (p195) Indulge in an evening tour of Rome's piazzas and fountains.

Arcult (p195) One for contemporary-architecture buffs.

GT Food & Travel (p195) Stroll through an outdoor market and discover the produce of Italy.

🗲 Spectator Sports

Stadio Olimpico   Stadium
(☎06 3685 7563; Viale dei Gladiatori 2, Foro
Italico; 🚇Lungotevere Maresciallo Cadorna) A
trip to Rome's impressive Stadio Olimpico
offers an unforgettable insight into Rome's
sporting heart. Throughout the football
season (September to May) there's a game
on most Sundays featuring one of the city's
two Serie A teams (Roma or Lazio), and
during the six nations rugby tournament
(February to March) it hosts Italy's home
games.

Foro Italico   Spectator Sport
(☎800 622662; www.foroitalicoticketing.it;
Viale del Foro Italico; 🚇Lungotevere Maresciallo
Cadorna) This grand Fascist-era sports
complex, built between 1928 and 1938, is
centred on Rome's 70,000-seat Stadio
Olimpico, home of the capital's two Serie A
football teams. It also hosts Italy's premier
tennis tournament, the Internazionali BNL
d'Italia, in May.

🗲 Tours

Taking a tour is a good way to see a lot
in a short time or investigate a sight in
depth. Several outfits run hop-on hop-off
bus tours, typically costing about €20 per
person. Both the Colosseum and Vatican
Museums offer official guided tours, but for
a more personalised service you'll be better
off with a private guide.

Roman Guy   Tours
(https://theromanguy.com) A professional setup
organising a wide range of group and private
tours. Packages, led by English-speaking
experts, include skip-the-line visits to the
Vatican Museums (US$89), foodie tours of
Trastevere and the Jewish Ghetto (US$84),
and an evening bar hop through the historic
centre's cocktail bars (US$225).

A Friend in Rome   Tours
(☎340 5019201; www.afriendinrome.it) Silvia
Prosperi and her team offer a range of
private tours covering the Vatican and main
historic centre as well as areas outside the
capital. They can also organise kid-friendly

Foro Italico

tours, food and wine itineraries, vintage car drives and horse rides along Via Appia Antica. Rates start at €165 for a basic three-hour tour for up to eight people; add €55 for every additional hour.

GT Food & Travel   Tours
(☑320 7204222; www.gtfoodandtravel.com; 3hr tour with tastings per person around €120) Small-group food lover tours, including a themed 'Cucina Povera & Roman Cuisine' tour in Monteverde. Gelato tours (with the option of an add-on gelato-making class), half- and full-day custom tours, cooking classes and in-home dining experiences are also on offer.

Casa Mia   Tours
(☑346 8001746; www.italyfoodandwinetours.com; 3hr tour with tastings 2/4 people €360/420) Serious food and wine tours, including a Trastevere and Jewish Quarter neighbourhood tour, with tastings and behind-the-scene meetings with local shop keepers, producers, chefs and restaurateurs. Bespoke tours, dining itineraries and reservations can also be arranged.

Eating Italy
Food Tours   Food & Drink
(☑06 9480 4492; www.eatingitalyfoodtours.com; €77-94) This cheery company offers informative food tours around Testaccio (the heartland of traditional Roman cooking) and Trastevere, with chances to taste various delicacies on the way. Prices start at €77 per person and there's a maximum of 12 people per tour.

Through Eternity
Cultural Association   Walking
(☑06 700 93 36; www.througheternity.com) A reliable operator offering private and group tours led by English-speaking experts. Popular packages include a twilight tour of Rome's piazzas and fountains (€39, 2½ hours), a night visit to the Vatican Museums (€69, 3½ hours), and a foodie tour of Testaccio (€79, four hours).

Arcult   Walking
(☑339 650 31 72; www.arcult.it) Run by architects, Arcult offers excellent customisable

 Football

In Rome you're either for AS Roma (*giallorossi* – yellow and reds; www.asroma.it) or Lazio (*biancazzuri* – white and blues; www.sslazio.it); both teams play in Serie A (Italy's premier league). A new Roma stadium is currently being built at Tor di Valle, due to be completed in time for the 2017/18 season. Both sets of supporters unfortunately have a controversial minority who have been known to cause trouble at matches.

From September to May there's a game at home for Roma or Lazio almost every weekend, and a trip to Rome's football stadium, the **Stadio Olimpico** (p194), is an unforgettable experience. Note that ticket purchase regulations are far stricter than they used to be. Tickets have to bear the holder's name and passport or ID number, and you must present a photo ID at the turnstiles when entering the stadium. Two tickets are permitted per purchase for Serie A, Coppa Italia and UEFA Champions League games. Tickets cost from about €16 to €250. Buy them from www.ticketone.it, www.listicket.it, from ticket agencies or at one of the A S Roma or Lazio stores around the city. To get to the stadium, take metro line A to Ottaviano–San Pietro and then bus 32.

Statue of football player, Foro Italico

group tours focusing on Rome's contemporary architecture. Prices depend on the itinerary but range from €250 to €370 for two to 10 people.

Rugby Union & Basketball

Italy's rugby team, the Azzurri (the Blues), entered the Six Nations rugby tournament in 2000, and has been the competition underdog ever since. It has scored some big wins in recent years, however, with shock triumphs over France in 2011 and 2013. In 2015 the team beat Scotland, but lost all other games.

Basketball is a popular spectator sport in Rome, though its support falls well short of the fervour inspired by football. Rome's team, Virtus Roma (www.virtusroma.it), plays throughout the winter months at the **Palalottomatica** (p189) in Southern Rome.

Italy versus Ireland rugby union match in Rome
MASSIMILIANO CARNABUCI/ALAMY STOCK PHOTO ©

Red Bicycle   Cycling
(Map p246; ☑327 5387148; www.theredbicycle. org; Via dei Santi Quattro 81; ☺9am-1pm & 3-7.30pm, closed Sun & Mon morning; ☐Via Labicana) A cycle shop offering bike hire (€10/15 per half/full day) and a range of cycling tours taking in the city's main neighbourhoods and environs. Prices start at €35 for a three-hour sunset tour, rising to €120 for the 80km ride up to Frascati and Castel Gandolfo.

Bici & Baci   Tours
(Map p252; ☑06 482 84 43; www.bicibaci.com; Via del Viminale 5; bike tours from €30, Vespa tours from €145; ☺8am-7pm; Ⓜ Repubblica) Bici & Baci runs a range of daily bike tours, taking in the main historical sites and Via Appia Antica, as well as tours on vintage

Vespas, in classic Fiat 500 cars or funky three-wheeled Ape Calessino. Its sparkling new flagship branch is near **Stazione Termini** (☑06 481 40 64; www.bicibaci.com; Via Rosmini 26; bike tours from €30, Vespa tours from €145; ☺8am-7pm Mon-Sat; Ⓜ Termini).

Vespa Style Roma   Tours
(☑06 446 62 68; www.vespastyleroma.it; Via Milazzo 3a; Vespa rental per hour/day €15/69, e-bikes per day €25; ☺9am-7pm; Ⓜ Termini) Wannabe Audrey Hepburns can rent a Vespa to scoot around town at Vespa Style Roma, across the road from Stazione Termini. It also rents e-bikes and organises guided Vespa/e-bike tours (starting from €70/40).

TopBike Rental & Tours   Cycling
(Map p255; ☑06 488 28 93; www.topbiker ental.com; Via Labicana 49; ☺10am-7pm; ☐Via Labicana) Offers a series of bike tours throughout the city, including a four-hour 16km exploration of the city centre (€45) and an all-day 30km ride through Via Appia Antica and environs (€79). Out-of-town tours take in Castel Gandolfo, Civita di Bagnoregio and Orvieto. Also offers bike hire from €15 per day.

Open Bus Cristiana   Bus
(☑06 69 89 61; www.operaromanapellegrinaggi. org; single tour €12, 24-/48-hr ticket €25/28) The Vatican-sponsored Opera Romana Pellegrinaggi runs a hop-on, hop-off bus departing from Piazza Pia and Termini. Stops are situated near to main sights including St Peter's Basilica, Piazza Navona, the Trevi Fountain and the Colosseum. Tickets are available onboard, online, or at the info point just off St Peter's Square.

Rome Boat Experience   Boating
(Map p250; ☑06 8956 7745; www.romeboat-experience.com; adult/reduced €18/12) From April to October, this outfit runs hop-on, hop-off cruises along the Tiber. From May to October there are also dinner cruises (€65, two hours) every Friday and Saturday, and a daily wine bar cruise (€30, 1½ hours) from Monday to Thursday. The main

embarkation point is Molo Sant'Angelo, over the river from Castel Sant'Angelo.

 Courses

Città di Gusto — Cooking

(☏06 5511 2211; www.gamberorosso.it; Via Ottavio Gasparri 13-17; 🚊Viale dei Colli Portuensi) Demonstrations, workshops, lessons and courses are held at the seat of the Italian food organisation, Gambero Rosso, in the Monteverde neighbourhood west of Testaccio. Reckon on around €60 for a three-hour course.

Vino Roma — Wine

(Map p246; ☏328 487 44 97; www.vinoroma.com; Via in Selci 84g; 2hr tastings per person €50; MCavour) With beautifully appointed century-old cellars and a chic tasting studio, Vino Roma guides novices and experts in tasting wine under the knowledgeable stewardship of sommelier Hande Leimer and her expert team. Also on offer is a wine-and-cheese dinner (€60) with snacks, cheeses and cold cuts to accompany the wines, and bespoke three-hour food tours. Book online.

Art Studio Lab — Art

(Map p253; ☏348 6099758, 344 0971721; box@ savellireligious.com; Via Paolo VI 27-29, c/o Savelli Arte e Tradizione; ⊙9.30am-7pm; 🚊Lungotevere in Sassia) This mosaic school, operating out of the Savelli Arte e Tradizione shop, offers individually tailored workshops and courses. In a basic three-hour workshop, which includes a bite to eat, you'll learn how to cut marble and enamels and make your own frames, mirrors or tiles. Reckon on €90/80 per adult/child for a group of one to three people.

Torre di Babele Centro di Lingua e Cultura Italiana — Language

(☏06 4425 2578; www.torredibabele.com; Via Cosenza 7; 🚊Via Bari) As well as language lessons, this school offers courses on cooking, art, architecture and several other subjects. Individual language lessons start at €39, with an enrolment fee of €80.

 Spas

Kami Spa — Spa

(Map p252; ☏06 4201 0039; www.kamispa.com; Via degli Avignonesi 11-12; massage €120-280; ⊙10am-10pm; MBarberini) A luxurious spa not far from the Trevi Fountain, this is a soothing place to recharge your batteries. Think hot stone massages, Balinese palm massages, massages with Moroccan rose petal oil, turmeric and sandalwood body wraps, and green tea body cocoons.

Hotel De Russie Spa — Spa

(Map p256; ☏06 3288 8820; www.roccoforte hotels.com/it; Via del Babuino 9; ⊙6.30am-10pm; MFlaminio) In one of Rome's top hotels, this glamorous and gorgeous day spa boasts a salt water pool, steam room, Finnish sauna and well-equipped gym. A wide choice of treatments are available (for him and her), including shiatsu and deep-tissue massages; count at least €100 for a 50-minute massage.

A LUXURIOUS ROOM AT BAGLIONI HOTEL REGINA. IMAGE COURTESY OF BAGLIONI HOTEL REGINA ©

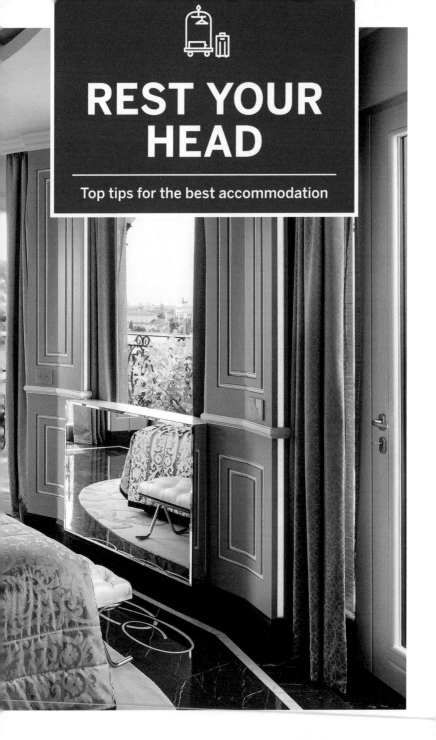

REST YOUR HEAD

Top tips for the best accommodation

Rest Your Head

Whether you're looking to splurge like royalty or spend modestly on budget stays, you'll find plenty of options among Rome's wide range of hotels, pensioni, B&Bs, hostels and convents. At the top end of the market, opulent five-star hotels occupy stately historic palazzi (mansions) and chic boutique guesthouses boast discreet luxury. Family-run B&Bs and pensioni offer character and a warm welcome, while religious houses cater to pilgrims and cost-conscious travellers. Hostel-goers can choose between party-loving hang-outs or quieter, more restrained digs.

In This Section

Accommodation Types......................202

Seasons & Rates................................203

Getting There 203

Useful Websites..................................204

Where to Stay.....................................205

Taxes

All guests must pay a per-night room-occupancy tax on top of the cost of accommodation. This amounts to €3 per person per night in one- and two-star hotels, €3.50 in B&Bs and room rentals, €4 in three-star hotels, €6 in four-star hotels and €7 in five-star hotels.

Tipping

Tipping is not necessary, but leaving up to €5 for porter, maid or room service in a top-end hotel is fine.

Hotel rooftop view over Rome

Reservations

○ Always try to book ahead, especially during the major religious festivals.

○ Ask for a *camera matrimoniale* for a room with a double bed or a *camera doppia* for twin beds.

Checking In & Out

○ When you check in you'll need to present your passport or ID card.

○ Checkout is usually between 10am and noon. In hostels it's around 9am.

○ Some guesthouses and B&Bs require you to arrange a time to check in.

📖 Accommodation Types

Pensioni & Hotels

The bulk of Rome's accommodation con-sists of *pensioni* and *alberghi* (hotels).

A *pensione* is a small family-run hotel, often in a converted apartment. Rooms are usually fairly simple, though most come with private bathroom.

Hotels are rated from one to five stars; this rating relates to facilities only and gives no indication of value, comfort, atmosphere or friendliness. Most hotels in Rome's *centro storico* (historic centre) are three-star and above. As a rule, a three-star room will come with a hairdryer, a minibar (or fridge), a safe, air-con and wi-fi. Some may also have satellite TV.

A common complaint in Rome is that ho-tel rooms are small. This is especially true in the *centro storico* and Trastevere, where many hotels are housed in centuries-old *palazzi*. Similarly, a spacious lift is a rare find, particularly in older *palazzi*, and you'll seldom find one that can accommodate more than one average-sized person with luggage.

Breakfast in cheaper hotels is rarely worth setting the alarm for, so if you have the option, pop into a bar for a coffee and *cornetto* (croissant) instead.

B&Bs & Guesthouses

Alongside traditional B&Bs, Rome has many boutique-style guesthouses offering chic, upmarket accommodation at mid- to top-end prices.

Breakfast in a Roman B&B usually consists of bread rolls, croissants, yoghurt, ham and cheese.

Hostels

Rome's hostels cater to everyone from backpackers to budget-minded fami-lies. Many offer smart hotel-style rooms (singles, doubles, even family rooms), with private bathrooms, alongside traditional dorms. Curfews are a thing of the past and some hostels even have 24-hour receptions.

Hotel poolside bar, Esquilino

Many hostels do not accept prior reservations for dorm beds; simply arrive after 10am and find a spot on a first come, first served basis.

Religious Accommodation

Unsurprisingly Rome is well furnished with religious institutions, a number of which offer good-value rooms for the night. Bear in mind, though, that many have strict curfews and that the accommodation, while spotlessly clean, tends to be short on frills. While there are a number of centrally located options, many convents are situated out of the centre, typically in the districts north and west of the Vatican. Book well in advance.

Rental Accommodation

For longer stays, renting an apartment will generally work out cheaper than an extended hotel sojourn. Bank on about €900 per month for a studio apartment or one-bedroom flat. For longer rentals, you'll probably have to pay bills plus a building maintenance charge.

Seasons & Rates

Rome doesn't have a low season as such but rates are at their lowest from November to March (excluding Christmas and New Year) and from mid-July to the end of August. Expect to pay top rates in spring (April to June) and autumn (September and October) and over the main holiday periods (Christmas, New Year and Easter).

Payment

Most midrange and top-end hotels accept credit cards. Budget places may do so too, but it's always best to check in advance.

Getting There

Most tourist areas are a bus ride or metro journey away from Stazione Termini. If you come by car, be warned that much of the

 Online Rentals

Holiday rentals are booming in Rome right now thanks to online outfits such as AirBnb and VRBO.

These sites offer a vast range of options, from single rooms in private houses to fully equipped apartments. They are often good value and will almost certainly save you money, especially in expensive areas such as the *centro storico* (historic centre) or Trastevere. They can also give you the chance to get away from touristy hot spots and see another side to the city – characterful neighbourhoods include Testaccio and Garbatella. Just be sure to research the location when you book and, if necessary, work out how to get there (eg public transport or organised pick-up from the property owner etc).

Always check the property's reviews for things such as noise (an issue in central locations) and privacy. You'll also need to check whether Rome's obligatory hotel tax is included in the rate or has to be paid separately (see p200).

Bed and breakfast, Quirinale

city centre is a ZTL (limited traffic zone) and is off-limits to unauthorised traffic. Note also that there is a terrible lack of on-site parking facilities in the city centre, although your hotel should be able to direct you to a private garage. Street parking is not recommended.

Interior of Hotel Art, by the Spanish Steps

🖳 Useful Websites

Lonely Planet (lonelyplanet.com/italy/rome/hotels) Consult a list of author-reviewed accommodation options and book online.

060608 (www.060608.it/en/accoglienza/dormire) Official Comune di Roma site with accommodation lists; details are not always up to date.

Bed & Breakfast Association of Rome (www.b-b.rm.it) Lists B&Bs and short-term apartment rentals.

Bed & Breakfast Italia (www.bbitalia.it) Rome's longest-established B&B network.

Rome As You Feel (www.romeasyoufeel.com) Apartment rentals, from cheap studio flats to luxury apartments.

Sleep in Italy (www.sleepinitaly.com) A reliable rental operator.

Where to Stay

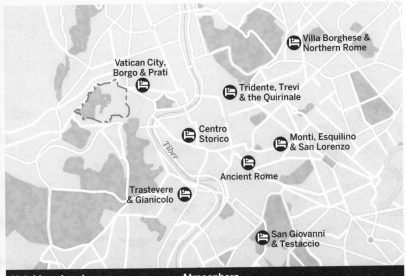

Neighbourhood	Atmosphere
Ancient Rome	Close to major sights such as Colosseum, Roman Forum and Capitoline Museums; quiet at night; not cheap; touristy restaurants.
Centro Storico	Atmospheric area with everything on your doorstep – Pantheon, Piazza Navona, restaurants, bars, shops; most expensive part of town; can be noisy.
Tridente, Trevi & the Quirinale	Good for Spanish Steps, Trevi Fountain and designer shopping; excellent midrange to top-end options; good transport links; subdued after dark.
Vatican City, Borgo & Prati	Near St Peter's Basilica; decent range of accommodation; some excellent shops and restaurants; on the metro; not much nightlife; sells out quickly for religious holidays.
Monti, Esquilino & San Lorenzo	Lots of budget accommodation around Stazione Termini; top eating in Monti and good nightlife in San Lorenzo; good transport links; some dodgy streets near Termini.
Trastevere & Gianicolo	Gorgeous, atmospheric area; party vibe with hundreds of bars, cafes and restaurants; some interesting sights; expensive; noisy, particularly on summer nights.
San Giovanni & Testaccio	Authentic atmosphere with good eating and drinking options; Aventino is a quiet, romantic area; Testaccio is a top food and nightlife district; not many big sights.
Villa Borghese & Northern Rome	Largely residential area good for the Auditorium and Stadio Olimpico; some top museums; generally quiet after dark.

Pantheon (p50)

In Focus

Rome Today   208
Political scandal, monumental clean-ups and conflict in the Vatican.

History   210
The lust for power lies at the heart of Rome's thrilling 3000-year history.

The Arts   218
Virgil, Michelangelo and Fellini are among the many poets, artists and auteurs to have found inspiration in Rome.

Architecture   222
Architecture's major developments are writ large on Rome's magnificent cityscape.

The Roman Way of Life   227
What is it really like to live in Italy's Eternal City?

Pope Francis

Rome Today

*From time immemorial, political turmoil has been part
and parcel of Roman life. On the surface, recent news
has been good: EU leaders met in town to celebrate 60
years of European unity; millions of pilgrims poured
into St Peter's for Pope Francis' Holy Year; and the
Colosseum was unveiled after a lengthy restoration.
But behind the scenes, the story has been one of controversy and crisis in City Hall and ferocious in-fighting
in the Vatican.*

Chaos in City Hall

In summer 2016 Rome elected its first ever woman mayor. Virginia Raggi, a 37-year-old city
councillor swept to victory in the June elections, taking 67% of the vote as candidate for
the populist Movimento 5 Stelle (5 Star Movement). Promising to take on corruption and
improve the city's dire public services, her message hit a real chord with a Roman public
weary of cutbacks and political scandal. Her honeymoon period didn't last long, though,
and within months her administration was mired in controversy.

By Christmas 2016 she'd had to deal with the resignation of several key appointees, including the manager she'd tasked with cleaning up the city. Then, in early 2017, she was placed
under investigation for abuse of office following the appointment of a city tourism official.

Belief Systems (% of population)

80 — Christian
20 — Other

if Rome were 100 people

87 would be Italian
5 would be East European
4 would be Asian
1 would be African
3 would be other

population per sq km

= 200 people

Rome
Italy

In the midst of this, she did, however, manage to make some big decisions. She withdrew Rome's bid for the 2024 Olympic Games and gave the go-ahead for a new football stadium in the city's southern reaches. She also passed a €5.3-billion budget, earmarking €430 million for upgrading the city's public transport network, including buying new buses and funding ongoing construction on the metro.

Jubilee & Vatican Intrigue

Over on the west bank of the Tiber at the Vatican, Pope Francis declared 2016 a Jubilee, or Holy Year, and millions made the pilgrimage to Rome. Twenty-one million people passed through the Holy Door at St Peter's Basilica according to Vatican estimates. Throughout the year several grand events were staged, including the canonisation of Mother Teresa in September 2016, which drew crowds of up to 120,000 to St Peter's Square.

Behind the scenes, however, the atmosphere within the Vatican has become increasingly toxic as internal opposition to Pope Francis' progressive politics grows. With his easy-going manner and popular charm, the Argentinean pontiff has won worldwide acclaim for giving the Church a friendlier face, but his liberal line has enraged conservatives within the Church. Central to this dispute, which some commentators have likened to a state of civil war, are the pope's efforts to reform teachings on issues surrounding family, marriage and divorce.

Monumental Makeovers

For several years now, Rome's cultural administrators have been courting private money to shore up municipal budgets and help cover the cost of maintaining the city's historic sites and monuments. This policy has often sparked heated debate, but it is now showing signs of fruition. Most notably, the Colosseum is looking better than it has in centuries after completion of a three-year clean-up. The scrub-down came as the first part of a comprehensive €25-million restoration project sponsored by Italian shoemaker Tod's. Similarly the Spanish Steps, which were reopened to the public in September 2016, are gleaming after a €1.5-million makeover financed by luxury jeweller Bulgari. Foreign organisations are also getting in on the act and, in March 2017, it was announced that the Danish Academy would donate €1.5 million towards work on the Foro di Cesare.

In addition to these high-profile projects, there have been other successes. At the Roman Forum, the Chiesa di Santa Maria Antiqua was recently re-opened after a lengthy restoration, while at the Circo Massimo a renovated section of the original stadium was opened to guided tours. Unfortunately, visits to these sites are often affected by a shortage of personnel, and you won't always find them open.

History

Rome's history spans three millennia, from the classical myths of vengeful gods to the follies of Roman emperors, from Renaissance excess to swaggering 20th-century fascism. Everywhere you go in this remarkable city, you're surrounded by the past. Martial ruins, Renaissance palazzi and flamboyant baroque basilicas all have tales to tell of family feuding, historic upheavals, artistic rivalries, dark intrigues and violent passions.

753 BC

According to legend, Romulus kills his twin brother Remus and founds Rome on the Palatino.

509 BC

The Roman Republic is founded, paving the way for Rome's rise to European domination.

15 March 44 BC

On the Ides of March, Julius Caesar is stabbed to death in the Teatro di Pompeo (on modern-day Largo di Torre Argentina).

Piazza del Campidoglio (p72)

JUSTIN FOULKES/LONELY PLANET ©

The Myth of Ancient Rome

As much a mythical construct as a historical reality, ancient Rome's image has been carefully nurtured throughout history.

Rome's original myth makers were the first emperors. Eager to reinforce the city's status as *caput mundi* (capital of the world), they turned to writers such as Virgil, Ovid and Livy to create an official Roman history. These authors, while adept at weaving epic narratives, were less interested in the rigours of historical research and frequently presented myth as reality. In the *Aeneid,* Virgil brazenly draws on Greek legends and stories to tell the tale of Aeneas, a Trojan prince who arrives in Italy and establishes Rome's founding dynasty.

Ancient Rome's rulers were sophisticated masters of spin; under their tutelage, art, architecture and elaborate public ceremony were employed to perpetuate the image of Rome as an invincible and divinely sanctioned power.

AD 67	**80**	**285**
St Peter and St Paul become martyrs as Nero massacres Rome's Christians in a ploy to win popularity after the great fire of AD 64.	The 50,000-seat Flavian Amphitheatre, better known as the Colosseum, is inaugurated by the emperor Titus.	Diocletian splits the Roman Empire in two. The eastern half later joins the Byzantine Empire; the western half falls to the barbarians.

Galata morente (Dying Gaul; p73), Capitoline Museums

★ Best Historical Sites

Palatino (p58)

Roman Forum (p78)

Pantheon (p50)

Ostia Antica (p92)

Capitoline Museums (p70)

Legacy of an Empire

Rising out of the bloodstained remnants of the Roman Republic, the Roman Empire was the Western world's first great superpower. At its zenith under Emperor Trajan (r AD 98–117), it extended from Britannia in the north to North Africa in the south, from Hispania (Spain) in the west to Palestina (Palestine) and Syria in the east. Rome itself had more than 1.5 million inhabitants. Decline eventually set in during the 3rd century and by the latter half of the 5th century Rome was in barbarian hands.

In AD 285 the emperor Diocletian, prompted by widespread disquiet across the empire, split the Empire into eastern and western halves – the west centred on Rome and the east on Byzantium (later called Constantinople) – in a move that was to have far-reaching consequences for centuries. In the west, the fall of the Western Roman Empire in AD 476 paved the way for the emergence of the Holy Roman Empire and the Papal States, while in the east, Roman (later Byzantine) rule continued until 1453 when the empire was finally conquered by Ottoman armies.

Christianity & Papal Power

For much of its history Rome has been ruled by the pope, and still today the Vatican wields immense influence over the city.

The ancient Romans were remarkably tolerant of foreign religions. They themselves worshipped a cosmopolitan pantheon of gods, ranging from household spirits and former emperors to deities appropriated from Greek mythology such as Jupiter, Juno, Neptune and Minerva. Religious cults were also popular – the Egyptian gods Isis and Serapis enjoyed a mass following, as did Mithras, a heroic saviour-god of vaguely Persian origin, who was worshipped by male-only devotees in underground temples.

476

The fall of Romulus Augustulus marks the end of the Western Empire.

754

Pope Stephen II and Pepin, king of the Franks, cut a deal resulting in the creation of the Papal States.

1084

Rome is sacked by a Norman army after Pope Gregory VII invites them in to help him against the besieging forces of Henry IV.

Emergence of Christianity

Christianity swept in from the Roman province of Judaea in the 1st century AD. Its early days were marred by persecution, most notably under Nero (r 54–68), but it slowly caught on, thanks to its popular message of heavenly reward.

However, it was the conversion of Emperor Constantine (r 306–37) that really set Christianity on the path to European domination. In 313 Constantine issued the Edict of Milan, officially legalising Christianity, and in 378, Theodosius (r 379–95) made Christianity Rome's state religion. By this time, the Church had developed a sophisticated organisational structure based on five major sees: Rome, Constantinople, Alexandria, Antioch and Jerusalem. At the outset, each bishopric carried equal weight, but in subsequent years Rome emerged as the senior party. The reasons for this were partly political – Rome was the wealthy capital of the Roman Empire – and partly religious – early Christian doctrine held that St Peter, founder of the Roman Church, had been sanctioned by Christ to lead the universal Church.

Romulus & Remus

The most famous of Rome's many legends is the story of Romulus and Remus, mythical twins said to have founded Rome.

Born to the vestal virgin Rhea Silva after she'd been seduced by Mars, Romulus and Remus were immediately sentenced to death by their great-uncle Amulius. The sentence was never carried out, however, and the twins were abandoned in a basket on the banks of the Tiber. The babies were saved by a she-wolf, who suckled them until a shepherd, Faustulus, found and raised them.

Years later, the twins decided to found a city on the site where they'd originally been saved. Not knowing the actual location, they consulted the omens: Remus, on the Aventino, saw six vultures; his brother on the Palatino saw 12. Unable to reach an accord, the two brothers argued and Romulus killed Remus, before going on to found his city.

Papal Control

But while Rome had control of Christianity, the Church had yet to conquer Rome. This it did in the dark days that followed the fall of the Roman Empire by skilfully stepping into the power vacuum created by the demise of imperial power. And although no one person can take credit for this, Pope Gregory the Great (r 590–604) did more than most to lay the groundwork. A leader of considerable foresight, he won many friends by supplying free bread to Rome's starving citizens and restoring the city's water supply. He also stood up to the menacing Lombards, who presented a very real threat to the city.

It was this threat that pushed the papacy into an alliance with the Frankish kings, resulting in the creation of the two great powers of medieval Europe: the Papal States and the Holy Roman Empire. In Rome, the battle between these two superpowers translated into endless feuding between the city's baronial families and frequent attempts by the French

1300
Pope Boniface VIII proclaims Rome's first ever Jubilee, offering a full pardon to anyone who makes the pilgrimage to the city.

1378–1417
Squabbling between factions in the Catholic Church leads to the Great Schism.

1527
Pope Clement VII hides in Castel Sant'Angelo as Rome is sacked by troops loyal to Charles V, king of Spain and Holy Roman Emperor.

Romulus and Remus (p213) statue, Piazza del Campidoglio (p72)

to claim the papacy for their own. This political and military fighting eventually culminated in the papacy transferring to the French city of Avignon between 1309 and 1377, and the Great Schism (1378–1417), a period in which the Catholic world was headed by two popes, one in Rome and one in Avignon.

As both religious and temporal leaders, Rome's popes wielded influence well beyond their military capacity. For much of the medieval period, the Church held a virtual monopoly on Europe's reading material (mostly religious scripts written in Latin) and was the authority on virtually every aspect of human knowledge.

Modern Influence

Almost 1000 years on and the Church is still a major influence on modern Italian life. In recent years, Vatican intervention in political and social debate has provoked fierce divisions within Italy. This relationship between the Church and Italy's modern political establishment is a fact of life that dates to the establishment of the Italian Republic in 1946. For much of the First Republic (1946–94), the Vatican was closely associated with Democrazia Cristiana (DC; Christian Democrat Party), Italy's most powerful party and an ardent opponent of communism. At the same time, the Church, keen to weed communism out of the political landscape, played its part by threatening to excommunicate anyone who voted for Italy's Partito Comunista Italiano (PCI; Communist Party). Today, no one political party has a monopoly on Church favour, and politicians across the spectrum tread warily around Catholic sensibilities.

Renaissance, a New Beginning

Bridging the gap between the Middle Ages and the modern age, the Renaissance (Rinascimento in Italian) was a far-reaching intellectual, artistic and cultural movement. It emerged in 14th-century Florence but quickly spread to Rome, where it gave rise to one of the greatest makeovers the city had ever seen.

1626	1798	1870
St Peter's Basilica is completed on 18 November after 150 years of construction.	Napoleon marches into Rome. A republic is announced, but it doesn't last long and in 1801 Pope Pius VII returns to Rome.	Nine years after Italian unification, Rome's city walls are breached at Porta Pia and Pope Pius IX cedes the city to Italy.

Humanism & Rebuilding

The movement's intellectual cornerstone was humanism, a philosophy that focused on the central role of humanity within the universe, a major break from the medieval world view, which placed God at the centre of everything. It was not anti-religious though. One of the most celebrated humanist scholars of the 15th century was Pope Nicholas V (r 1447–84), who is considered the harbinger of the Roman Renaissance.

When Nicholas became pope in 1447, Rome was not in a good state. Centuries of medieval feuding had reduced the city to a semi-deserted battleground. In political terms, the papacy was recovering from the trauma of the Great Schism and attempting to face down Muslim encroachment in the east.

The Madness of Caligula

Of all ancient Rome's cruel and insane leaders, few are as notorious as Caligula. Later to become a byword for depravity, he was first hailed as a saviour when he inherited the empire from his hated great-uncle Tiberius in AD 37. But this optimism was soon to prove ill-founded, and after a bout of serious illness, Caligula began showing disturbing signs of mental instability. He made his senators worship him and infamously tried to make his horse a senator. By AD 41 everyone had had enough of him, and on 24 January the leader of his own Praetorian Guard stabbed him to death.

Against this background, Nicholas decided to rebuild Rome as a showcase of Church power, setting off an enormous program that would see the building of the Sistine Chapel and St Peter's Basilica.

Sack of Rome & Protestant Protest

But outside Rome an ill wind was blowing. The main source of trouble was the long-standing conflict between the Holy Roman Empire, led by the Spanish Charles V, and the Italian city-states. This simmering tension came to a head in 1527 when Rome was invaded by Charles' marauding army and ransacked as Pope Clement VII (r 1523–34) hid in Castel Sant'Angelo. The sack of Rome, regarded by most historians as the nail in the coffin of the Roman Renaissance, was a hugely traumatic event. It left the papacy reeling and gave rise to the view that the Church had been greatly weakened by its own moral shortcomings. That the Church was corrupt was well known, and it was with considerable public support that Martin Luther pinned his famous 95 Theses to a church door in Wittenberg in 1517, thus sparking off the Protestant Reformation.

Counter-Reformation

The Catholic reaction to the Reformation was strong. The Counter-Reformation was marked by a second wave of artistic and architectural activity, as the Church once again turned to bricks and mortar to restore its authority. But in contrast to the Renaissance,

1922	1929	1946
Some 40,000 fascists march on Rome. King Vittorio Emanuele III invites the 39-year-old Mussolini to form a government.	The Lateran Treaty is signed, creating the state of Vatican City. To celebrate, Via della Conciliazione is bulldozed through the medieval Borgo.	The Italian republic is born after a vote to abolish the monarchy.

Festa della Repubblica (p11)

★ **Best Historical Celebrations**

Carnevale Romano (p7)

Natale di Roma (p9)

Festa de'Noantri (p12)

Festa della Liberazione (p9)

Festa della Repubblica (p11)

the Counter-Reformation was a period of persecution and official intolerance. With the full blessing of Pope Paul III, Ignatius Loyola founded the Jesuits in 1540, and two years later the Holy Office was set up as the Church's final appeals court for trials prosecuted by the Inquisition. In 1559 the Church published the *Index Librorum Prohibitorum* (Index of Prohibited Books) and began to persecute intellectuals and freethinkers.

Despite, or perhaps because of, the Church's policy of zero tolerance, the Counter-Reformation was largely successful in re-establishing papal prestige. From being a rural backwater with a population of around 20,000 in the mid-15th century, Rome had grown to become one of Europe's great 17th-century cities, home to Christendom's most spectacular churches and a population of 100,000 people.

The First Tourists

While Rome has a long past as a pilgrimage site, its history as a modern tourist destination can be traced back to the late 1700s and the fashion for the Grand Tour. The 18th-century version of a gap year, the Tour was considered an educational rite of passage for wealthy young men from northern Europe, and Britain in particular.

Rome, enjoying a rare period of peace, was perfectly set up for this English invasion. The city was basking in the aftermath of the 17th-century baroque building boom, and a craze for all things classical was sweeping Europe. Rome's papal authorities were also crying out for money after their excesses had left the city coffers bare, reducing much of the population to abject poverty.

Thousands came, including German writer Goethe, who stopped off to write his travelogue *Italian Journey* (1817), and English poets Byron, Shelley and Keats, who all fuelled their Romantic sensibilities in the city's vibrant streets.

Artistically, rococo was all the rage. The Spanish Steps, built between 1723 and 1726, proved a major hit with tourists, as did the exuberant Trevi Fountain.

1957	1978	2005
The Treaty of Rome is signed in the Capitoline Museums and establishes the European Economic Community.	Former prime minister Aldo Moro is kidnapped and shot by a cell of the extreme left-wing *Brigate Rosse* (Red Brigades).	Pope John Paul II dies after 27 years on the papal throne. He is replaced by his long-standing ally Josef Ratzinger (Benedict XVI).

Ghosts of Fascism

Rome's fascist history is a deeply sensitive subject, and in recent years historians on both sides of the political spectrum have accused each other of recasting the past to suit their views.

Mussolini

Benito Mussolini was born in 1883 in Forlì, a town in Emilia-Romagna. As a young man he was a member of the Italian Socialist Party, rising through the ranks to become editor of the party's official newspaper. However, service in WWI and Italy's subsequent descent into chaos led to a change of heart and in 1919 he founded the Italian Fascist Party.

In 1921 Mussolini was elected to the Chamber of Deputies. His parliamentary support was limited, but on 28 October 1922 he marched on Rome with 40,000 black-shirted followers. The march was largely symbolic but it had the desired effect: King Vittorio Emanuele III, fearful of a civil war between the fascists and socialists, invited Mussolini to form a government. By the end of 1925 the king had seized control of Italy. In order to silence the Church Mussolini signed the Lateran Treaty in 1929, which made Catholicism the state religion and recognised the sovereignty of the Vatican State.

Abroad, Mussolini invaded Abyssinia (now Ethiopia) in 1935 and sided with Hitler in 1936. In 1940, from the balcony of Palazzo Venezia, he announced Italy's entry into WWII to a vast, cheering crowd. The good humour didn't last: Rome suffered, first at the hands of its own Fascist regime, then, after Mussolini was ousted in 1943, at the hands of the Nazis. Rome was finally liberated from German occupation on 4 June 1944.

Postwar Period

Defeat in WWII didn't kill off Italian fascism, and in 1946 hard-line Mussolini supporters founded the Movimento Sociale Italiano (MSI; Italian Social Movement). For close on 50 years this overtly fascist party participated in mainstream Italian politics, while on the other side of the spectrum the PCI grew into Western Europe's largest communist party. The MSI was finally dissolved in 1994, when Gianfranco Fini rebranded it as the post-fascist Alleanza Nazionale (AN; National Alliance). AN remained an important political player until it was incorporated into Silvio Berlusconi's Popolo della Libertà party in 2009.

Outside the political mainstream, fascism (along with communism) was a driving force of the domestic terrorism that rocked Rome and Italy during the *anni di piombo* (years of lead), between the late 1960s and the early '80s.

Roman Roads

The ancient Romans were the expert engineers of their day, and the ability to travel quickly was an important factor in their power to rule. The queen of all ancient roads was Via Appia Antica, which connected Rome with the southern Adriatic port of Brindisi, named after Appius Claudius Caecus, the Roman censor who initiated its construction in 312 BC. Via Appia survives to this day, as do many of the other consular roads: Via Aurelia, Via Cassia, Via Flaminia and Via Salaria among them.

2013

Pope Benedict XVI becomes the first pope to resign since 1415. Argentinian cardinal Jorge Mario Bergoglio is elected as Pope Francis.

2014

Ex-mayor Gianni Alemanno and up to 100 other public officials are investigated as the Mafia Capitale scandal rocks Rome.

2015–16

Pope Francis declares an Extraordinary Jubilee of Mercy, a special period of prayer running from 8 December 2015 to 20 November 2016.

Trevi Fountain (p84)

The Arts

Rome's turbulent history and magical cityscape have long provided inspiration for painters, sculptors, film-makers, writers and musicians. The great classical works of Roman antiquity fuelled the imagination of Renaissance artists; Counter-Reformation persecution led to baroque art and popular street satire; and the trauma of Mussolini and WWII found expression in neorealist cinema.

Painting & Sculpture

Home to some of the Western world's most recognisable art, Rome is a visual feast. Its churches alone contain more masterpieces than many small countries possess, and the city's galleries are laden with works by world-famous artists.

Etruscan Groundwork

Laying the groundwork for much later Roman art, the placed great importance on their funerary rites and they developed sepulchral decoration into a highly sophisticated art form. Elaborate stone sarcophagi were often embellished with a reclining figure or a couple, typically depicted with a haunting, enigmatic smile. An important example is the *Sarcofago degli sposi* (Sarcophagus of the Betrothed) in the Museo Nazionale Etrusco di Villa Giulia. The Etruscans were also noted for their bronze work and filigree jewellery. One of Rome's most iconic sculptures, the 5th-century-BC *Lupa capitolina* (Capitoline Wolf), held in the Capitoline Museums, is an Etruscan bronze.

Roman Developments

In terms of decorative art, the Roman use of mosaics and wall paintings was derived from Etruscan funerary decoration. By the 1st century BC, floor mosaics were a popular form of home decor. Typical themes included landscapes, still lifes, geometric patterns and depictions of gods. In the Museo Nazionale Romano: Palazzo Massimo alle Terme, you'll find some spectacular wall mosaics and 1st-century-BC frescoes.

Sculpture was an important element of Roman art, and was largely influenced by Greek styles. Indeed, early Roman sculptures were often made by Greek artists or were copies of Greek works. Works were largely concerned with visions of male beauty; classic examples are the *Apollo Belvedere* and the *Laocoön* in the Museo Pio-Clementino of the Vatican Museums.

From the time of Augustus (r 27 BC–AD 14), Roman art was increasingly used to serve the state, and artists came to be regarded as little more than state functionaries. A new style of narrative art developed, which often took the form of relief decoration – the *Ara Pacis Augustae,* Augustus' peace monument now in the Museo dell'Ara Pacis, is a stunning example.

Early Christian Art

The earliest Christian art in Rome are the traces of biblical frescoes in the Catacombe di Priscilla and the Catacombe di San Sebastiano.

With the legalisation of Christianity in the 4th century, these images began to move into the public arena, appearing in mosaics across the city and in churches such as the Basilica di Santa Maria Maggiore.

Eastern influences became much more pronounced between the 7th and 9th centuries, when Byzantine styles swept in from the east; you can see such brighter, golden works in the Basilica di Santa Maria in Trastevere.

The Renaissance

The Renaissance arrived in Rome in the latter half of the 15th century, and was to have a profound impact on the city, as the top artists of the day were summoned to decorate the many new buildings going up around town.

Rome's most celebrated works of Renaissance art are Michelangelo's paintings in the Sistine Chapel – his cinematic ceiling frescoes, painted between 1508 and 1512, and the *Giudizio Universale* (Last Judgment), which he worked on between 1536 and 1541.

Central to the *Last Judgment* and much Renaissance art was the human form. This led artists to develop a far greater appreciation of perspective. But while early Renaissance painters made great strides in formulating rules of perspective, they still struggled to paint harmonious arrangements of figures. And it was this that Raffaello Sanzio (Raphael; 1483–1520) tackled in his great masterpiece *La Scuola di Atene* (The School of Athens; 1510–11) in the Vatican Museums.

Neoclassicism

Emerging in the late 18th and early 19th centuries, neoclassicism signalled a departure from the emotional abandon of the baroque and a return to the clean, sober lines of classical art. Its major exponent was the sculptor Antonio Canova (1757–1822), whose study of Paolina Bonaparte Borghese as *Venere Vincitrice* (Venus Victrix) in the Museo e Galleria Borghese is typical of the mildly erotic style for which he became known.

San Luigi dei Francesi (p65)

★ **Art Churches**

St Peter's Basilica (p46)

Santa Maria in Trastevere (p104)

Santa Maria Maggiore (p102)

San Luigi dei Francesi (p65)

Santa Maria del Popolo (p86)

Counter-Reformation & the Baroque

The baroque burst onto Rome's art scene in the early 17th century. Combining a dramatic sense of dynamism with highly charged emotion, it was enthusiastically appropriated by the Catholic Church, which used it as a propaganda tool in its persecution of Counter-Reformation heretics. The powerful popes of the day eagerly championed the likes of Caravaggio, Gian Lorenzo Bernini, Domenichino, Pietro da Cortona and Alessandro Algardi.

Unsurprisingly, much baroque art has a religious theme and you'll often find depictions of martyrdoms, ecstasies and miracles.

A premier exponent was Milan-born Caravaggio (1573–1610), whose realistic interpretations of religious subjects often outraged his patrons. In contrast, the exquisite sculptural works of Gian Lorenzo Bernini (1598–1680) proved an instant hit.

Literature

Rome has a rich literary tradition, encompassing everything from ancient satires to dialect poetry, anti-fascist prose and contemporary thrillers.

Classics

Famous for his blistering oratory, Marcus Tullius Cicero (106–43 BC) was the Roman Republic's preeminent author. His contemporary, Catullus (c 84–54 BC) cut a very different figure with his epigrams and erotic verse.

On becoming emperor, Augustus (aka Octavian) encouraged the arts, and Virgil (70–19 BC), Ovid, Horace and Tibullus all enjoyed freedom to write.

Rome as Inspiration

Rome has provided inspiration for legions of foreign authors. In the 18th century, historians and Grand Tourists poured into Rome from northern Europe. The German author Goethe captures the elation of discovering ancient Rome in his travelogue *Italian Journey* (1817). The city was also favoured by the Romantic poets: John Keats, Lord Byron, Percy Bysshe Shelley, Mary Shelley and other writers all spent time here. More recently, Rome has provided settings for many a literary blockbuster, including Dan Brown's thriller *Angels and Demons* (2001).

Writing Today

Born in Rome in 1966, Niccolò Ammaniti is the best known of the city's crop of contemporary authors. In 2007 he won the Premio Strega, Italy's top literary prize for his novel *Come Dio comanda* (As God Commands). Another name to look out for is Andrea Bajani (b 1975), who has already scooped an impressive number of awards in his short writing career.

Cinema

Rome has a long cinematic tradition, spanning the works of the postwar neorealists and film-makers as diverse as Federico Fellini, Sergio Leone, Nanni Moretti, and Paolo Sorrentino, the Oscar-winning director of *La grande belleza* (The Great Beauty).

The 1940s was Roman cinema's golden age, when Roberto Rossellini (1906–77) produced a trio of neorealist masterpieces, most notably *Roma città aperta* (Rome Open City; 1945). Also important was Vittorio de Sica's 1948 *Ladri di biciclette* (Bicycle Thieves).

Federico Fellini (1920–94) took the creative baton from the neorealists, producing his era-defining hit *La Dolce Vita* in 1960. The films of Pier Paolo Pasolini (1922–75) are similarly demanding in their depiction of Rome's gritty underbelly in the postwar period.

Idiosyncratic and whimsical, Nanni Moretti continues to make films that fall outside of mainstream tradition, including *Habemus Papam*, his 2011 portrayal of a pope having a crisis of faith.

Sergio Leone

Best known for almost single-handedly creating the spaghetti western, Roman-born Sergio Leone (1929–89) is a hero to many. The son of a silent-movie director, Leone cut his teeth as a screenwriter, before working as assistant director on *Quo Vadis?* (1951) and *Ben-Hur* (1959). He made his directorial debut three years later on *Il Colosso di Rodi* (The Colossus of Rhodes; 1961).

It was with his famous dollar trilogy, however – *Per un pugno di dollari* (A Fistful of Dollars; 1964), *Per qualche dollari in piu* (For a Few Dollars More; 1965) and *Il buono, il brutto, il cattivo* (The Good, the Bad and the Ugly; 1966) – that he really hit the big time.

Stylistically, Leone introduced a series of innovations that were later to become trademarks. Chief among these was his use of musical themes to identify his characters. In this he was brilliantly supported by his old schoolmate Ennio Morricone, another Roman-born legend of the arts.

Recently the big news in cinema circles has been the return of international film-making to Rome. In 2015 Daniel Craig charged around town filming another 007 outing, *Spectre,* while Ben Stiller was camping it up for *Zoolander 2*. Down in the city's southern reaches, a remake of *Ben-Hur* was filmed at the Cinecittà film studios, the very same place where the original sword-and-sandal epic was shot in 1959.

Music

Despite years of austerity-led cut-backs, Rome's music scene is bearing up well. International orchestras perform to sell-out audiences, jazz greats jam in steamy clubs, and rappers rage in underground venues.

Jazz has long been a mainstay of Rome's music scene, while recent years have seen the emergence of a vibrant rap and hip-hop culture. Opera is served up at the Teatro dell'Opera and, in summer, at the spectacular Terme di Caracalla.

La Nuvola (The Cloud; p226) by architect Massimiliano Fuksas

Architecture

*From ancient ruins and Renaissance basilicas
to baroque churches and hulking fascist* palazzi
*(mansions), Rome's architectural legacy is unparal-
leled. Michelangelo, Bramante, Borromini and Bernini,
as well as contemporary stars, such as Renzo Piano
and Zaha Hadid, are among the architects who have
stamped their genius on Rome's remarkable cityscape.*

The Ancients

Architecture was central to the success of the ancient Romans. In building their great capital, they were pioneers in using architecture to tackle problems of infrastructure, urban management and communication. For the first time, architects and engineers designed houses, roads, aqueducts and shopping centres alongside temples, tombs and imperial palaces. To do this, the Romans advanced methods devised by the Etruscans and Greeks, developing construction techniques and building materials that allowed them to build on a massive and hitherto unseen scale.

Etruscan Roots

By the 7th century BC the Etruscans were the dominant force on the Italian peninsula, with important centres at Tarquinia, Caere (Cerveteri) and Veii (Veio). They built with wood and brick, however, which didn't age well, and much of what we now know about the Etruscans derives from their impressive cemeteries. These were constructed outside the city walls and harboured richly decorated stone vaults covered by mounds of earth.

Roman Developments

When Rome was founded in 753 BC (or even earlier according to recent archaeological findings), the Etruscans were at the height of their power and Greek colonists were establishing control over southern Italy. Against this background, Roman architects borrowed heavily from Greek and Etruscan traditions, gradually developing their own styles and techniques.

Ancient Roman architecture was monumental in form and often propagandistic in nature. Huge amphitheatres, aqueducts and temples joined muscular and awe-inspiring basilicas, arches and thermal baths in trumpeting the skill and vision of the city's early rulers and the nameless architects who worked for them.

Temples

Early Republican-era temples were based on Etruscan designs, but over time the Romans turned to the Greeks for their inspiration. Whereas Greek temples had steps and colonnades on all sides, however, the classic Roman temple had a high podium with steps leading up to a deep porch.

The Roman use of columns was also Greek in origin, even if the Romans favoured the more slender Ionic and Corinthian columns over the plain Doric pillars. To see how these differ, study the exterior of the Colosseum, which incorporates all three styles.

Aqueducts & Sewers

One of the Romans' crowning architectural achievements was the development of a water supply infrastructure.

To meet the city's water demand, the Romans constructed a complex system of aqueducts to bring water in from the hills of central Italy and distribute it around town. The first aqueduct to serve Rome was the 16.5km Aqua Appia, which became fully operational in 312 BC. Over the next 700 years or so, up to 800km of aqueducts were built in the city, a network capable of supplying up to one million cubic metres of water per day.

At the other end of the water cycle, waste water was drained away via an underground sewerage system known as the Cloaca Maxima (Great Sewer) and emptied downstream into the Tiber.

Residential Housing

While Rome's emperors and aristocrats lived in luxury on the Palatino (Palatine Hill), the city's poor huddled together in large residential blocks called *insulae*. These poorly built structures were sometimes up to six or seven storeys high, accommodating hundreds of people in dark, unhealthy conditions. Near the foot of the steps that lead up to the Chiesa di Santa Maria in Aracoeli, you can still see a section of what was once a typical city-centre *insula*.

★ **Best Ancient Sites**

Colosseum (p36)
Pantheon (p50)
Palatino (p58)
Roman Forum (p78)
Ostia Antica (p92)

Ostia Antica (p92)

BILL PERRY/SHUTTERSTOCK ©

Concrete & Monumental Architecture

Grandiose structures such as the Colosseum, the Pantheon and the Forums are not only reminders of the sophistication and scale of ancient Rome – just as they were originally designed to be – but also monuments to the vision and bravura of the city's ancient architects.

One of the key breakthroughs the Romans made was the invention of concrete in the 1st century BC. Made by mixing volcanic ash with lime and an aggregate, often tufa rock or brick rubble, concrete was quick to make, easy to use and cheap. It allowed the Romans to develop vaulted roofing, which they used to span the Pantheon's ceiling and the huge vaults at the Terme di Caracalla.

Early Christian

The most startling reminders of early Christian activity are the catacombs, a series of underground burial grounds built under Rome's ancient roads. Christian belief in the resurrection meant that the Christians could not cremate their dead, as was the custom in Roman times, and with burial forbidden inside the city walls they were forced to go outside the city.

The Christians began to abandon the catacombs in the 4th century and increasingly opted to be buried in the churches that the emperor Constantine was building in the city. The most notable of the many churches he commissioned is the Basilica di San Giovanni in Laterano, the model on which many subsequent basilicas were based. Other period showstoppers include the Basilica di Santa Maria in Trastevere and the Basilica di Santa Maria Maggiore.

A second wave of church-building hit Rome in the period between the 8th and 12th centuries. As the early papacy battled for survival against the threatening Lombards, its leaders took to construction to leave some sort of historical imprint, resulting in churches such as the Chiesa di Santa Maria in Cosmedin, home of the Bocca della Verità (Mouth of Truth).

The Renaissance

Many claim it was the election of Pope Nicholas V in 1447 that sparked the Renaissance in Rome. Nicholas believed that as head of the Christian world Rome had a duty to impress, a theory that was endorsed by his successors, and it was at the behest of the great papal dynasties – the Barberini, Farnese and Pamphilj – that the leading artists of the day were summoned to Rome.

Bramante & the High Renaissance

It was under Pope Julius II that the Roman Renaissance reached its peak, thanks largely to a classically minded architect from Milan, Donato Bramante.

Considered the high priest of Renaissance architecture, Bramante arrived in Rome in 1499 and developed a hugely influential, refined classical style. His 1502 Tempietto, for example, perfectly illustrates his innate understanding of proportion. In 1506 Julius commissioned him to start work on his greatest project – the rebuilding of St Peter's Basilica. The fall of Constantinople's Aya Sofya (Church of the Hagia Sofia) to Islam in the mid-14th century had pricked Nicholas V into ordering an earlier revamp, but the work had never been completed and it wasn't until Julius took over the project that progress was made. Bramante died in 1514, however, and he never got to see how his original Greek-cross design was developed.

St Peter's Basilica occupied most of the other notable architects of the High Renaissance, including Giuliano da Sangallo, Baldassarre Peruzzi and Antonio da Sangallo the Younger. Michelangelo eventually took over in 1547, modifying the layout and creating the basilica's crowning dome. Modelled on Brunelleschi's cupola for the Duomo in Florence, this is considered the artist's finest architectural achievement and one of the most important works of the Roman Renaissance.

Rococo Frills

In the early days of the 18th century, as baroque began to fade and neoclassicism was still to come, the rococo burst into life. Drawing on the excesses of the baroque, it was a short-lived, theatrical fad but one that left several iconic monuments.

Built between 1723 and 1726 by Francesco de Sanctis, the Spanish Steps provided a focal point for the many Grand Tourists who were busy discovering Rome's classical past. A short walk to the southwest, Piazza Sant'Ignazio was designed by Filippo Raguzzini to provide a suitably melodramatic setting for the Chiesa di Sant'Ignazio di Loyola, Rome's second most important Jesuit church. Most spectacular of all was the Trevi Fountain, one of the city's most exuberant and enduringly popular monuments. It was designed in 1732 by Nicola Salvi and completed three decades later.

The Baroque

As the principal motor of the Roman Renaissance, the Catholic Church became increasingly powerful in the 16th century. But with power came corruption and calls for reform. These culminated in the far-reaching Protestant Reformation, which prompted the Counter-Reformation, a vicious campaign to get people back into the Catholic fold. In the midst of this great offensive, baroque art and architecture emerged as a highly effective form of propaganda. Stylistically, baroque architecture aims for a dramatic sense of dynamism, an effect that it often achieves by combining spatial complexity with clever lighting and a flamboyant use of decorative painting and sculpture.

One of the first great Counter-Reformation churches was the Jesuit Chiesa del Gesù, designed by the leading architect of the day, Giacomo della Porta. In a move away from the style of earlier Renaissance churches, the facade has pronounced architectural elements that create a contrast between surfaces and a play of light and shade.

The end of the 16th century and the papacy of Sixtus V marked the beginning of major urban-planning schemes. Domenico Fontana and other architects created a network of major thoroughfares to connect previously disparate parts of the sprawling medieval city.

Palazzo Barberini (p69)

★ **Best Baroque**

St Peter's Square (p49)

Fontana dei Quattro Fiumi (p64)

Chiesa di Sant'Agnese in Agone (p64)

Palazzo Barberini (p69)

Fontana also designed the main facade of Palazzo del Quirinale, the immense palace that served as the pope's summer residence for almost three centuries.

Bernini Versus Borromini

No two people did more to fashion the face of Rome than Gian Lorenzo Bernini and Francesco Borromini, the great figures of the Roman baroque. Naples-born Bernini, confident and suave, is best known for his work in the Vatican, where he designed St Peter's Square and was chief architect at St Peter's Basilica from 1629.

Under the patronage of the Barberini pope Urban VIII, Bernini was given free rein to transform the city, and his churches, *palazzi,* piazzas and fountains remain landmarks to this day. His fortunes nose-dived, however, when the pope died in 1644. Urban's successor, Innocent X, wanted as little contact as possible with the favourites of his hated predecessor, and instead turned to Borromini.

Borromini, a solitary, peculiar man from Lombardy, created buildings involving complex shapes and exotic geometry, including the Chiesa di Sant'Agnese in Agone on Piazza Navona.

Rationalism & Fascism

Rome entered the 20th century in good shape. During the late 19th century it had been treated to one of its periodic makeovers – this time after being made capital of the Kingdom of Italy in 1870. Piazzas were built, including Piazza Vittorio Emanuele II and Piazza della Repubblica, and roads were laid. To celebrate unification and pander to the ruling Savoy family, the ostentatious Vittoriano monument was built.

The 1920s saw the emergence of architectural rationalism. Its main Italian proponents, the Gruppo Sette, combined classicism with modernism, which tied in perfectly with Mussolini's vision of fascism as the modern bearer of ancient Rome's imperialist ambitions. Mussolini's most famous architectural legacy is Rome's southern EUR district, an Orwellian quarter of wide boulevards and huge linear buildings, built for the Esposizione Universale di Roma in 1942.

Modern Rome

The 21st century has witnessed a flurry of architectural activity in Rome as a clutch of 'starchitects' have made their mark. Italian Renzo Piano worked on the acclaimed Auditorium Parco della Musica; American Richard Meier built a controversial new pavilion for the 1st-century-AD Ara Pacis; Anglo-Iraqi Zaha Hadid won plaudits for the Museo Nazionale delle Arti del XXI Secolo (MAXXI); and Roman-born Massimiliano Fuksas recently put the final touches on a striking conference centre in the EUR, known as the Nuvola (Cloud).

Football spectators at Stadio Olimpico (p194)

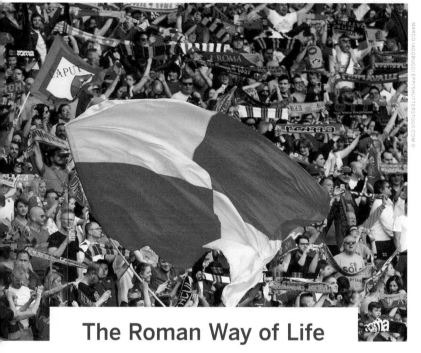

The Roman Way of Life

As a visitor, it's often difficult to see beyond Rome's spectacular veneer to the large, modern city that lies beneath: a living, breathing capital that's home to almost three million people. So how do the Romans live in their city? Where do they work? Who do they live with? And how do they let their hair down?

Work

Employment in the capital is largely based on Italy's bloated state bureaucracy. Every morning armies of suited civil servants pour into town and disappear into vast ministerial buildings to keep the machinery of government ticking over. Other important employers include the tourist sector, finance, media and culture. As Italy's economy continues to stagnate, however, it's tough for young people to get a foot on the career ladder. To land it lucky, it helps to know someone. Official figures are impossible to come by, but it's a widely held belief that having personal or political connections is the best way of landing a job.

Like everywhere in Italy, Rome's workplace remains predominantly male. Female unemployment is an ongoing issue and Italian women continue to earn less than their male

Caffè Sant'Eustachio (p122)

★ Best Local Haunts

Caffè Sant'Eustachio (p122)

Doppiozeroo (p140)

Stadio Olimpico (p194)

Nuovo Mercato di Testaccio (p161)

Villa Borghese (p56)

counterparts. That said, recent signs have been positive. Half of Prime Minister Matteo Renzi's 2014 cabinet was made up of women, and in June 2016 Rome elected its first-ever female mayor.

Home Life & Family

Romans, like most Italians, live in apartments, which are often small and expensive. House prices in central Rome are among the highest in the country and many first-time buyers are forced to move out of town or to distant suburbs. Rates of home ownership are relatively high in Rome – about 65%. People do rent, but the rental market is largely targeted at Rome's huge student population.

Italy's single most successful institution is the family. It's still the rule rather than the exception for young Romans to stay at home until they marry, which they typically do at around 30. But while faith in the family remains, the family unit is shrinking – Italian women are giving birth later than ever and having fewer children.

Play

Despite the high cost of living in Rome, few Romans would swap their city for anywhere else, and they enjoy it with gusto. You only have to look at the city's pizzerias and trattorias to see that eating out is a much-loved local pastime. Drinking, in contrast, is not a traditional Roman activity – an evening out in Rome is as much about flirting and looking gorgeous as it is about consuming alcohol.

Clothes shopping is a popular Roman pastime, alongside cinema-going and football; a trip to the Stadio Olimpico to watch the Sunday game is considered an afternoon well spent. Romans are inveterate car-lovers and on hot summer weekends they will often drive out to the coast or surrounding countryside for a fresh breeze or a pocket of green.

Religion

Rome is packed with churches. And with the Vatican in the centre of town, the Church is a constant presence in Roman life. Yet the role of religion in modern Roman society is an ambiguous one. On the one hand, most people consider themselves Catholic, but on the other, church attendance is in free fall, particularly among the young.

Catholicism's hold on the Roman psyche is strong, but an increase in the city's immigrant population has led to a noticeable Muslim presence. This has largely been a pain-free process, but friction has flared on occasion and there were violent scenes in summer 2015 when far-right anti-immigration protestors clashed with police in the Casale San Nicola neighbourhood in north Rome.

Colosseum (p36)

SBORISOV/GETTY IMAGES ©

Survival Guide

DIRECTORY A–Z 230

Customs Regulations 230
Electricity 230
Emergency 230
Health 230
Internet Access 230
Legal Matters 231
LGBT Travellers 231
Money 231

Opening Hours 231
Public Holidays 231
Safe Travel 232
Telephone 232
Time 232
Toilets 232
Tourist Information 233
Travellers with
Disabilities 233

Visas 233
Women Travellers 233

TRANSPORT 233

Arriving in Rome 233
Getting Around 235

LANGUAGE 238

Directory A–Z

Customs Regulations

If you're arriving from a non-EU country you can import, duty free, 200 cigarettes, 1L of spirits (or 2L fortified wine), 4L wine, 60ml perfume, 16L beer, and goods, including electronic devices, up to a value of €300 if arriving by land or €430 arriving by air or sea; anything above this value must be declared on arrival and the duty paid. Non-EU residents can reclaim value-added tax (VAT) on expensive purchases on leaving the EU.

Electricity

Type F
230V/50Hz

Type L
220V/50Hz

Emergency

Ambulance	118
Fire	115
Police	112, 113

Health

• EU nationals are entitled to reduced-cost, sometimes free, medical care with a European Health Insurance Card (EHIC), available from your home health authority; non-EU citizens should take out medical insurance.

• For emergency treatment, you can go to the *pronto soccorso* (casualty) section of an *ospedale* (public hospital). For less serious ailments call the **Guardia**

Medica Turistica (☏06 7730 6650; Via Emilio Morosini 30; ⏰8am-8pm Mon-Fri; 🚋Viale di Trastevere, 🚊Viale di Trastevere). More convenient, if you have insurance and can afford to pay up front, would be to call a private doctor for a home visit. Try **International Medical Centre '84** (☏06 488 23 71; www.imc84.com/roma; Via Firenze 47; GP call-out & treatment fee €140, 8pm-9am & weekends €200; ⏰24hr; Ⓜ Repubblica).

• Marked by a green cross, *farmacie* (pharmacies) open from 8.30am to 1pm and 4pm to 7.30pm Monday to Friday and on Saturday mornings. Outside these hours they open on a rotational basis, and all are legally required to post a list of places open in the vicinity.

Internet Access

• Free wi-fi is widely available in hostels, B&Bs and hotels; signals are of varying quality. Many bars and cafes also offer wi-fi.

• There are many public wi-fi hotspots across town run by Roma Wireless (https://captivik.uni.it/romawireless) and WiFimetropolitano (www.cittametropolitana roma.gov.it/wifimetropolitano). To use these you'll need to register online using a credit card or an Italian mobile phone number.

Legal Matters

The most likely reason for a brush with the law is if you need to report a theft. If you have something stolen and you want to claim it on insurance, you must make a statement to the police; insurance companies won't pay up without official proof of a crime.

LGBT Travellers

o Homosexuality is legal (above the age of 16) and even widely accepted, but Rome is fairly conservative in its attitudes, largely in keeping with the Vatican's line on social issues, and discretion is still wise.

o The city has a thriving, if low-key, gay scene. There are relatively few queer-only venues but the Colosseum end of Via di San Giovanni in Laterano is a favourite hang-out and many clubs host regular gay and lesbian nights.

Money

o Italy's currency is the euro. The seven euro notes come in denominations of €500, €200, €100, €50, €20, €10 and €5. Euro coins are in denominations of €2

and €1, and 50, 20, 10, five, two and one cents.

o You can change money in banks, at post offices or at a *cambio* (exchange office). There are exchange booths at Stazione Termini and at Fiumicino and Ciampino airports.

ATMs

ATMs (*bancomat*, in Italian) are widely available and most will accept cards tied into the Visa, Master-Card, Cirrus and Maestro systems. The daily limit for cash withdrawal is €250.

Credit Cards

Credit cards are widely accepted but it is still a good idea to carry a cash back-up. Virtually all midrange and top-end hotels accept cards, as do most restaurants and large shops. You can also use credit cards to obtain cash advances at some banks. Some of the cheaper *pensioni* (guest-houses), trattorias and pizzerias only accept cash.

Opening Hours

Banks 8.30am to 1.30pm and 2.45pm to 4.30pm Monday to Friday.

Bars & cafes 7.30am to 8pm, sometimes until 1am or 2am.

Clubs 10pm to 4am or 5am.

Restaurants noon to 3pm and 7.30pm to 11pm (later in summer).

Shops 9am to 7.30pm or 10am to 8pm Monday to Saturday, some 11am to 7pm Sunday; smaller shops 9am to 1pm and 3.30pm to 7.30pm Monday to Saturday; some shops closed Monday mornings.

Public Holidays

Most Romans take their annual holiday in August. Many businesses and shops close for at least part of the month. Public holidays include the following:

Capodanno (New Year's Day) 1 January

Epifania (Epiphany) 6 January

Roma Pass

A comprehensive discount card, the Roma Pass comes in two forms:

72-hour Roma Pass (€38.50) Provides free admission to two museums or sites, as well as reduced entry to extra sites, unlimited city transport, and discounted entry to other exhibitions and events for 72 hours.

48-hour Roma Pass (€28) Gives free admission to one museum or site as well as reduced entry to extra sites, unlimited city transport, and discounted entry to other exhibitions and events for 48 hours.

Pasquetta (Easter Monday) March/April

Giorno della Liberazione (Liberation Day) 25 April

Festa del Lavoro (Labour Day) 1 May

Festa della Repubblica (Republic Day) 2 June

Festa dei Santi Pietro e Paolo (Feast of St Peter & St Paul) 29 June

Ferragosto (Feast of the Assumption) 15 August

Festa di Ognisanti (All Saints' Day) 1 November

Festa dell'Immacolata Concezione (Feast of the Immaculate Conception) 8 December

Natale (Christmas Day) 25 December

Festa di Santo Stefano (Boxing Day) 26 December

Safe Travel

Rome is a safe city but petty theft can be a problem; pickpockets are active

in touristy areas and on crowded public transport. Be particularly vigilant around the bus stops on Via Marsala, where thieves prey on travellers fresh in from Ciampino airport. Use common sense and watch your valuables.

Telephone

● Rome's area code is ☎06, which must be dialled even when calling locally. Mobile phone numbers are nine or 10 digits long and begin with a three-digit prefix starting with a 3.

● To call abroad from Italy dial ☎00, then the country and area codes, followed by the telephone number.

Mobile Phones

Italian mobile phones operate on the GSM 900/1800 network, which is compatible with the rest of Europe

and Australia but not always with the North American GSM or CDMA systems – check with your service provider.

If you can unlock your phone, it can cost as little as €10 to activate a *prepagato* (prepaid) SIM card in Italy. TIM (Telecom Italia Mobile; www.tim.it), Wind (www.wind.it) and Vodafone (www.vodafone.it) all offer SIM cards and have retail outlets across town. Note that by Italian law all SIM cards must be registered, so make sure you have a passport or ID card with you when you buy one.

Time

Italy is in a single time zone, one hour ahead of GMT, and operates on a 24-hour clock. Daylight-saving time, when clocks move forward one hour, starts on the last Sunday in March. Clocks are put back an hour on the last Sunday in October.

Toilets

Public toilets are not widespread but you'll find them at St Peter's Square and Stazione Termini (€1). If you're caught short, the best thing to do is to go into a cafe or bar.

Practicalities

● **Newspapers** Key national dailies include centre-left *La Repubblica* and its right-wing rival *Corriere della Sera*. For the Vatican's take on affairs, *L'Osservatore Romano* is the Holy See's official paper.

● **Smoking** Banned in enclosed public spaces, which includes restaurants, bars, shops and public transport. Also banned in Villa Borghese and all other public parks during summer (June to September).

● **TV** The main terrestrial channels are RAI 1, 2 and 3 run by Rai (www.rai.it), Italy's state-owned national broadcaster, and Canale 5, Italia 1 and Rete 4 run by Mediaset (www.mediaset.it).

● **Weights and measures** Italy uses the metric system.

Tourist Information

○ The Comune di Roma runs a free multilingual tourist information line (☑06 06 08).

○ Tourist information points at **Fiumicino** (Fiumicino Airport; International Arrivals, Terminal 3; ⊙8am-8.45pm) and **Ciampino** (Arrivals Hall; ⊙8.30am-6pm) airports, and across the city:

Piazza Navona (Piazza delle Cinque Lune; ⊙9.30am-7pm; ☐Corso del Rinascimento)

Stazione Termini (☑06 06 08; www.turismoroma.it; Via Giovanni Giolitti 34; ⊙9am-5pm; ⓂTermini)

Fori Imperiali (Via dei Fori Imperiali; ⊙9.30am-7pm; ☐Via dei Fori Imperiali)

Minghetti (Via Marco Minghetti; ⊙9.30am-7pm; ☐Via del Corso)

Via Nazionale (☑06 06 08; www.turismoroma.it; Via Nazionale 184; ⊙9.30am-7pm; ☐Via Nazionale)

○ For information about the Vatican, contact **Centro Servizi Pellegrini e Turisti** (☑06 6988 1662; St Peter's Square; ⊙8.30am-6.30pm Mon-Sat; ☐Piazza del Risorgimento, ⓂOttaviano-San Pietro).

○ Useful tourist websites: **060608** (www.060608.it) Good information on sites, upcoming events, transport etc. **Roma Turismo** (www.turismoroma.it) Rome's official tourist website with listings and up-to-date information.

Travellers with Disabilities

Cobbled streets, blocked pavements, tiny lifts and bad traffic make Rome a difficult city for travellers with disabilities.

○ On metro line B all stations have wheelchair access except for Circo Massimo, Colosseo and Cavour; 11 stops on line A have lifts. Bus 590 covers the same route as metro line A and is wheelchair accessible. Newer buses and trams have disabled access; bus stops indicate which routes are accessible for wheelchairs.

○ Contact ADR Assistance (www.adrassistance.it) for assistance at Fiumicino or Ciampino airports.

○ Some taxis are equipped to carry passengers in wheelchairs; ask for a taxi for a *sedia a rotelle* (wheelchair).

○ Download Lonely Planet's free Accessible Travel guide from http://lptravel.to/AccessibleTravel.

Visas

○ EU citizens do not need a visa to enter Italy. Nationals of some other countries, including Australia, Canada, Israel, Japan, New Zealand, Switzerland and the USA, do not need a visa for stays of up to 90 days.

○ Italy is one of the 26 European countries to make up the Schengen area. There are no customs controls when travelling between Schengen countries, so the visa rules that apply to Italy apply to all Schengen countries.

Women Travellers

Sexual harassment can be an issue in Rome; if you get groped, a loud *'che schifo!'* (how disgusting!) will draw attention to the incident. Women should take the same precautions as they would in any large city and, as in most places, avoid wandering around alone late at night, especially in the area around Termini.

Transport

Arriving in Rome

Most people arrive in Rome by plane, landing at one of its two airports: Leonardo da Vinci, better known as Fiumicino; or Ciampino, the hub for European low-cost carrier Ryanair. Flights from New York take around nine hours; from London 2¾ hours; from Sydney at least 22 hours.

As an alternative to short-haul flights, trains serve Rome's main station, Stazione Termini, from a number of European destinations, including Paris (about 15 hours), as well as cities across Italy.

Ferries serve Civitavecchia, some 80km north of the city, from a number of Mediterranean ports.

Flights, cars and tours may be booked online at lonelyplanet.com/bookings.

Leonardo da Vinci Airport

Rome's main international airport, **Leonardo da Vinci** (Fiumicino; ☑ 06 59 51; www.adr.it/fiumicino), aka Fiumicino, is 30km west of the city. It's divided into four terminals: Terminals 1, 2 and 3 are for domestic and international flights; Terminal 5 is for American and Israeli airlines flying to the US and Israel.

Terminals 1, 2 and 3 are within easy walking distance of each other in the main airport building; Terminal 5 is accessible by shuttle bus from Terminal 3.

The easiest way to get into town is by train. There are also buses and private shuttle services.

Train

Leonardo Express (one way €14) Runs to/from Stazione Termini. Departures from the airport every 30 minutes between 6.23am and 11.23pm; from Termini between 5.35am and 10.35pm. Journey time is 30 minutes.

FL1 (one way €8) Connects to Trastevere, Ostiense and Tiburtina stations, but not Termini. Departures from the airport every 15 minutes (half-hourly on Sundays and public holidays) between 5.57am and 10.42pm; from Tiburtina every 15 minutes between 5.01am and 7.31pm, then half-hourly until 10.01pm.

Bus

SIT (☑ 06 591 68 26; www.sitbusshuttle.it; one way/return €6/11) Regular departures from the airport to Stazione Termini (Via Marsala) from 8.30am to 12.30am; from Termini between 5am and 8.30pm. All buses stop at the Vatican en route. Tickets are available on the bus. Journey time is approximately one hour.

Cotral (☑ 800 174471; www.cotralspa.it; one way €5, if bought on the bus €7) Runs to/from Fiumicino from Stazione Tiburtina via Termini. Eight daily departures including night services from the airport at 1.15am, 2.15am, 3.30am and 5am, and from Tiburtina at 12.30am, 1.15am, 2.30am and 3.45am. Journey time is one hour.

Schiaffini Rome Airport Bus

(☑ 06 713 05 31; www.romeairportbus.com; one way/return €5.90/7.90) Regular services from the airport to Stazione Termini between 6.05am and 8.25pm; from Termini between 5.10am and 9.30pm. Allow about an hour for the journey.

Private Shuttle

Airport Connection Services
(☑ 06 2111 6248; www.airportconnection.it) Transfers to/from the city centre start at €22 per person.

Airport Shuttle (☑ 06 420 13 469; www.airportshuttle.it) Transfers to/from your hotel for €25 for one person, then €6 for each additional passenger up to a maximum of eight.

Climate Change & Travel

Every form of transport that relies on carbon-based fuel generates CO_2, the main cause of human-induced climate change. Modern travel is dependent on aeroplanes, which might use less fuel per kilometre per person than most cars but travel much greater distances. The altitude at which aircraft emit gases (including CO_2) and particles also contributes to their climate change impact. Many websites offer 'carbon calculators' that allow people to estimate the carbon emissions generated by their journey and, for those who wish to do so, to offset the impact of the greenhouse gases emitted with contributions to portfolios of climate-friendly initiatives throughout the world. Lonely Planet offsets the carbon footprint of all staff and author travel.

Taxi

The set fare to/from the city centre is €48, which is valid for up to four passengers including luggage. Journey time is approximately 45 minutes to an hour depending on traffic.

Ciampino Airport

Ciampino (✆06 6 59 51; www.adr.it/ciampino), 15km southeast of the city centre, is used by Ryanair. It's not a big airport but there's a steady flow of traffic and at peak times it can get extremely busy.

To get into town, the best option is to take one of the dedicated bus services.

Bus

Schiaffini Rome Airport Bus (✆06 713 05 31; www.rome airportbus.com; Via Giolitti; one way/return €4.90/7.90) Regular departures to/from Via Giolitti outside Stazione Termini. From the airport, services run between 4am and 10.50pm; from Via Giolitti, buses run from 4.50am to midnight. Buy tickets onboard, online, at the airport, or at the bus stop. Journey time is approximately 40 minutes.

SIT (✆06 591 68 26; www. sitbusshuttle.com; from/to airport €5/6, return €9) Regular departures from the airport to Stazione Termini (Via Marsala) between 7.45am and 11.15pm; from Termini between 4.30am and 9.30pm. Get tickets on the bus. Journey time is 45 minutes.

Atral (www.atral-lazio.com) Runs buses to/from Anagnina metro station (€1.20) and

Ciampino train station (€1.20), where you can get a train to Termini (€1.50).

Private Shuttle

Airport Shuttle (✆06 420 13 469; www.airportshuttle.it) Transfers to/from your hotel for €25 for one person, then €6 for each additional passenger up to a maximum of eight.

Taxi

The set rate to/from the airport is €30. Journey time is approximately 30 minutes depending on traffic.

Termini Train Station

Almost all trains arrive at and depart from **Stazione Termini** (www.romatermini. com; Piazza dei Cinquecento; Ⓜ Termini), Rome's main train station and principal transport hub. There are regular connections to other European countries, all major Italian cities and many smaller towns.

Train information is available from the customer service area on the main concourse to the left of the ticket desks. Alternatively, check www.trenitalia.com or phone ✆892021.

From Termini, you can connect with the metro or take a bus from Piazza dei Cinquecento out the front. Taxis are outside the main entrance/exit.

Civitavecchia Port

The nearest port to Rome is at Civitavecchia, about 80km north of town. Ferries sail here from Barcelona

and Tunis, as well as Sicily and Sardinia. Check www. traghettiweb.it for route details, prices and to book.

From Civitavecchia half-hourly trains run to Stazione Termini (€5 to €16, 45 minutes to 1½ hours). Civitavecchia's station is about 700m from the entrance to the port.

Getting Around

Rome is a sprawling city, but the *centro storico* (historic centre) is relatively compact and it's quite possible to explore much of it on foot. The city's public transport system includes buses, trams, a metro and a sub-urban train system. Tickets, which come in various forms, are valid for all forms of transport.

Metro

○ Rome has two main metro lines, A (orange) and B (blue), which cross at Stazione Termini. A branch line, 'B1', serves the northern suburbs, and line C runs through the southeastern outskirts, but you're unlikely to use these.

○ Trains run between 5.30am and 11.30pm (to 1.30am on Friday and Saturday).

○ Take line A for the Trevi Fountain (Barberini), Spanish Steps (Spagna) and St Peter's (Ottaviano–San Pietro).

Public Transport Tickets

Public transport tickets are valid on all of Rome's bus, tram and metro lines, except for routes to Fiumicino airport. Children under 10 travel free.

Buy tickets at *tabacchi* (tobacconists), newsstands and from vending machines at main bus stops and metro stations. Tickets must be purchased before you start your journey and be validated in the machines on buses, at the entrance gates to the metro, or at train stations. Ticketless riders risk a fine of at least €50.

Tickets come in various forms:

BIT (*biglietto integrato a tempo;* a single ticket valid for 100 minutes and one metro ride) €1.50

Roma 24h (valid for 24 hours) €7

Roma 48h (valid for 48 hours) €12.50

Roma 72h (valid for 72 hours) €18

CIS (*carta integrata settimanale;* a weekly ticket) €24

○ Take line B for the Colosseum (Colosseo).

Bus

○ The main bus station is in front of Stazione Termini on Piazza dei Cinquecento, where there's an **information booth** (Piazza dei Cinquecento; ⊗8am-8pm). Other important hubs are at Largo di Torre Argentina and Piazza Venezia.

○ Buses generally run from about 5.30am until midnight, with limited services throughout the night.

○ Rome's night bus service comprises more than 25 lines, many of which pass Termini and/or Piazza Venezia. Buses are marked with an 'n' before the number and bus stops have a blue owl symbol. Departures are usually every 15 to 30 minutes between about 1am and 5am.

The most useful routes:

n1 Follows the route of metro line A.

n2 Follows the route of metro line B.

n7 Piazzale Clodio, Piazza Cavour, Via Zanardelli, Corso del Rinascimento, Corso Vittorio Emanuele II, Largo di Torre Argentina, Piazza Venezia, Via Nazionale and Stazione Termini.

Taxi

○ Official licensed taxis are white with an ID number and have *Roma Capitale* on the sides.

○ Always go with the metered fare, never an arranged price (the set fares to/from the airports are exceptions).

○ In town (within the ring road) flag fall is €3 between 6am and 10pm on weekdays, €4.50 on Sundays and holidays, and €6.50 between 10pm and 6am. It's €1.10 per kilometre thereafter. Official rates are posted in taxis and at https://roma mobilita.it/it/servizi/taxi/tariffe.

○ You can hail a taxi from the street, but it's often easier to wait at a rank or phone for one. There are taxi ranks at the airports, Stazione Termini, Piazza della Repubblica, Piazza Barberini, Piazza di Spagna, the Pantheon, the Colosseum, Largo di Torre Argentina, Piazza Belli, Piazza Pio XII and Piazza del Risorgimento.

○ Note that when you call for a cab, the meter is switched on straight away and you pay for the cost of the journey from wherever the driver receives the call.

Pronto Taxi (☎06 66 45; www.6645.it)

Radiotaxi 3570 (☎06 35 70; www.3570.it)

Samarcanda (☎06 55 51; www.samarcanda.it)

Taxi Tevere (☎06 41 57; www.taxitevere.it)

Car & Motorcycle

○ Driving around Rome is not recommended. Riding a scooter or motorbike is faster and makes parking easier, but Rome is no place for learners, so if you're not an experienced rider give it a miss. Hiring a car for a day trip out of town is worth considering.

○ Most of Rome's historic centre is closed to unauthorised traffic from 6.30am to 6pm Monday to Friday, and from 2pm to 6pm (10am to 7pm in some places) Saturday. Evening restrictions also apply in Trastevere, San Lorenzo, Monti and Testaccio, typically from 9.30pm or 11pm to 3am on Friday and Saturday.

○ All streets accessing the 'Limited Traffic Zone' (ZTL) are monitored by electronic-access detection devices. If you're staying in this zone, contact your hotel. For further information, check www.agenziamobilita.roma.it.

Driving Licence

○ All EU driving licences are recognised in Italy. Holders of non-EU licences should get an International Driving Permit (IDP) to accompany their national licence. Apply to your national motoring association.

○ A licence is required to ride a scooter. A car licence is acceptable for bikes up to 125cc; for anything over 125cc you'll need a motorcycle licence.

○ **Automobile Club d'Italia** (ACI; ☑roadside assistance from Italian mobile 803 116, roadside assistance from foreign mobile 800 116 800; www.aci.it), Italy's national motoring organisation, is a good source of information.

Hire

To hire a car you'll require a driving licence (plus IDP if necessary) and a credit card. Age restrictions vary,

but generally you'll need to be 21 or older.

Car hire is available at both Fiumicino and Ciampino airports and at Stazione Termini. Reckon on at least €40 per day for a small car. Note also that most Italian hire cars have manual gear transmission.

Avis (☑06 45210 8391; www.avisautonoleggio.it)

Europcar (☑199 307030; www.europcar.it)

Hertz (☑Stazione Termini office 06 488 39 67; www.hertz.it)

Maggiore National (☑Termini office 06 488 00 49, central reservations 199 151120; www.maggiore.it; Via Giolitti 34, Stazione Termini; Ⓜ Termini)

Scooter hire ranges from about €30 to €120 per day depending on the size of the vehicle. Reliable operators:

Bici & Baci (☑06 482 84 43; www.bicibaci.com; Via del Viminale 5; bike tours from €30, Vespa tours from €145; ⊙8am-7pm; Ⓜ Repubblica)

Eco Move Rent (☑06 4470 4518; www.ecomoverent.com; Via Varese 48-50; bike/scooter/Vespa hire per day from €8/40/110; ⊙8.30am-7.30pm; Ⓜ Termini)

Parking

○ Blue lines denote pay-and-display parking – get tickets from meters (coins only) and *tabacchi* (tobacconists).

○ Expect to pay up to €1.20 per hour between 8am and 8pm (11pm in some places). After 8pm (or 11pm) parking

is free until 8am the next morning.

○ Traffic wardens are vigilant and fines are not uncommon. If your car gets towed away, call ☑06 67691.

Useful car parks:

Piazzale dei Partigiani (per hr €0.77; ⊙6am-11pm; Ⓜ Piramide)

Stazione Termini (Piazza dei Cinquecento; per hr/day €2.20/18; ⊙6am-1am; 🚇Piazza dei Cinquecento)

Villa Borghese (☑06 322 59 34; www.sabait.it; Viale del Galoppatoio 33; per hr/day €2.20/18; ⊙24hr; 🚇Via Pinciana)

Train

Apart from connections to Fiumicino airport, you'll probably only need the overground rail network if you head out of town.

○ Train information is available from the customer service area on the main concourse. Alternatively, check www.trenitalia.com or phone ☑892021.

○ Buy tickets on the main station concourse, from automated ticket machines, or from an authorised travel agency – look for an FS or *biglietti treni* sign in the window.

○ Rome's second train station is Stazione Tiburtina, four stops from Termini on metro line B. Of the capital's eight other train stations, the most important are Stazione Roma-Ostiense and Stazione Trastevere.

Language

Italian pronunciation isn't difficult as most sounds are also found in English. The pronunciation of some consonants depends on which vowel follows, but if you read our pronunciation guides below as if they were English, you'll be understood just fine. Just remember to pronounce double consonants as a longer, more forceful sound than single ones. The stressed syllables in words are in italics in our pronunciation guides.

To enhance your trip with a phrasebook, visit **lonelyplanet.com**. Find Lonely Planet iPhone phrasebooks in the Apple App store.

Basics

Hello.
Buongiorno./Ciao. (pol/inf) bwon·*jor*·no/chow

How are you?
Come sta? ko·me sta

I'm fine, thanks.
Bene, grazie. be·ne *gra*·tsye

Excuse me.
Mi scusi. mee *skoo*·zee

Yes./No.
Sì./No. see/no

Please. (when asking)
Per favore. per fa·*vo*·re

Thank you.
Grazie. *gra*·tsye

Goodbye.
Arrivederci./Ciao. (pol/inf) a·ree·ve·*der*·chee/chow

Do you speak English?
Parla inglese? *par*·la een·*gle*·ze

I don't understand.
Non capisco. non ka·*pee*·sko

How much is this?
Quanto costa? *kwan*·to *ko*·sta

Accommodation

I'd like to book a room.
Vorrei prenotare vo·*ray* pre·no·*ta*·re
una camera. *oo*·na *ka*·me·ra

How much is it per night?
Quanto costa per *kwan*·to *kos*·ta per
una notte? *oo*·na *no*·te

Eating & Drinking

I'd like ..., please.
Vorrei ..., per favore. vo·*ray* ... per fa·*vo*·re

What would you recommend?
Cosa mi consiglia? *ko*·za mee kon·*see*·lya

That was delicious!
Era squisito! e·ra skwee·*zee*·to

Bring the bill/check, please.
Mi porta il conto, mee *por*·ta eel *kon*·to
per favore. per fa·*vo*·re

I'm allergic (to peanuts).
Sono allergico/a so·no a·*ler*·jee·ko/a
(alle arachidi). (m/f) (a·le a·*ra*·kee·dee)

I don't eat ...
Non mangio ... non *man*·jo ...

fish	*pesce*	*pe*·she
meat	*carne*	*kar*·ne
poultry	*pollame*	po·*la*·me

Emergencies

I'm ill.
Mi sento male. mee *sen*·to *ma*·le

Help!
Aiuto! a·*yoo*·to

Call a doctor!
Chiami un medico! *kya*·mee oon *me*·dee·ko

Call the police!
Chiami la polizia! *kya*·mee la po·lee·*tsee*·a

Directions

I'm looking for (a/the) ...
Cerco ... *cher*·ko ...

bank
la banca la *ban*·ka

... embassy
la ambasciata de ... la am·ba·*sha*·ta de ...

market
il mercato eel mer·*ka*·to

museum
il museo eel moo·*ze*·o

restaurant
un ristorante oon rees·to·*ran*·te

toilet
un gabinetto oon ga·bee·*ne*·to

tourist office
l'ufficio del turismo loo·*fee*·cho del too·*reez*·mo

Behind the Scenes

Acknowledgements

Climate map data adapted from Peel MC, Finlayson BL & McMahon TA (2007) 'Updated World Map of the Köppen-Geiger Climate Classification', Hydrology and Earth System Sciences, 11, 1633–44.

Illustration pp82–3 by Javier Martinez Zarracina.

This Book

This guidebook was researched and written by Duncan Garwood and curated by Saralinda Turner. The previous edition was researched and written by Duncan Garwood and Abigail Blasi. This guidebook was produced by the following:

Curator Saralinda Turner

Destination Editor Anna Tyler

Product Editor Alison Ridgway

Senior Cartographer Anthony Phelan

Book Designer Lauren Egan

Assisting Editors Katie Connolly, Melanie Dankel, Kate Mathews, Jenna Myers, Susan Paterson, Sarah Reid

Assisting Book Designer Virginia Moreno

Cover Researcher Naomi Parker

Thanks to Grace Dobell, Liz Heynes, Mark Griffiths, Carly Hall, Robert Jennings, Indra Kilfoyle, Katherine Marsh, Catherine Naghten , Kirsten Rawlings, Tony Wheeler

Send Us Your Feedback

We love to hear from travellers – your comments keep us on our toes and help make our books better. Our well-travelled team reads every word on what you loved or loathed about this book. Although we cannot reply individually to postal submissions, we always guarantee that your feedback goes straight to the appropriate authors, in time for the next edition. Each person who sends us information is thanked in the next edition, the most useful submissions are rewarded with a selection of digital PDF chapters.

Visit lonelyplanet.com/contact to submit your updates and suggestions or to ask for help. Our award-winning website also features inspirational travel stories, news and discussions.

Note: We may edit, reproduce and incorporate your comments in Lonely Planet products such as guidebooks, websites and digital products, so let us know if you don't want your comments reproduced or your name acknowledged. For a copy of our privacy policy visit lonelyplanet.com/privacy.

Index

A

accommodation 19, 199-205
activities 4-17, 29, 191-7
air travel 233-5
airports
Ciampino Airport 235
Leonardo da Vinci Airport 234-5
Ancient Rome **246-7**
drinking & nightlife 168
food 122
history 211
itineraries 20-1
aqueducts 223
archaeological sites, *see also* ruins
Colosseum 36-9
Imperial Forums 81
Museo Nazionale Romano: Terme di Diocleziano 69
Ostia Antica 92-3
Palatino 58-61
Roman Forum 78-83
Terme di Caracalla 96-7
Via Appia Antica 74-7
architecture 31, 98-101, 222-6
area codes 232
art 31, 218-20, *see also* museums & galleries, *individual artists*
art courses 197
art galleries, *see* museums & galleries
arts 218-21
ATMs 231
Auditorium Parco della Musica 100

000 Map pages

B

bars, *see* drinking & nightlife
Basilica di San Clemente 94-5
Basilica di San Giovanni in Laterano 88-9
Basilica di Santa Maria del Popolo 86-7
Basilica di Santa Maria in Trastevere 104-5
Basilica di Santa Maria Maggiore 102-3
basilicas, *see* churches & basilicas
basketball 196
bathrooms 232
beer 30, 166, 172
Bernini, Giano Lorenzo 47 49, 54, 55, 64, 69, 87, 103, 107, 220
bicycle travel, *see* cycling
boat travel 235
Bocca della Verità 73
books 114-15, 147, 220-1
Borgo, *see* Vatican City, Borgo & Prati
Bramante 86, 225
budgeting 18
bus travel 19, 234, 236
business hours 145, 164, 231

C

Campo de' Fiori 65
Capitoline Museums 70-3
car travel 236-7
Caravaggio 55, 65, 73, 86, 220
Carnevale Romano 7
Castel Sant'Angelo 49
catacombes 76-7
cell phones 18, 232
centri sociali 178
Centro Storico **250-1**
drinking & nightlife 168-9
entertainment 184

food 122-7
itineraries 22-3
shopping 148-53
walking tour 112-13, **112-13**
children, travel with 32-3
churches & basilicas
art 220
Basilica dei SS Quattro Coronati 95
Basilica di San Clemente 94-5
Basilica di San Giovanni in Laterano 88-9
Basilica di San Pietro in Vincoli 103-4
Basilica di Santa Maria del Popolo 86-7
Basilica di Santa Maria in Trastevere 104-5
Basilica di Santa Maria Maggiore 102-3
Basilica di Santa Maria Sopra Minerva 53
Basilica di Santa Sabina 97
Chiesa del Gesù 107
Chiesa di San Luigi dei Francesi 65
Chiesa di Santa Maria della Vittoria 69
Chiesa di Sant'Ignazio di Loyola 107
Chiesa di Santo Stefano Rotondo 95
Sistine Chapel 43-5
St Peter's Basilica 46-9
cinema 221
climate 4-17, 19
climate change 234
Colosseum 36-9
cooking courses 197
costs 18
courses 197
credit cards 231

culture 208-9, 227-8
currency 18
customs regulations 230
cycling 196

D

dance 187
dangers, *see* safety
desserts 30
disabilities, travellers with 233
discount cards 231
drinking & nightlife 163-79, **165**,
    *see also individual
    neighbourhoods*
drivers licences 237
driving, *see* car travel

E

economy 209
electricity 230
emergencies 230, 238
entertainment 181-9, *see also
    individual neighbourhoods*
Esquilino, *see* Monti, Esquilino &
    San Lorenzo
Estate Romana 11
Etruscans 218-19, 223
events 4-17

F

family travel 32-3
fascism 217, 226
ferry travel 235
festivals 4-17
film 221
food 117-41, **119**, *see also
    individual neighbourhoods*
    desserts 30
    for children 33
    gelato 121, 140
    grattachecca 135
    kosher 124
    offal 132
    pastry 121

pizza 30, 120, 126
    Roman 123
football 194, 195
Forum, Roman 78-83
free attractions 31

G

Galleria Doria Pamphilj 106-7
galleries, *see* museums &
    galleries
gardens, *see* parks & gardens
Garibaldi 174
gay travellers 167, 177, 231
gelato 121, 140
Gianicolo, *see* Trastevere &
    Gianicolo
grattachecca 135

H

health 230
history 28, 32, 210-17
holidays 231-2

I

Il Vittoriano 73
immigration 233
insurance 230, 231
internet access 230
internet resources 18
itineraries 20-7, *see also
    individual neighbourhoods*

L

language 18, 238
    courses 197
    drinking 165, 238
    eating 238
    food 119, 238
    shopping 144
legal matters 231
Leone, Sergio 221
lesbian travellers 167, 177, 231
lifestyle 227-8

literature 114-15, 220-1
Lungo il Tevere 13

M

markets 157
Mausoleo di Cecilia Metella 77
measures 232
medical services 230
metro travel 19, 235-6
Michelangelo 43-5, 46, 47, 103,
    219-20
Miracle Players 189
mobile phones 18, 232
money 18, 231
Monti, Esquilino & San Lorenzo
    252, **255**
    drinking & nighlife 171-5
    entertainment 186
    food 132-4
    itineraries 26-7
    shopping 157-9
motorcycle travel 236-7
Museo Nazionale delle Arti del
    XXI Secolo (MAXXI) 100
Museo Nazionale Romano:
    Palazzo Massimo alle Terme
    66-9
museums & galleries 29
    Capitoline Museums 70-3
    Casa di Goethe 109
    Galleria Doria Pamphilj 106-7
    Keats-Shelley House 91
    La Galleria Nazionale 57
    Mercati di Traiano Museo dei
       Fori Imperiali 81
    Museo Carlo Bilotti 57
    Museo d'Arte Contemporanea
       di Roma 101
    Museo dell'Ara Pacis 101
    Museo e Galleria Borghese
       54-7
    Museo Nazionale delle Arti del
       XXI Secolo 100
    Museo Nazionale Etrusco di
       Villa Giulia 56

museums & galleries
continued
Museo Nazionale Romano:
Palazzo Altemps 65
Museo Nazionale Romano:
Palazzo Massimo alle Terme
66-9
Museo Nazionale Romano:
Terme di Diocleziano 69
Palazzo Barberini 69
Vatican Museums 40-5
music 183, 221
Mussolini, Benito 217

N

Natale di Roma 9
neoclassicism 219
newspapers 232
nightlife, *see* drinking &
nightlife
Northern Rome, *see* Villa
Borghese & Northern Rome

O

offal 132
opening hours 145, 164, 231
opera 187
Ostia Antica 92-3
Ostiense 179
outdoor activities 29

P

painting 218-21
Palatino 58-61
Palazzo del Quirinale 85
Palazzo della Civiltà Italiana 101
Pantheon 50-3
parks & gardens 31
Pincio Hill Gardens 57
Villa Borghese 56
Villa Celimontana 97
passports 233
perfumes 155
pharmacies 230

Pianostrada 30
Piazza del Popolo 87
Piazza Navona 62-5
piazzas 31
pizza 30, 120, 126
planning
budgeting 18
calendar of events 4-17
children, travel with 32-3
climate 4-17, 19
internet resources 18
itineraries 20-7
repeat visitors 30
politics 208-9
Pope Francis 209
population 209
Porta del Popolo 87
Prati, *see* Vatican City, Borgo
& Prati
public holidays 231-2
public transport 236

Q

Quirinale, the, *see* Tridente, Trevi
& the Quirinale

R

Raphael 41, 43, 53, 55, 87, 106,
220
rationalism 226
religion 209, 212-14, 228
Renaissance, the 214-16, 219-20,
224-5
Roma Pass 31, 231
RomaEuropa 14
Roman Empire 212
Roman Forum 78-83
romantic places 29
Romulus and Remus 213
rugby union 196
ruins
Mausoleo di Cecilia Metella 77
Museo Nazionale Romano:
Terme di Diocleziano 69

Ostia Antica 92-3
Palatino 58-61
Roman Forum 78-83
Terme di Caracalla 96-7
Via Appia Antica 74-7
Villa Adriana 111
Villa di Massenzio 77

S

safety 232
San Giovanni & Testaccio **255**
drinking & nightlife 177-8
entertainment 187
food 138-9
shopping 161
San Lorenzo, *see* Monti,
Esquilino & San Lorenzo
sculpture 218-21
shopping 143-61, **145**, *see
also individual neighbourhoods*
Sistine Chapel 43-5
smoking 232
soccer 194, 195
Southern Rome
drinking & nightlife 179
entertainment 188-9
food 140-1
itineraries 26-7
Spanish Steps 90-1
spas 197
sports 192, 193, 194
St Peter's Basilica 46-9
St Peter's Square 49

T

taxes 149, 200
taxis 235, 236
telephone services 18, 232
Terme di Caracalla 96-7
Testaccio, *see* San Giovanni &
Testaccio
theatres 185
time 18, 232
tipping 118, 165, 200

Tivoli 110-11
toilets 232
tourist information 18, 233
tours 31, 194-7, *see also* walking
 tours
train travel
 from airports 234
 metro travel 19, 235-6
 to/from Rome 235
 within Rome 237
Trastevere & Gianicolo **254**
 drinking & nightlife 175-7
 entertainment 186-7
 food 134-8
 itineraries 26-7
 shopping 159-61
travel to/from Rome 19, 233-5
travel within Rome 19, 235-7
Trevi, *see* Tridente, Trevi & the
 Quirinale
Trevi Fountain 84-5
Tridente, Trevi & the Quirinale
 252
 drinking & nightlife 170
 entertainment 184
 food 127-9

itineraries 24-5
 shopping 153-6
 walking tour 114-15, **114-15**
Triumphs and Laments 30, 65
TV 232

vacations 231-2
Vatican City, Borgo & Prati **253**
 drinking & nightlife 170-1
 entertainment 184
 food 129-32
 itineraries 22-3
 shopping 156-7
Vatican Museums 40-5
vegetarian travellers 139
Via Appia Antica 74-7
Via Margutta 108-9
Villa Borghese & Northern
 Rome **256**
 drinking & nightlife 178-9
 entertainment 187-8
 food 139-40
 itineraries 24-5
 shopping 161

Villa del Priorato di Malta 97
Villa di Massenzio 77
Villa Medici 109
visas 18, 233

walking tours 193
 Centro Storico 112-13, **112-13**
 literature 114-15, **114-15**
 Tridente 114-15, **114-15**
weather 4-17, 19
websites 18
weights 232
wi-fi 31
wine 172
wine courses 197
women travellers 233
work 227-8
WWI 217
WWII 217

Yellow Square 30

View over St Peter's Square (p49) from St Peter's Basilica (p46)

NIKADA/GETTY IMAGES ©

Rome Maps

Ancient Rome 246

Centro Storico 250

Trevi & Esquilino 252

Vatican City, Borgo & Prati 253

Trastevere & Gianicolo 254

San Giovanni & San Lorenzo 255

Villa Borghese 256

Ancient Rome

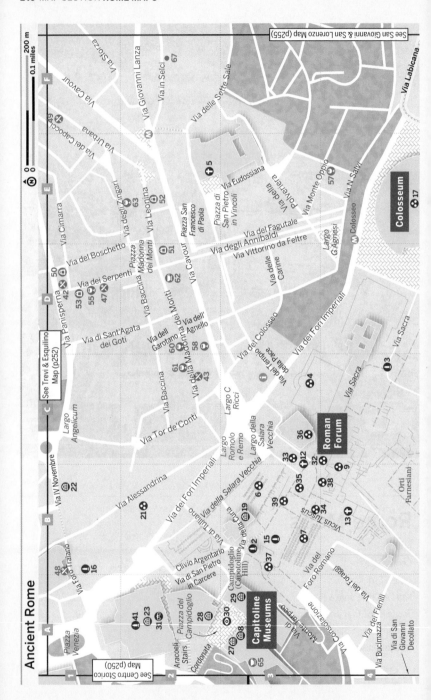

Piazza Venezia

See Centro Storico Map (p250)

See Trevi & Esquilino Map (p252)

See San Giovanni & San Lorenzo Map (p255)

Colosseum

Roman Forum

Capitoline Museums

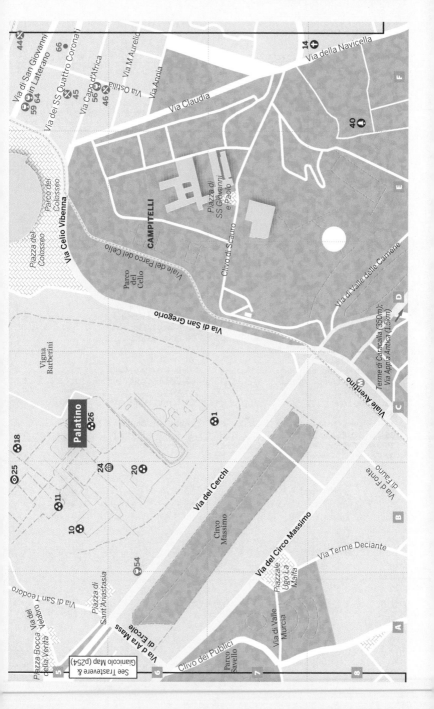

Ancient Rome

◎ Sights

1 Arcate Severiane C7
2 Arco di Settimio Severo B3
3 Arco di Tito C4
4 Basilica di Massenzio C3
5 Basilica di San Pietro in Vincoli...............E2
6 Basilica Fulvia Aemilia...............................B3
7 Basilica Giulia B3
8 Capitoline Museums...................................A3
9 Casa delle Vestali.......................................B4
10 Casa di Augusto B5
11 Casa di Livia...B5
12 Chiesa di San Lorenzo in Miranda........... C3
13 Chiesa di Santa Maria Antiqua................. B4
14 Chiesa di Santo Stefano Rotondo F8
15 Colonna di Foca..B3
16 Colonna Traiana.. B1
17 Colosseum..E4
18 Criptoportico Neroniano............................C5
19 Curia B3
20 Domus Augustana.. B6
21 Imperial Forums..B2
22 Mercati di Traiano Museo dei Fori
    Imperiali B1
23 Museo Centrale del Risorgimento............A2
24 Museo Palatino B6
25 Orti Farnesiani..B5
26 Palatino C5
27 Palazzo dei Conservatori...........................A3
28 Palazzo Nuovo...A2
29 Palazzo Senatorio.......................................A3
30 Piazza del Campidoglio..............................A3
31 Roma dal Cielo A2
32 Roman Forum C4
33 Tempio di Antonino e Faustina................. C3
34 Tempio di Castore e Polluce B3
35 Tempio di Giulio Cesare.............................B3
36 Tempio di Romolo.. C3
37 Tempio di Saturno.......................................B3

38 Tempio di Vesta B4
39 Via Sacra B3
40 Villa Celimontana F8
41 Vittoriano...A2

◎ Eating

42 Ai Tre Scalini...D1
43 Alle Carette C2
44 Aroma F5
45 Cafè Cafè..F5
46 Il Bocconcino F5
47 Temakinho D1
48 Terre e Domus...B1
49 Trieste Pizza F1

◎ Shopping

50 Fabio Piccioni..D1
51 La Bottega del Cioccolato.........................D2
52 Mercato Monti Urban Market.................... E2
53 Podere Vecciano D1

◎ Drinking & Nightlife

54 0,75 ....B6
55 Al Vino al Vino D1
56 Bibenda Wine Concept...............................F5
57 BrewDog Roma E4
58 Cavour 313 ....D2
59 Coming Out...F5
60 Fafiuché D2
61 Ice Club...C2
62 La Casetta a Monti D2
63 Libreria Caffè Bohemien E2
64 My Bar...F5
65 Terrazza Caffarelli......................................A3

◎ Activities, Courses & Tours

66 The Red Bicycle...F5
67 Vino Roma..F2

Centro Storico

◎ Sights

1 Basilica di Santa Maria Sopra Minerva	E6
2 Campo de' Fiori	C7
3 Castel Sant'Angelo	A3
4 Chiesa del Gesù	F7
5 Chiesa di San Luigi dei Francesi	D5
6 Chiesa di Sant'Agnese in Agone	C5
7 Chiesa di Sant'Ignazio di Loyola	F5
8 Fontana dei Quattro Fiumi	C5
9 Fontana del Moro	C6
10 Fontana del Nettuno	C5
11 Galleria Doria Pamphilj	F6
12 Museo dell'Ara Pacis	D1
13 Museo Nazionale Romano: Palazzo Altemps	C4
14 Palazzo Pamphilj	C6
15 Pantheon	E5
16 Piazza Colonna	F4
17 Piazza di Pietra	F5
18 Piazza di Sant'Ignazio Loyola	F5
19 Piazza Navona	C5
20 Stadio di Domiziano	C4
21 Triumphs and Laments	A7

✹ Eating

22 Alfredo e Ada	A5
23 Antico Forno Urbani	D8
24 Armando al Pantheon	D5
25 Caffetteria Chiostro del Bramante	C5
26 Casa Bleve	D6
27 Casa Coppelle	D4
28 Cremeria Romana	E8
29 Ditirambo	C6
30 Emma Pizzeria	D7
31 Forno di Campo de' Fiori	C7
32 Forno Roscioli	D7
33 Gelateria del Teatro	B4
34 La Ciambella	E6
35 Mercato di Campo de' Fiori	C7
36 Osteria dell'Ingegno	F5
37 Palatium	F2
38 Pasticceria De Bellis	C7
39 Pianostrada	C8
40 Renato e Luisa	D7
41 Ristorante L'Arcangelo	A1
42 Salumeria Roscioli	D8
43 Supplizio	A6
44 Tiramisù Zum	C7
45 Venchi	E5

⊜ Shopping

46 A S Roma Store	F4
47 Alberta Gloves	E7
48 Aldo Fefè	D4
49 Atelier Patrizia Pieroni	B6
50 Bartolucci	E5
51 Borini	C8
52 C.U.C.I.N.A.	F1
53 Casali	A4
54 Confetteria Moriondo & Gariglio	F6
55 De Sanctis	E5
56 Enoteca Costantini	B2
57 Fausto Santini	F2
58 Federico Buccellati	F2
59 Feltrinelli	E7
60 Fendi	E2
61 Flumen Profumi	E2
62 Fratelli Fabbi	F1
63 Galleria Alberto Sordi	F4
64 I Colori di Dentro	A5
65 Ibiz – Artigianato in Cuoio	D7
66 La Rinascente	F4
67 Le Artigiane	D6
68 Le Tartarughe	E6
69 Luna & L'Altra	C6
70 Manila Grace	F3
71 Mercato delle Stampe	D3
72 Mondello Ottica	B6
73 namasTèy	E6
74 Nardecchia	B7
75 Officina Profumo Farmaceutica di Santa Maria Novella	C5
76 Pelletteria Nives	F2
77 Rachele	C6
78 Re(f)use	E2
79 Salumeria Focacci	F1
Salumeria Roscioli	(see 42)
80 SBU	C6
81 Tempi Moderni	B5
82 Tod's	E2
83 Vertecchi Art	F1

❾ Drinking & Nightlife

84 Antico Caffè Greco	F2
85 Barnum Cafe	B6
86 Caffè Sant'Eustachio	D6
87 Circus	B5
88 Etablì	B5
89 Il Goccetto	A6
90 Jerry Thomas Project	A6
91 La Casa del Caffè Tazza d'Oro	E5
92 L'Angolo Divino	C7
93 Open Baladin	D8
94 Roscioli Caffè	D8
95 Salotto 42	F5
96 The Gin Corner	D3
97 Zuma Bar	E2

✪ Entertainment

98 Teatro Argentina	D7

✪ Activities, Courses & Tours

99 Rome Boat Experience	A4

Centro Storico

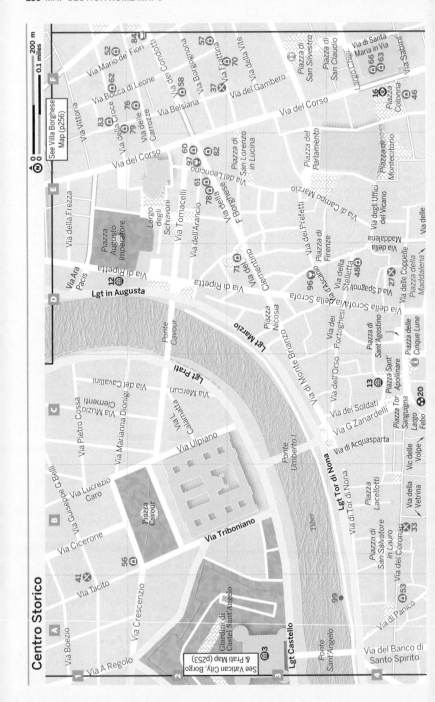

See Villa Borghese Map (p256)

200 m
0.1 miles

See Vatican City, Borgo & Prati Map (p253)

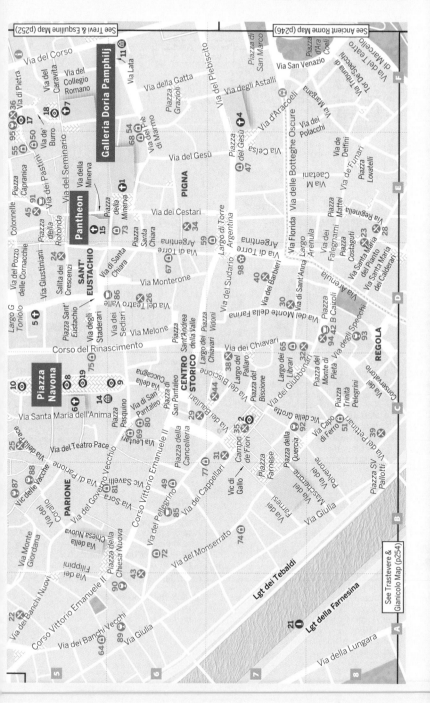

See Trevi & Esquiline Map (p252)

See Ancient Rome Map (p246)

See Trastevere & Gianicolo Map (p254)

Galleria Doria Pamphilj

Pantheon

Piazza Navona

Via del Corso

Via di Pietra

Via del Caravita

Via del Collegio Romano

Via della Gatta

Piazza di San Marco

Piazza d'Ara Coeli

Via del Teatro di Marcello

Via delle Tre Pile

Via de' Specchi

Tor De' Specchi

Via della Tribuna di Tor de'Specchi

Via Margana

Via San Venazio

Via degli Astalli

Via del Plebiscito

Piazza Grazioli

Via della Minerva

Via del Seminario

Via dei Pastini

Via di Pie' di Marmo

Via del Gesù

Via d'Aracoeli

Via dei Polacchi

Via delle Botteghe Oscure

Via M Caetani

Via de' Delfini

Via de'Funari

Piazza Lovatelli

Piazza Mattei

Via Reginella

Via Florida

Largo Arenula

PIGNA

Piazza del Gesù

Via Celsa

Piazza della Minerva

Via dei Cestari

Largo di Torre Argentina

Via di Torre Argentina

Via dei Falegnami

Piazza Costaguti

Via Santa Maria del Pianto

Via Santa Maria dei Calderari

Piazza della Rotonda

Colonnelle

Piazza Capranica

Via dei Pastini

Via Giustiniani

Via del Pozzo delle Cornacchie

Salita dei Crescenzi

Piazza Santa Chiara

Via di Santa Chiara

Via Monterone

Via del Teatro Valle

Via dei Sediari

Via Melone

Piazza Sant'Andrea della Valle

Via del Sudario

Via di Torre Argentina

Via di Sant'Anna

Via del Monte della Farina

Via dei Barbieri

Via dei Chiavari

Via del Biscione

Via del Pianto

SANT'EUSTACHIO

Piazza Sant'Eustachio

Via degli Staderari

Corso del Rinascimento

Largo G Toniolo

CENTRO STORICO

Largo dei Chiavari

Piazza Vidoni

Via dei Giubbonari

Largo dei Librari

Piazza del Paradiso

Via dei Chiavari

Piazza della Valle

Via dei Baullari

Largo del Pallaro

Via di San Pantaleo

Via della Cuccagna

Piazza Pasquino

Via Leutari

Via di San Pantaleo

Via del Teatro Pace

Via di Parione

Vic delle Vacche

Via del Corallo

Via della Pace

Via Santa Maria dell'Anima

PARIONE

Via del Governo Vecchio

Vic Savelli

Via Sora

Via del Pellegrino

Piazza della Cancelleria

Corso Vittorio Emanuele II

Campo de' Fiori

Via dei Cappellari

Vic di Gallo

Piazza della Quercia

Piazza Farnese

Via dei Baullari

Via del Monserrato

Via dei Banchi Nuovi

Via Monte Giordana

Via della Chiesa Nuova

Piazza della Chiesa Nuova

Via dei Filippini

Corso Vittorio Emanuele II

Via di Banchi Vecchi

Via Giulia

Via del Mascherone

Via dei Farnesi

Lgt dei Tebaldi

Lgt della Farnesina

Via della Lungara

Via della Polverone

Via Capo di Ferro

Piazza della Trinità dei Pellegrini

Via di Pettinari

Piazza Trinità dei Pellegrini

Piazza SV Pallotti

Via del Conservatorio

Via degli Specchi

Piazza B Cairoli

REGOLA

Piazza delle Grotte

Piazza del Monte di Pietà

Via delle Zoccolette

Via Arenula

See Trastevere & Gianicolo Map (p254)

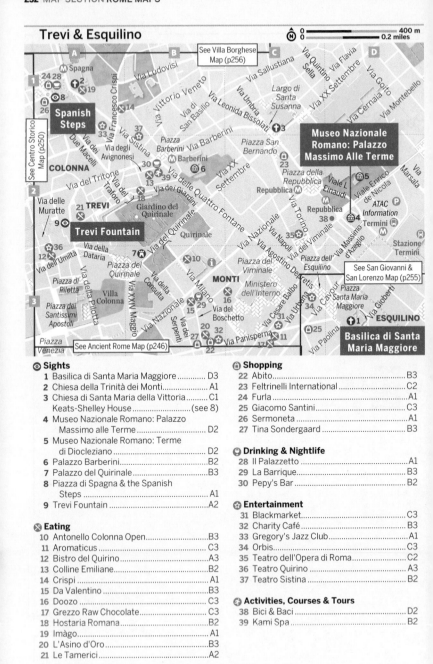

Trevi & Esquilino

See Villa Borghese Map (p256)

0 — 400 m
0 — 0.2 miles

⊙ **Sights**

1 Basilica di Santa Maria Maggiore	D3
2 Chiesa della Trinità dei Monti	A1
3 Chiesa di Santa Maria della Vittoria	C1
Keats-Shelley House	(see 8)
4 Museo Nazionale Romano: Palazzo Massimo alle Terme	D2
5 Museo Nazionale Romano: Terme di Diocleziano	D2
6 Palazzo Barberini	B2
7 Palazzo del Quirinale	B3
8 Piazza di Spagna & the Spanish Steps	A1
9 Trevi Fountain	A2

⊗ **Eating**

10 Antonello Colonna Open	B3
11 Aromaticus	C3
12 Bistro del Quirino	A3
13 Colline Emiliane	B2
14 Crispi	A1
15 Da Valentino	B3
16 Doozo	C3
17 Grezzo Raw Chocolate	C3
18 Hostaria Romana	B2
19 Imàgo	A1
20 L'Asino d'Oro	B3
21 Le Tamerici	A2

⊕ **Shopping**

22 Abito	B3
23 Feltrinelli International	C2
24 Furla	A1
25 Giacomo Santini	C3
26 Sermoneta	A1
27 Tina Sondergaard	B3

⊕ **Drinking & Nightlife**

28 Il Palazzetto	A1
29 La Barrique	B3
30 Pepy's Bar	B2

⊕ **Entertainment**

31 Blackmarket	C3
32 Charity Café	B3
33 Gregory's Jazz Club	A1
34 Orbis	C3
35 Teatro dell'Opera di Roma	C2
36 Teatro Quirino	A3
37 Teatro Sistina	B2

⊕ **Activities, Courses & Tours**

38 Bici & Baci	D2
39 Kami Spa	B2

Vatican City, Borgo & Prati

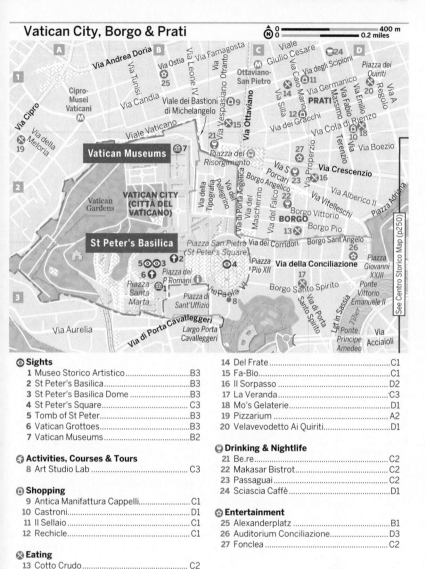

◎ Sights

1 Museo Storico Artistico	B3
2 St Peter's Basilica	B3
3 St Peter's Basilica Dome	B3
4 St Peter's Square	C3
5 Tomb of St Peter	B3
6 Vatican Grottoes	B3
7 Vatican Museums	B2

✪ Activities, Courses & Tours

8 Art Studio Lab	C3

🛍 Shopping

9 Antica Manifattura Cappelli	C1
10 Castroni	D1
11 Il Sellaio	C1
12 Rechicle	C1

✕ Eating

13 Cotto Crudo	C2

14 Del Frate	C1
15 Fa-Bìo	C1
16 Il Sorpasso	D2
17 La Veranda	C3
18 Mo's Gelaterie	D1
19 Pizzarium	A2
20 Velavevodetto Ai Quiriti	D1

🍷 Drinking & Nightlife

21 Be.re	C2
22 Makasar Bistrot	C2
23 Passaguai	C2
24 Sciascia Caffè	D1

✪ Entertainment

25 Alexanderplatz	B1
26 Auditorium Conciliazione	D3
27 Fonclea	C2

Trastevere & Gianicolo

⊚ Sights
1 Basilica di Santa Maria in Trastevere	B2
2 Basilica di Santa Sabina	D3
3 Bocca della Verità	D2
4 Piazza di Santa Maria in Trastevere	B2
5 Villa del Priorato di Malta	C3

🛍 Shopping
6 Almost Corner Bookshop	B1
7 Antica Caciara Trasteverina	B2
8 Benheart	B1
9 Biscottificio Innocenti	C2
10 La Cravatta su Misura	C2
11 Leone Limentani	D1
12 Les Vignerons	A2
13 Officina della Carta	B1
14 Open Door Bookshop	C2
15 Porta Portese Market	C3
16 Roma-Store	B2
17 Scala Quattordici	A1

🍴 Eating
18 Buff	B2
19 Da Augusto	B1
20 Da Enzo	C2
21 Da Olindo	A1
22 Don	B3
23 Fatamorgana Trastevere	B2
24 Fior di Luna	B2

26 La Gensola	C2
27 La Prosciutteria	A1
28 Le Levain	A2
29 Locanda del Gelato	B3
30 Mercato di Piazza San Cosimato	B2
31 Nonna Betta	D1
32 Paris in Trastevere	B2
33 Piperno	C1
34 Ristorante Roof Garden Circus	D2
35 Roma Sparita	C2
36 Sora Mirella Caffè	C2
37 Trattoria degli Amici	B1

🍷 Drinking & Nightlife
38 Bar San Calisto	B2
39 Big Star	A2
40 Bir & Fud	B1
41 Freni e Frizioni	B1
42 Hýbris	C2
43 Il Baretto	A2
44 Keyhole	B2
45 Ma Che Siete Venuti a Fà	B1
46 Mescita Ferrara	B1
47 Ombre Rosse	B1
48 Pimms' Good	A1

🎭 Entertainment
49 Big Mama	B3
50 Isola del Cinema	D1
Lettere Caffè	(see 22)

San Giovanni & San Lorenzo

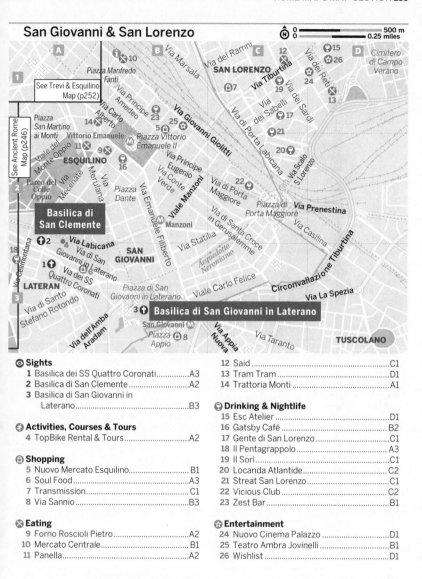

See Trevi & Esquilino Map (p252)

See Ancient Rome Map (p246)

Sights

◎ **Sights**	
1 Basilica dei SS Quattro Coronati	A3
2 Basilica di San Clemente	A2
3 Basilica di San Giovanni in Laterano	B3

Activities, Courses & Tours

4 TopBike Rental & Tours	A2

Shopping

5 Nuovo Mercato Esquilino	B1
6 Soul Food	A3
7 Transmission	C1
8 Via Sannio	B3

Eating

9 Forno Roscioli Pietro	A2
10 Mercato Centrale	B1
11 Panella	A2
12 Said	C1
13 Tram Tram	D1
14 Trattoria Monti	A1

Drinking & Nightlife

15 Esc Atelier	D1
16 Gatsby Café	B2
17 Gente di San Lorenzo	C1
18 Il Pentagrappolo	A3
19 Il Sorì	C1
20 Locanda Atlantide	C2
21 Streat San Lorenzo	C1
22 Vicious Club	C2
23 Zest Bar	B1

Entertainment

24 Nuovo Cinema Palazzo	D1
25 Teatro Ambra Jovinelli	B1
26 Wishlist	D1

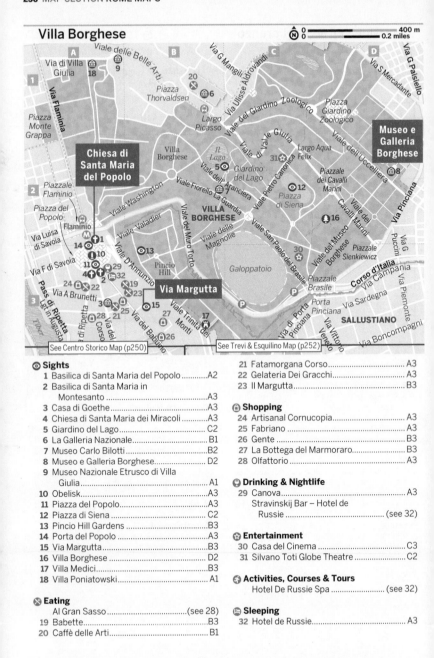

Villa Borghese

See Centro Storico Map (p250)
See Trevi & Esquilino Map (p252)

◎ Sights
1 Basilica di Santa Maria del Popolo A2
2 Basilica di Santa Maria in
  Montesanto A3
3 Casa di Goethe...A3
4 Chiesa di Santa Maria dei Miracoli A3
5 Giardino del Lago...C2
6 La Galleria Nazionale..................................B1
7 Museo Carlo Bilotti.....................................B2
8 Museo e Galleria Borghese.......................D2
9 Museo Nazionale Etrusco di Villa
  Giulia..A1
10 Obelisk..A3
11 Piazza del Popolo...A3
12 Piazza di Siena...C2
13 Pincio Hill Gardens......................................B3
14 Porta del Popolo...A3
15 Via Margutta..B3
16 Villa Borghese..D2
17 Villa Medici..B3
18 Villa Poniatowski...A1

❸ Eating
Al Gran Sasso ....(see 28)
19 Babette..B3
20 Caffè delle Arti..B1

21 Fatamorgana Corso.....................................A3
22 Gelateria Dei Gracchi.................................A3
23 Il Margutta..B3

ⓐ Shopping
24 Artisanal Cornucopia A3
25 Fabriano A3
26 Gente B3
27 La Bottega del Marmoraro......................... B3
28 Olfattorio... A3

ⓓ Drinking & Nightlife
29 Canova... A3
Stravinskij Bar – Hotel de
  Russie .... (see 32)

ⓔ Entertainment
30 Casa del Cinema C3
31 Silvano Toti Globe Theatre C2

ⓐ Activities, Courses & Tours
Hotel De Russie Spa .... (see 32)

ⓢ Sleeping
32 Hotel de Russie.. A3

Symbols & Map Key

Look for these symbols to quickly identify listings:

- ◉ Sights
- ✚ Activities
- ⊜ Courses
- ⊙ Tours
- ✸ Festivals & Events
- ✖ Eating
- ⊖ Drinking
- ✪ Entertainment
- 🔒 Shopping
- ❶ Information & Transport

These symbols and abbreviations give vital information for each listing:

- 🍃 Sustainable or green recommendation
- **FREE** No payment required

- ☏ Telephone number
- ⊙ Opening hours
- Ⓟ Parking
- ⊖ Nonsmoking
- ❄ Air-conditioning
- @ Internet access
- 🔊 Wi-fi access
- ⊠ Swimming pool
- ⊠ Bus
- ⊕ Ferry
- ⊠ Tram
- ⊠ Train
- ⊡ English-language menu
- ⊘ Vegetarian selection
- ⊕ Family-friendly

Find your best experiences with these Great For... icons.

 Art & Culture

 Beaches

Budget

Cafe/Coffee

🚲 Cycling

 Detour

Drinking

 Entertainment

Events

Family Travel

Food & Drink

 History

 Local Life

 Nature & Wildlife

 Photo Op

 Scenery

Shopping

Short Trip

Sport

Walking

Winter Travel

Sights

- 🏖 Beach
- 🐦 Bird Sanctuary
- 🛕 Buddhist
- 🏰 Castle/Palace
- ✝ Christian
- 🛕 Confucian
- 🕉 Hindu
- ☪ Islamic
- 🛕 Jain
- ✡ Jewish
- ❶ Monument
- 🏛 Museum/Gallery/ Historic Building
- ⊙ Ruin
- ⛩ Shinto
- ☬ Sikh
- ☯ Taoist
- 🍇 Winery/Vineyard
- 🐾 Zoo/Wildlife Sanctuary
- ◉ Other Sight

Points of Interest

- Bodysurfing
- Camping
- Cafe
- Canoeing/Kayaking
- Course/Tour
- Diving
- Drinking & Nightlife
- Eating
- Entertainment
- Sento Hot Baths/ Onsen
- Shopping
- Skiing
- Sleeping
- Snorkelling
- Surfing
- Swimming/Pool
- Walking
- Windsurfing
- Other Activity

Information

- $ Bank
- Embassy/Consulate
- Hospital/Medical
- @ Internet
- Police
- Post Office
- Telephone
- Toilet
- ❶ Tourist Information
- • Other Information

Geographic

- Beach
- Gate
- Hut/Shelter
- Lighthouse
- Lookout
- ▲ Mountain/Volcano
- Oasis
- Park
-)(Pass
- Picnic Area
- Waterfall

Transport

- Airport
- BART station
- Border crossing
- Boston T station
- Bus
- Cable car/Funicular
- Cycling
- Ferry
- Metro/MRT station
- Monorail
- Ⓟ Parking
- Petrol station
- Subway/S-Bahn/ Skytrain station
- Taxi
- Train station/Railway
- Tram
- Tube Station
- Underground/ U-Bahn station
- • Other Transport

Our Story

A beat-up old car, a few dollars in the pocket and a sense of adventure. In 1972 that's all Tony and Maureen Wheeler needed for the trip of a lifetime – across Europe and Asia overland to Australia. It took several months, and at the end – broke but inspired – they sat at their kitchen table writing and stapling together their first travel guide, *Across Asia on the Cheap*. Within a week they'd sold 1500 copies. Lonely Planet was born.

Today, Lonely Planet has offices in Franklin, London, Melbourne, Oakland, Dublin, Beijing and Delhi, with more than 600 staff and writers. We share Tony's belief that 'a great guidebook should do three things: inform, educate and amuse'.

Our Writer

Duncan Garwood

From facing fast bowlers in Barbados to sidestepping hungry pigs in Goa, Duncan's travels have thrown up many unique experiences. These days he largely dedicates himself to Italy, his adopted homeland where's he's been living since 1997. From his base in the Castelli Romani hills outside Rome, he's clocked up endless kilometres exploring the country's well-known destinations and far-flung reaches, working on guides to Rome, Sardinia, Sicily, Piedmont, and Naples and the Amalfi Coast. Other LP titles include *Italy's Best Trips*, the *Food Lover's Guide to the World*, and *Pocket Bilbao & San Sebastián*. He also writes on Italy for newspapers, websites and magazines.

STAY IN TOUCH LONELYPLANET.COM/CONTACT

AUSTRALIA The Malt Store, Level 3, 551 Swanston St, Carlton, Victoria 3053
☏03 8379 8000,
fax 03 8379 8111

IRELAND Unit E, Digital Court. The Digital Hub, Rainsford St, Dublin 8, Ireland

USA 124 Linden Street, Oakland, CA 94607
☏ 510 250 6400,
toll free 800 275 8555,
fax 510 893 8572

UK 240 Blackfriars Road, London SE1 8NW
☏ 020 3771 5100,
fax 020 3771 5101

 twitter.com/
lonelyplanet

 facebook.com/
lonelyplanet

 instagram.com/
lonelyplanet

 youtube.com/
lonelyplanet

 lonelyplanet.com/
newsletter